DESTINATION COMPETITIVENESS, THE ENVIRONMENT AND SUSTAINABILITY

Challenges and Cases

FSC
www.fsc.org

MIX

Paper from
responsible sources

FSC® C013604

CABI Series in Tourism Management Research

General Editors:
Professor Eric Laws, Professor of Tourism, Siam University, Bangkok
Professor Noel Scott, Griffith Institute for Tourism, Griffith University, Australia

Since the mid-20th century, modern tourism has grown rapidly in extent and diversity, becoming increasingly competitive and volatile as it is impacted by climate change, new technologies, changing distribution systems and the opening of new markets. As a result, governments, tourism destinations and businesses need to improve their management capability and adopt best practices to survive. The purpose of this series is to provide tourism managers, administrators, specialists and advanced students with state-of-the-art research and strategic knowledge to enable them to thrive in dynamic and unpredictable environments. Contributions are based on critical and interdisciplinary research that combines relevant theory and practice, while placing case studies from specific destinations into an international context. The series presents research on the development and diffusion of best practice in business and destination management that fulfils the objective of environmental, sociocultural and economic sustainability at both the local and global scale.

The cover design for this series depicts a generalized mosaic composed of many tiles. Metaphorically, this illustrates our philosophies that while the various elements of tourism require specific study, it is the overall picture that is most significant, and that tourism is a very dynamic, complex and evolving industry. This series seeks to build a coherent approach to future tourism research through each individual title.

Titles available

1. *Tourism Crisis and Disaster Management in the Asia-Pacific*
Edited by Brent W. Ritchie and Kom Campiranon.
2. *Destination Competitiveness, the Environment and Sustainability: Challenges and Cases*
Edited by Andrés Artal-Tur and Metin Kozak.

DESTINATION COMPETITIVENESS, THE ENVIRONMENT AND SUSTAINABILITY

Challenges and Cases

Edited By

Andrés Artal-Tur

Technical University of Cartagena, Spain

and

Metin Kozak

Dokuz Eylul University, Turkey

www.cabi.org

CABI is a trading name of CAB International

CABI
Nosworthy Way
Wallingford
Oxfordshire OX10 8DE
UK

CABI
745 Atlantic Avenue
8th Floor
Boston, MA 02111
USA

Tel: +44 (0)1491 832111
Fax: +44 (0)1491 833508
E-mail: info@cabi.org
Website: www.cabi.org

Tel: +1 (617) 682-9015
E-mail: cabi-nao@cabi.org

A catalogue record for this book is available from the British Library, London, UK.

Library of Congress Cataloging-in-Publication Data

Names: Artal-Tur, Andres, author. | Kozak, Metin, 1968- author.
Title: Destination competitiveness, the environment and sustainability :
    challenges and cases / Andres Artal-Tur, Metin Kozak.
Description: Oxfordshire OX, UK ; Boston, MA : CABI, 2015. | Series: CABI
    series in tourism management research | Includes bibliographical
    references and index.
Identifiers: LCCN 2015027437 | ISBN 9781780646978 (hbk)
Subjects: LCSH: Tourism--Environmental aspects. | Sustainable development. |
    Tourism--Management--Case studies. | Tourism--Marketing--Case studies.
Classification: LCC G156.5.E58 A78 2015 | DDC 910.68--dc23 LC record available at
    http://lccn.loc.gov/2015027437

ISBN-13: 978 1 78064 697 8

Commissioning editor: Claire Parfitt
Editorial assistant: Emma McCann
Production editor: Lauren Povey

Typeset by SPi, Pondicherry, India.
Printed and bound in the UK by CPI Group (UK) Ltd, Croydon, CR0 4YY.

Contents

Contributors

Ángela Aguiló, Faculty of Economics and Business, University of the Balearic Islands, Carretera de Valldemossa, Km 7.5, 07122, Palma de Mallorca, Spain. E-mail: angela.aguilo@uib.es

Margarita Alemany, Faculty of Economics and Business, University of the Balearic Islands, Carretera de Valldemossa, Km 7.5, (07122), Palma de Mallorca, Spain. E-mail: marga.alemany@uib.es

Habib Alipour, Faculty of Tourism, Eastern Mediterranean University, Via Mersin 10, Gazimagusa/KKTC, 99450, Turkey. E-mail: habib.alipour@emu.edu.tr

Andrés Artal-Tur, Faculty of Business Studies, Technical University of Cartagena, C\ Real 3, Cartagena, 30201, Spain. E-mail: andres.artal@upct.es

Ibrahim Birkan, Department of Tourism and Hotel Management, Atilim University, Kizilcasar Mahallesi, 06836 Incek, Ankara, Turkey. E-mail: ibrahim.birkan@atilim.edu.tr

Kimberley Blackwood, Mona School of Business, University of the West Indies, 4A Widcombe Road, T/H#2, Kingston 6, Jamaica, West Indies. E-mail: kimberleyvblackwood@gmail.com

Zélia Breda, Department of Economy, Management and Industrial Engineering, University of Aveiro, Campus Universitário de Santiago, 3810-193 Aveiro, Portugal. E-mail: zelia@ua.pt

Antonio Juan Briones-Peñalver, Faculty of Business Studies, Technical University of Cartagena, Cartagena, 30201, Spain. E-mail: aj.briones@upct.es

Pablo Juan Cárdenas-García, Laboratory of Analysis and Innovation in Tourism (LAInnTUR), Department of Economics, University of Jaén, Campus Las Lagunillas s/n, Building D3-231, 23071, Spain. E-mail: pcgarcia@ujaen.es

Adriana Fumi Chim-Miki, CAPES Foundation, Ministry of Education of Brazil, Brasilia-DF (70040-020), Brazil, and Faculty of Economics, Business and Tourism (FEET), University of Las Palmas de Gran Canaria (ULPGC), Edificio CC, Tafira (35017), Las Palmas de Gran Canaria, Spain. E-mail: adriana.chimmiki@gmail.com

José David Cisneros-Martínez, Facultad de Turismo, Universidad de Málaga, Calle León Tolstoi, 4, 29071, Málaga, Spain. E-mail: joscismar@uma.es

José María Nácher Escriche, Faculty of Economics, University of Valencia, Avenida de los Naranjos s/n, 46022, Valencia, Spain. E-mail: jose.m.nacher@uv.es

Antonio Fernández-Morales, Facultad de Ciencias Económicas y Empresariales, Universidad de Málaga, Calle El Ejido, 6, 29071, Málaga, Spain. E-mail: afdez@uma.es

Jose Manoel Gândara, Programme of Post-Graduation in Tourism, Federal University of Paraná (UFPR), Campus Reitoria, Rua Dr Faivre, 405, Ed. D. Pedro II, 3a. andar (80060-000), Curitiba-PR, Brazil. E-mail: jmggandara@yahoo.com.br

Maria Antonia García, Faculty of Economics and Business, University of the Balearic Islands, Carretera de Valldemossa km 7.5, 07122, Palma de Mallorca, Spain. E-mail: garcia.sastre@uib.es

Antonio García Sánchez, Faculty of Business Studies, Technical University of Cartagena, Cartagena, Murcia, Spain. E-mail: a.garciasanchez@upct.es

Siyanda Jonas, Economic Performance and Development, Human Sciences Research Council, 134 Pretorius Street, Pretoria 0002, South Africa. E-mail: sjonas@hsrc.ac.za

Selma Karuaihe, Economic Performance and Development, Human Sciences Research Council, 134 Pretorius Street, Pretoria 0002, South Africa. E-mail: skaruaihe@hsrc.ac.za

Metin Kozak, School of Tourism and Hospitality Management, Dokuz Eylul University, 35680, Foca, Izmır, Turkey. E-mail: metin.kozak@deu.edu.tr

Tanja Mihalič, Faculty of Economics, University of Ljubljana, Kardeljeva pl. 17, 1000 Ljubljana, Slovenia. E-mail: tanja.mihalic@ef.uni-lj.si

Gerardo Novo Espinosa de los Monteros, El Colegio Mexiquense, A.C. Exhacienda Santa Cruz de los Patos s/n, Zinacantepec, 51350, México. E-mail: novogerardo@hotmail.com

Charles Nhemachena, International Water Management Institute, Southern Africa, 141 Cresswell Street, Weavind Park 0184, Pretoria, South Africa. E-mail: cnhemachena@gmail.com; c.nhemachena@cgiar.org

Hossein G.T. Olya, Faculty of Tourism, British University of Nicosia, Via Mersin 10, Girne/KKTC, 99450, Turkey. E-mail: hossein.olya@bun.edu.tr

Maribel Osorio García, Facultad de Turismo, Universidad Autónoma del Estado de México, Ciudad Universitaria, Cerro de Coatepec s/n, Toluca, 50100, México. E-mail: maribelosorio2@gmail.com

Musa Pinar, College of Business Administration, Valparaiso University, Valparaiso, Indiana, 46383, USA. E-mail: musa.pinar@valpo.edu

Juan Ignacio Pulido-Fernández, Laboratory of Analysis and Innovation in Tourism (LAInnTUR), Department of Economics, University of Jaén, Campus Las Lagunillas s/n, Building D3-273, 23071, Spain. E-mail: jipulido@ujaen.es

David Siles López, Faculty of Business Studies, Technical University of Cartagena, Cartagena, Murcia, Spain. E-mail: dsl0@upct.es

Paula Simó Tomás, Faculty of Economics, University of Valencia, Avenida de los Naranjos s/n, 46022, Valencia, Spain: E-mail: pausito@alumni.uv.es

Mariya Stankova, Faculty of Economics, South-West University 'Neofit Rilski', 2 'Krali Marko' str., 2700 Blagoevgrad, Bulgaria. E-mail: mzlstan@yahoo.com

Ivana Stević, Department of Economy, Management and Industrial Engineering, University of Aveiro, Campus Universitário de Santiago, 3810-193 Aveiro, Portugal. E-mail: ivana.stevic87@ua.pt

Gamze Tanil, Dogus University, Acibadem, Kadikoy, 34722, İstanbul, Turkey. E-mail: gtanil@dogus.edu.tr

Muzaffer Uysal, Department of Hospitality and Tourism Management, Pamplin College of Business, Virginia Polytechnic Institute and State University, Blacksburg, VA 24061-0429, USA. E-mail: samil@vt.edu

Nadine Valentine, University of the West Indies, Mona Campus, School of Education, Mona, Kingston 7, Jamaica, West Indias. E-mail: nadstwo@yahoo.com

Juley Wynter-Robertson, Mona School of Business and Management, University of the West Indies, Mona, Cheapside District, Cobbla P.A., Manchester, Jamaica, West Indies. E-mail: jujuwynter@hotmail.com

1   Introduction

ANDRÉS ARTAL-TUR[1]* AND METIN KOZAK[2]

[1]*Technical University of Cartagena, Cartagena, Spain; [2]Dokuz Eylul University, Foca, Turkey*

At the beginning of the 21st century, tourism has become a global industry. International tourism revenues exceed US$1 trillion, and today's 1.1 bn travellers are expected to reach 1.8 bn in 2030, according to the forecasts of the United Nations World Tourism Organization (UNWTO). As a result, in recent years, destinations have faced some crucial questions with respect to maintaining sustainability. Destinations must be cleaner, greener and safer in order to safeguard the life quality not only of holiday-makers but also of local residents. This is also important for attracting investments and promoting the development of tourism, which will lead to economic benefits and staying tuned to rival destinations. Therefore, the most important considerations are environmentally sustainable tourism applications and asset management (Ratcliffe and Flanagan, 2004). Recent developments exert pressure on the cultural, natural and economic resources of tourism; for example, the rapid increase in the number of both domestic and international tourists and the number of vehicles allocated for tourists, such as cars, buses and aircraft (Davidson and Maitland, 1997).

This poses enormous challenges for the future of the industry as a whole, and for destinations in particular. In this context, the present book provides new insights on the topic of *tourism destination management*, focusing on the analysis of three main issues: *competitiveness*, *the role of the environment* and *sustainability*. Maintaining competitiveness is a key issue for the future of tourism destinations. Environmental issues directly affect destination opportunities, particularly in regards to the question of climate change. Sustainability, on its own, occupies a central place in the current literature and practice of destination management. All three issues conform to a set of prominent topics in today's tourism analysis. Moreover, they are closely interrelated, as the environmental dimension is pivotal for the sustainability of a tourism destination and also constitutes a cornerstone for building its competitive position for the future.

*E-mail: andres.artal@upct.es

The present book on *Destination Competitiveness, the Environment and Sustainability: Challenges and Cases* is structured into three parts comprising 15 main chapters. Each part constitutes a monographic view on every topic analysed through the book. The chapters employ case studies in order to illustrate their contributions. Given the global nature of the cases presented, the book provides an up-to-date perspective of the worldwide challenges and solutions arising in the management of tourism destinations. The analysis presents an interdisciplinary approach, including contributions from economists, managers, geographers and marketing professionals. All these features make the book an appealing text for academics and professionals of management in the tourism industry, offering new strands of knowledge on the subject.

Part I pursues the analysis of factors influencing the *competitiveness of destinations* through four chapters. The first two chapters follow the mainstream focus of the literature, as pointed out, for example, in the well-known contribution of Ritchie and Crouch (2003). Particular attention is paid to identifying the role played by conceptual blocks fostering competitiveness, including natural and cultural inherited resources, created and supporting resources, situational conditions and demand factors. The concept of competitiveness pillars and its relationship to the tourism destination is also reviewed (WEF, 2013). These two chapters seek to refine the analysis employing competitiveness indicators; in particular, they focus on identifying the most relevant factors inside a number of resources conferring competitive capacity to a destination. The final two chapters of Part I investigate other emerging sources of competitiveness, including that of creativity at destinations or the role played by visual semantics when developing new sources of competitiveness. Creativity is yet to be recognized as a driving force for urban and cultural development in tourism (Richards, 2011). The capacity of communication policy in shaping the international image of a destination, and by then building new competitive resources, is an interesting new topic of the literature (Rakic and Chambers, 2012).

In more detail, Chapter 2 by García Sánchez and Siles López focuses on competitiveness and innovation, with an application to the Spanish Mediterranean region. Building on a wide range of indicators, the authors seek to identify the main sources of tourism destination competitiveness. In doing so, they follow the theoretical approach of Crouch and Ritchie (1999) in their conceptual model and the integrated model of Dwyer and Kim (2003) as the conceptual basis of their study. As a natural link with competitiveness, they extend the research to accommodate for the incidence of innovation in tourism. They also link the concepts of innovation and competitiveness, defining how the former variable can enhance the latter one. In Chapter 3, Gândara and Fumi Chim-Miki present an analysis based on the tourism competitiveness pillars defined by the Ministry of Tourism in Brazil. The relevance of each pillar is evaluated through a focus group technique with the participation of national tourism stakeholders. Building on the qualitative results of the group of tourism experts, the authors can evaluate the efficiency of factors of competitiveness at destinations. It allows them to identify prioritizing actions for improving destination competitiveness from a policy point of view.

Chapters 4 and 5 widen the scope of the analysis of destination competiveness by introducing new trends in the literature, as the role of creativity, and the effects of promotional and marketing efforts in establishing new tourism products at traditional destinations. In Chapter 4, Nácher Escriche and Simó Tomás investigate the capacity of creativity in reshaping the city tourism product for Valencia, Spain, an emerging creative destination in European urban space. Creative activities induce an urban interaction between visitors and residents. Urban planning strategies show a growing interest of public authorities in promoting creative districts of the city as tourism destinations, given the boost experienced by cultural and city tourism in the past years. In this context, and focusing on creative neighbourhoods or urban clusters of the city, the chapter develops and implements a methodology to characterize better the interaction of creative districts and urban travellers.

Closing the first part of the book, in Chapter 5, Novo Espinosa de los Monteros and Osoria García analyse how visual semantics in tourism marketing can be employed to foster the competitiveness of a destination. They apply this methodological framework to investigate wedding tourism in Mexico. While this country has not positioned itself explicitly as a wedding destination, it has started to capitalize on the attributes making it an attractive destination for such purposes, placing particular emphasis on promotion campaigns for the North American market. Marketing efforts, as those using visual communication of destination weddings, have featured Mexican destinations as ideal backdrops for such celebrations. Analysing tourism by the images used to depict the product or destination is becoming a new strand of research in tourism analysis. The visual information received by visitors through the media help them to create their own imagery of destinations. In this chapter, the authors investigate how the systematized use of schemas provides meaning to tourism communication, with new iconic elements being added to the images used to represent tourism. The connotative functions of the images communicate multiple concrete and symbolic possibilities of the destination. At the same time, the representation of social interactions provides expressive strength to the elements of communication, while also helping to generate a social image of the destination. All these issues open new possibilities for enhancing tourism competitiveness at destinations.

Part II of the book concentrates on the study of the environmental dimension of tourism. The environment and climate change have become central topics in the tourism literature, for obvious reasons. The literature on the impact of tourism on the natural environment is nowadays well established (Holden, 2008). The rapid growth in the demand for international tourism has brought environmental issues to the forefront of any debate on tourism destination planning. The profound impact of human activity on global resources transcends particular disciplines of research, with special impact on those industries highly dependent on the natural medium, as is the tourism industry (Gössling, 2002). Articulating the collective response of the tourism industry regarding the environmental challenge is not an easy task. The range of stakeholders involved, the different dimensions at play (sociological, psychological, geographical, financial, etc.), or even the lack of consensus in the definition of key conceptual themes, make a shared response extremely difficult (Holden, 2009). The role of education in spreading environmental sensitiveness in both the demand and supply agents in the tourism industry is becoming a common point in the literature (Fidgeon, 2010; Ballantyne *et al.*, 2011; Chou, 2014).

The effect of climate change also occupies a salient place in the industry's discussions (UNWTO and UNEP, 2008). The UNWTO organized *The First International Conference on Climate Change and Tourism* in 2003 (UNWTO, 2003). Sea level rise, alterations in the weather, impact on biodiversity or water stress highly condition the perspectives of the tourism industry. The loss of destination attractiveness and the decline in demand levels are being recognized as the potential threats of climate change (Rosselló-Nadal, 2014). The necessity of responding to the effects of climate variability has triggered stakeholders and the academic community to develop generic adaptation frameworks for tourism destinations (Simpson *et al.*, 2008). These frameworks serve to guide the choices of policy makers seeking to reduce the vulnerability of destinations while increasing their resilience. Further attempts are being made to propose an enhanced Regional Tourism Sustainable Adaptation Framework (Njoroge, 2014). Other authors have wondered about the importance of understanding how tourism stakeholders perceive the impact of climate change, and how this influences the cooperative action among them (Hall, 2006; Wyss, 2013).

This second part of the book investigates how to address some of these key issues in the tourism industry's daily practices. It investigates the level of awareness shown by stakeholders on environmental practices, and elaborates on the capacity of environmental management to build new competitive advantages for the hospitality industry. It reviews the importance of education in order to increase the environmental consciousness of the students who will form the future labour force of the tourism industry. The scope of the green practices used at the tourism industry level is also analysed. This part consists of five chapters, including case studies for Europe, the Caribbean and South Africa.

Starting with Chapter 6, Pinar *et al.* investigate the potential effects of climate change and global warming in Turkey. The chapter begins by reviewing the perceptions of hotel managers on the impact of these two salient issues on the tourism industry. They also analyse the measures launched by the industry in order to face the situation. Further, the study tests for the linkage between managers' perceptions and their demographic profile. By employing a factor analysis, the authors identify five individual factors, suggesting five different areas of concern of the managerial staff about the impact of climate change on the evolution of business. Some policy recommendations emerge from results of the study for the hotel industry. In Chapter 7, Blackwood *et al.* investigate how tourism activities can be used to improve the awareness of people of the effects of climate change, focusing on the Caribbean. As they note, tourism is a highly climate-sensitive industry, and the evolution of business at destinations is extremely dependent on the weather conditions. This becomes particularly true for all destinations exploiting their natural comparative advantages as seaside resources and wildlife and biodiversity destinations. In this context of extreme interdependence between business and climate conditions, the tourism industry in the Caribbean is highly interested in improving the understanding of all stakeholders and related personnel of the necessity to undertake real measures against the sources of global warming. The same industry, which receives visits from multiple international tourists, could be playing an instructive role regarding such a global issue. In this way, Caribbean governments can build on the tourism industry as a defender against climate change. This chapter analyses the main tools and policies available to this extent, providing insights into the incentives helping to pursue responsible tourism initiatives that minimize the impact of tourism on the environment.

The next three chapters in this part explore the relationship between tourism and the environment in a wider sense. They include investigations on green economy practices in tourism, the role of environmental resources in fostering the competitiveness of the hotel industry and the salient issue of environmental education for future generations. In Chapter 8, Nhemachena *et al.* explore the degree of understanding of the green economy, its concepts and practices, undertaken by the tourism industry of the Limpopo Province, South Africa. The chapter begins by reviewing the structure and main components of the green economy as indicated by national and international legislations and recommendations. Further, and building on survey data collected from business tourists and key local actors, they investigate the degree of comprehension and implementation of green economy practices in this province. As a complement, the authors explore the emerging limits to the environmental approach in the region, as well as the formative and qualification needs identified in this region for the future of the green management strategy in tourism. In Chapter 9, Mihalič explores the capacity of environmental resources to become a competitive advantage for the hotel industry, making an application to Slovenia. The author investigates whether hotel managers perceive environmental management techniques as a competitive factor of this business, and the level of priority they confer to these tools. The distinction between the actions of environmental quality management (EQM) and environmental impact management (EIM) is also investigated. In this context, the competitive advantage factor (CAF) model is expanded by a new factor, the environmental management and EQM and EIM components. The model is tested empirically in the case of the Slovenian hotel industry. The investigation provides a benchmark to measure the competitive advantages provided by environmental management techniques. Closing Part II of the book, Alipour and Olya's Chapter 10 investigates the role of environmental education for a sustainable tourism horizon, with an application to Turkey. The chapter explores how educational institutions help to conform to an environmental attachment in students, as a way of introducing and enlarging the presence of environmental convictions at the tourism industry level. The theory of ecological modernization is employed as a theoretical basis in promoting an environmentally conscious stance, in the context of a knowledge-based platform. Further, building on survey data, the chapter assesses the scope of environmentally related education, as well as the students' general knowledge on environmental issues. The results identify some weaknesses still present in the educative process design for students to develop a truly environmental awareness. Protocols for improvement are then explored and prescribed.

Part III of the book is devoted to the general topic of destination sustainability. The concept of sustainable development has become commonplace in the literature. In what refers to a sustainable tourism development definition, the three-pillar framework promoted by UNWTO became the original standard. This included a broad focus on the environmental, sociocultural and economic responsibility of the tourism industry, and of the tourists themselves. Regarding the academic approach, researchers show a basic consensus on the aim of sustainable practices to minimize environmental impacts and preserve cultural heritage while providing learning opportunities, resulting in positive benefits for local residents (Weaver, 2005). Tourism policy and private management occupy a central role in defining, promoting and controlling sustainable strategies for destinations, including the objective to integrate the local community, and achieving a responsible tourist demand management (Kastenholz, 2004; Wang and Pizam, 2011). In a broader sense, sustainable tourism policy and management appear as emerging forces influencing the dynamics of destination competitiveness. In fact, empirical evidence shows that sustainability has become a core dimension of destination competitiveness (Cucculelli and Goffi, 2015).

Despite the current extension of tourism sustainability as an appealing conceptual idea across the profession, the reality still shows an alarmingly slow penetration of action and practice in the tourism industry (Mihalic, 2014). As a response, this book intends to provide a deeper knowledge of sustainability issues in tourism through the six chapters composing Part III. Chapters 11 and 12 cope with the issue of seasonality of demand. Finding new sources of demand for low-season months would help to build more sustainable tourism destinations. It would also help to attract other types of tourists at coastal destinations, increasing the diversity of demand, and hence the specialization in new and more sustainable activities. Chapters 13 and 14 analyse the economic sustainability of destinations, focusing on the expenditure and stay behaviour of tourists. A deeper knowledge of tourist behaviour allows destination managers to find an optimal combination between economic profits and a lower environmental impact of tourism activities. Finally, Chapter 15 contributes to the study of tourism sustainability by exploring the cultural product and heritage-based tourism, while Chapter 16 provides a broader view when analysing the search for a sustainability approach in the development of an emerging destination, the country of Bulgaria in former Eastern Europe.

In more detail, the seasonality pattern of tourism is always a matter of concern for destination managers. Excess demand in some particular months of the year can be followed by a shortage of visitors in other seasons, critically affecting the evolution of the tourism business. At the destination level, seasonality patterns can lead to common negative outcomes, i.e. unstable labour conditions or low-qualified personnel, limits to the profitability of investments, reduction in business revenue, a mismatch in load capacity, fluctuation of prices, environmental degradation and congestion problems, and various sociocultural effects among visitors and residents (Butler, 2001). In some way, all tourism destinations have to face the problem of seasonality, this being a key variable to be addressed when defining a sustainability strategy for the future. In Chapter 11, Cisneros-Martínez and Fernández-Morales analyse the seasonal concentration of tourism in the region of Andalusia, in southern Spain. Employing microdata based on tourist surveys, the authors seek to identify segments of visitors showing a clear counter-seasonal behaviour. They build on statistical techniques to extract these types of collectives from data panels. In particular, they focus on establishing the role that cultural tourism can play in confronting the seasonality of demand, attracting new visitors in low-season periods to the five coastal destinations under study. Expanding on this line of research, in Chapter 12, Alemany *et al.* study the role of tourism policy in providing adequate responses to the challenge of seasonality at a crowded coastal destination in Spain, the Balearic Islands. In particular, they start by developing a qualitative review of the evolution of successive marketing plans in the Balearics in the framework of tourism policies. Strategies based on product, price and communication policies conform to the main approach of the public policies to this matter. Further, the authors test for a statistical correlation between the policy stimuli set out in the regional plans and the evolution of the seasonal behaviour of tourists.

The expenditure and stay behaviour of tourists, and the capacity of these two variables in improving the sustainability of a nature-based destination such as Costa Rica, is explored by Artal-Tur and Briones-Peñalver in Chapter 13. Tourism is a growing industry in Central America, with nature-related activities leading the product specialization of this region. Green forest and wildlife richness attract international visitors to this place, one of the most important world reserves of the biosphere. Throughout the chapter, the authors identify the personal characteristics of the tourists coming to these destinations, and building on survey data, deduce their individual behaviour. In carrying out the analysis, they estimate two equations explaining the expenditure and stay patterns of international tourists arriving in the country. In particular, they test for the role played by time and budget restrictions, socio-economic features of visitors, destination characteristics and previous knowledge of the country. All these findings help to improve the knowledge on visitors' behaviour arriving in a nature-based tourist location, obtaining interesting conclusions to improve the management of the destination on a sustainable basis. In Chapter 14, Cárdenas-García and Pulido-Fernández study the profile of sustainable tourists and expenditure patterns at destinations, applying this methodology to Andalusia, Spain. The study begins by identifying the profile of what they call a 'sustainable tourist'. Then, by means of a regression model, the authors estimate the determinants of expenditure on the basis of the sociodemographic characteristics of such sustainable tourists. The analysis is developed for particular destinations inside this region, the mid-sized cities. The chapter concludes by establishing a number of tourism policy proposals aimed at improving the tourism management of emerging mid-sized urban cultural destinations.

Culture is also the key variable in the analysis of Chapter 15. In this study, Stević and Breda elaborate on the networking nature of sustainable cultural tourism activities and dynamics in Oporto, Portugal. Tourism consists of a large number of interrelated entities forming a complex system, with a vast range of stakeholders playing different roles. The tourism industry is constantly changing and evolving, forcing destinations to become involved in sustainable strategies for a sustainable product. In this context, the need for an effective management destination model, through the definition of World Heritage Sites, requires a networking strategy that enables destinations to collaborate and share knowledge. The specific objectives of the chapter include: first, to understand and discuss the importance of networking at the cultural tourism level; second, to identify if there is an official network of stakeholders involved in management, planning, organization, strategic decisions and protection of the heritage site, or merely collaboration among them; and third, to identify the main difficulties and challenges when it comes to management, preservation and protection of cultural heritage and sustainable tourism development at the World Heritage Site. Finally, Chapter 16 closes Part III of the book. In this chapter, Stankova reviews the broader challenges of defining sustainability issues for a particular destination, in this case that of an emerging tourism country in Europe, Bulgaria. The search for an increasing level of revenues and development in an emerging destination is confronted in this chapter, along with the necessary sustainability issues that should be guiding the tourism life cycle of the destination. The review of previous experiences and the current situation underlines the need for the conscious and purposeful cooperation of all stakeholders, notably through the development of sustainable tourism strategic initiatives. In this way, the approach to tourism destination sustainability in a wider sense brings to a close this part of the book devoted to the study of sustainability in tourism.

This book, then, brings to our attention the centrality of the environmental dimension in tourism and how it is currently reshaping the subjects of destination competitiveness and sustainability. The work shows how the challenges posed by human development can be seen as an opportunity to build a truly responsible tourism model that is capable of responding to the increasing environmental sensitivity characterizing the millions of people arriving annually at worldwide destinations.

References

Ballantyne, R., Packer, J. and Falk, J. (2011) Visitors' learning for environmental sustainability: testing short- and long-term impacts of wildlife tourism experiences using structural equation modelling. *Tourism Management* 32(6), 1243–1252.

Butler, R. (2001) Seasonality in tourism: issues and implications. In: Baum, T. and Lundtorp, C. (eds) *Seasonality in Tourism*. Pergamon, New York, pp. 5–22.

Chou, C.J. (2014) Hotels' environmental policies and employee personal environmental beliefs: interactions and outcomes. *Tourism Management* 40, 436–446.

Crouch, G.I. and Ritchie, J.R.B. (1999) Tourism, competitiveness, and societal prosperity. *Journal of Business Research* 44, 137–152.

Cucculelli, M. and Goffi, G. (2015) Does sustainability enhance tourism destination competitiveness? Evidence from Italian destinations of excellence. *Journal of Cleaner Production* 53, 1–13.

Davidson, R. and Maitland, R. (1997) *Tourism Destinations.* Hodder and Stoughton, London.

Dwyer, L. and Kim, C. (2003) Destination competitiveness: determinants and indicators. *Current Issues in Tourism* 6(5), 369–414.

Fidgeon, P.R. (2010) Tourism education and curriculum design: a time for consolidation and review? *Tourism Management* 31(6), 699–723.

Gössling, S. (2002) Global environmental consequences of tourism. *Global Environmental Change* 12(4), 283–302.

Hall, C.M. (2006) New Zealand tourism entrepreneur attitudes and behaviours with respect to climate change adaptation and mitigation. *International Journal of Innovation and Sustainable Development* 1(3), 229–237.

Holden, A. (2008) *Environment and Tourism*, 2nd edn. Routledge, London.

Holden, A. (2009) The environment–tourism nexus. Influence of market ethics. *Annals of Tourism Research* 36(3), 373–389.

Kastenholz, E. (2004) 'Management of demand' as a tool in sustainable tourist destination development. *Journal of Sustainable Tourism* 12(5), 388–408.

Mihalic, T. (2014) Sustainable–responsible tourism discourse – towards 'responsustable' tourism. *Journal of Cleaner Production* 52, 1–10.

Njoroge, J.M. (2014) An enhanced framework for regional tourism sustainable adaptation to climate change. *Tourism Management Perspectives* 12, 23–30.

Rakic, T. and Chambers, D. (eds) (2012) *An Introduction to Visual Search Methods in Tourism*. Routledge, New York.

Ratcliffe, J. and Flanagan, S. (2004) Enhancing the vitality and viability of town and city centres: the concept of the business improvement district in the context of tourism enterprise. *Property Management* 22(5), 377–395.

Richards, G. (2011) Creativity and tourism: the state of the art. *Annals of Tourism Research* 38(4), 1225–1253.

Ritchie, J.R.B. and Crouch, G.I. (2003) *The Competitive Destination: A Sustainable Tourism Perspective.* CAB International, Wallingford, UK.

Rosselló-Nadal, J. (2014) How to evaluate the effects of climate change on tourism. *Tourism Management* 42, 334–340.

Simpson, M.C., Gössling, S., Scott, D., Hall, C.M. and Gladin, E. (2008) *Climate Change Adaptation and Mitigation in the Tourism Sector: Frameworks, Tools and Practices.* UNEP, University of Oxford, UNWTO, WMO, Paris.

UNWTO (2003) Climate change and tourism. *Proceedings of the First International Conference on Climate Change Tourism,* Djerba, Tunisia, 9–11 April. United Nations World Tourism Organization, Madrid.

UNWTO and UNEP (2008) *Climate Change and Tourism: Responding to Global Challenges.* World Tourism Organization, Madrid.

Wang, Y. and Pizam, A. (eds) (2011) *Destination Marketing and Management. Theories and Applications.* CAB International, Wallingford, UK.

Weaver, D. (2005) *Sustainable Tourism.* Elsevier Butterworth-Heinemann, Oxford, UK.

WEF (2013) *The Travel & Tourism Competitiveness Report 2013.* World Economic Forum, Geneva, Switzerland.

Wyss, R. (2013) Cooperation for climate adaptation in tourism. An agenda for the Alps based on structuration theory. *Journal of Alpine Research/Revue de Géographie Alpine* Dossier 101(4).

Part I Managing Destination Competitiveness

2

Tourism Destination Competitiveness and Innovation: The Case of the Spanish Mediterranean Coast

Antonio García Sánchez* and David Siles López

Technical University of Cartagena, Cartagena, Spain

2.1   Introduction

Tourism is one of the most valuable industries in a country's economy today; it adds value to the country's GDP, resulting in increased well-being for the country's inhabitants. According to the World Data Bank, there were 1.076 million tourist arrivals around the world in 2012, and these tourists contributed large expenditures to their destinations' economies (World Data Bank, 2012). Tourism is important for economies and is common in developed countries, and can be a determinant in developing countries to ensure their economic growth. For many countries, tourism is a good option for growth, and during economic slowdowns, tourism offers an excellent boost to local economies. According to the World Travel and Tourism Council (WTTC), tourism has contributed 10% to world GDPs over the past 20 years (WTTC, n.d.).

In Spain, tourism has contributed approximately 10% to the GDP since 2000 (National Statistics Institute (INE), 2000–2012). Spain is ranked fourth in tourist arrivals, according to the competitiveness report from the World Economic Forum (WEF, 2013). Spain's tourism has been developing rapidly since the 1980s, and today the country offers a consolidated tourism product based on sun and sand. According to the World Data Bank (2012), Spain received 5.36% of international tourist arrivals and 57.7 million tourists in 2012, and the country ranked third in tourism expenditures.

In 2008, Spain experienced an economic crisis. Spain's economy grew based on building and real estate speculation, and financial liquidity risks drove the country into the crisis; Spain had been growing by a mean of 3.5% between 2000 and 2007, but showed a growth by a mean of −1% between 2008 and 2013 (European Commission, 2000–2013). In this context, Spain has depended on other industries to grow, one of

*E-mail: a.garciasanchez@upct.es

© CAB International 2016. *Destination Competitiveness, the Environment and Sustainability: Challenges and Cases* (eds A. Artal-Tur and M. Kozak)

which has been tourism, and today Spain is supporting this industry through schemes such as the National and Integral Tourism Plan 2012–2015 (PNIT; TourSpain, 2012–2015). Tourism development involves increasing the supply, which must be broad and varied and which introduces competitiveness into the tourism concept: destinations compete against each other to attract tourists.

The relevance of tourism is growing. Data from the WEF (WEF, 2011) show that in 1950 almost all international arrivals (97%) were concentrated in only 15 destination countries; this share had fallen to 56% by 2009, indicating that other countries had developed their tourism offerings.

We analyse tourism competitiveness in the context of Spain expanding on its sun and sand tourism options, and the main objective of the chapter is to obtain a range of tourism competitiveness indicators for the Mediterranean provinces and conduct statistical tests to determine their efficiency. In this way, we can establish the best-performing indicators and use those to increase destination competitiveness through improvement and innovation.

For this analysis, we selected the Mediterranean coast, because the Mediterranean provinces receive more than 50% of Spain's tourists (INE, 2000–2012). Moreover, all of the provinces share common characteristics (they all offer the 'sun and sand' tourism product), and thus, the relatively homogeneous sample allows us to analyse and interpret the results.

2.2   Literature Review

The *Oxford English Dictionary* defines competitiveness as an agent's ability to sell products on markets and obtain revenue. Porter (1980, 1990) observes that enterprises' characteristics allow them to surpass their rivals, but that to do so, these enterprises must exploit their comparative and competitive advantages. At the global level, countries compete on international markets to sell their goods and services, and thus, the competitiveness concept applies both nationally and internationally.

Competitiveness has been studied and defined by many tourism researchers. For instance, Kozak and Rimmington (1999) classify the determinants of tourism competitiveness into two categories: primary and secondary factors. Mihalic (2000) offers contributions about management and organization. Gooroochurn and Sugiyarto (2005) present a model of eight pillars based on 23 tourism competitiveness indicators. Craigwell (2007) explains small islands' competitiveness using indicators that affect tourist arrivals and expenditures.

Among all of the contributions to the tourism competitiveness literature, we based our model on two relevant articles. In the first of the studies we used to build our model, Crouch and Ritchie (1999) developed a theoretical tourism competitiveness model that they referred to as a 'conceptual model'. The authors found a range of tourism competitiveness indicators and established that these indicators must result in prosperity, the most relevant outcome of tourism destination competitiveness. Buhalis (2000) similarly notes that prosperity increases inhabitants' well-being and is measured through indicators such as tourism gross value added, per capita income and employment.

The second study that influenced our model development was by Dwyer and Kim (2003), who developed an 'integrated model' in which a variety of indicators were grouped to comprise tourism competitiveness, including supply and demand indicators. This model was also required to result in prosperity as an outcome of tourism destination competitiveness. We base our model on this integrated model because we believe that it encompasses all aspects of tourism competitiveness. The authors review all of the previous literature to create a general model that includes demand indicators as well, which are very important because demand reflects satisfaction.

One way of measuring tourism competitiveness, according to many authors (Kozak and Rimmington, 1999; Hassan, 2000; Ritchie and Crouch, 2003; Enright and Newton, 2004), is through tourist arrivals, and our aim is to identify the wide variety of indicators that explain tourist arrivals. The tourism competitiveness blocks included in the integrated model are the following: inherited, created and supporting resources, situational conditions and demand.

2.3   Methodology

Beginning with Dwyer and Kim's (2003) integrated model, we select 57 relevant destination-related variables and indicators, and group them into the competitiveness blocks (natural and cultural inherited resources, created and supporting resources, situational conditions and demand) to arrive at 31 variables that are significant to explain tourism competitiveness (Table 2.1): these variables are similar to the ones that have been included in the integrated model.

We focus our model on Spain's Mediterranean provinces because the country's Mediterranean destinations all offer the same sun and sand product; all of the provinces are coastal and have similar characteristics, which simplifies the search for common indicators. Moreover, Spain's Mediterranean provinces account for 56% of the country's tourism; as such, they are representative of Spanish tourism and they are relevant to Spain's economy. The selected provinces are: Alicante, Almería, Baleares, Barcelona, Cádiz, Castellón, Gerona, Granada, Málaga, Murcia, Tarragona and Valencia (Fig. 2.1). The year of reference for the analysis is 2010, because this is the last year with common available data.

We began with all 12 provinces and 31 variables for each, but to arrive at a solution while minimizing the loss of information, it was necessary to reduce the number of variables, taking into account that the parameters we were estimating had to be equal to or less than the number of observations (i.e. the liberty degrees had to equal 0 or more). A simple dimensional reduction procedure is principal component analysis (PCA), a method that has been used often in the tourism destination competitiveness literature (Gooroochurn and Sugiyarto, 2005; Crouch, 2011). Using PCA, we were able to reduce the original 31 variables to seven new variables (factors) that represented the principal tourism competitiveness components following the integrated model of Dwyer and Kim (2003); in addition, we avoided multicollinearity. Each competitiveness component resulted in one factor, but the natural resources resulted in two (Weather and Natural).

Table 2.1. Competitiveness variables, factors and conceptual blocks.

Variables	Factor	Block
Average temperature	Weather	Natural resources
Sunlight hours		
Cultural places of interest	Natural	
Beaches		
Libraries	Cultural	Cultural resources
Museums		
Edited books		
UNESCO sites		
Tennis courts	Attractiveness	Created resources
Hotel beds		
Golf courses		
Commercial centres		
Zoos		
LFP soccer teams[a]		
Theme parks		
Music festivals		
Bank branches	Services	Supporting resources
Saving bank branches		
Central bank branches		
Hospitals		
Flight lines		
Cruise layover		
Road kilometres		
Port authorities		
Foreign tourism weight	Specialization	Situational conditions
Tourism quote above national		
Hotel occupancy rates		
Price index hotels–pubs–restaurants		
Beach satisfaction	Assessment	Demand
Restaurant satisfaction		
Environment satisfaction		

[a]LFP = Liga de Futbol Profesional (Spanish football league).

Fig. 2.1. Spain's Mediterranean provinces.

The model of competitiveness we propose has been developed using García Sánchez and Siles (2014) as a reference, and has the following structure:

$$\text{ARRIVALS}_i = \beta_0 + \beta_1 \text{NATURAL}_i + \beta_2 \text{WEATHER}_i + \beta_3 \text{CULTURAL}_i$$
$$+ \beta_4 \text{ATTRACTIVENESS}_i + \beta_5 \text{SERVICES}_i$$
$$+ \beta_6 \text{SPECIALIZATION}_i + \beta_7 \text{ASSESSMENT}_i + u_i$$

The subscript 'i' denotes the provinces and 'u' is the error term.

We needed to know how the analysed variables influenced competitiveness, and which competitiveness components could be strengthened by which variables, for the purpose of increasing tourism competitiveness in the destinations. Thus, we ran an ordinary least squares linear regression that would explain arrivals by tourists who spent at least one night at a hotel. We selected this dependent variable because, as Pavlyuk (2010) suggested, staying in a hotel reflected attraction to the tourism destination and contributed to tourism expenditures, and thus it was a more complete measure of tourism competitiveness.

2.4   Results

We use PCA to reduce the 31 significant variables to seven factors that represent tourism competitiveness, and we show the linear regression results in Table 2.2. We can observe that each independent variable has a positive sign and all significant factors have a confidence level of at least 90%, except for Natural. The theory we reviewed previously confirmed that all of the variables we used in the analysis were

Table 2.2. Linear regression OLS results.

Variable	Coefficient	S.D.	t-statistic	Probability
C	5.84E-08	0.015508	3.77E-06	1.0000
WEATHER	0.095449	0.034976	2.729001	0.0525
NATURAL	0.020100	0.028761	0.698848	0.5231
CULTURAL	0.242570	0.058494	4.146945	0.0143
ATTRACTIVENESS	0.187267	0.087871	2.131173	0.1001
SERVICES	0.372170	0.113328	3.284018	0.0304
SPECIALIZATION	1.430116	0.070130	20.39228	0.0000
ASSESSMENT	0.299318	0.041246	7.256852	0.0019
R^2	0.998951	Var mean depend.	1.000000	
Adjusted R^2	0.997114	SD var depend.	−2.775318	
SE regression	0.053721	Akaike criterion	−2.452046	
Square sum of resid.	0.011544	Schwarz criterion	−2.895004	
Enter probability	24.65191	Hannan–Quinn criterion	2.110855	
F-statistic	543.9469	Durbin–Watson statistic		
Probability (F-statistic)	0.000009			

Notes: OLS = ordinary least squares; S.D. = standard deviation; SE = standard error; E = *10 exp, i.e.
5.84E-08 = 5.84*10^{-8}; Var mean depend. = variance mean dependent; SD var depend. = standard deviation
variance dependent; Square sum of resid. = square sum of residuals.

important for the tourism competitiveness model. The sun and sand product singularities, statistical limitations and our particular model specification did not allow us to confirm the Natural factor as significant, but it did at least have the expected sign; however, the variables that comprised the factor did not confirm robustly Nature's contribution to Spain's tourism destination competitiveness.

The overall result of the analysis, however, is robust, as the tests confirm, and the independent variables explain the dependent variable in a consistent way. The most important factor for competitiveness is Specialization, followed by Services, Assessment, Culture, Attractiveness and Weather. We renamed the factors according to the variables that comprised them. Specialization comprised variables such as tourism quotes, foreign tourism weight and prices. Services comprised destination-related variables such as financial, health and transport services. Assessment entailed tourists' assessments of destination characteristics such as the environment, restaurants and beaches. Culture factor variables included destinations' cultural offerings such as museums, libraries and UNESCO sites. Attractiveness related to destinations' leisure offerings, such as sport facilities, commercial centres, theme parks, etc. The Weather factor comprised variables such as temperature and hours of sunlight.

Other authors confirm our results: we agree with Sánchez-Rivero (2006) on the importance of the Specialization and Services indicators. We obtained results similar to those of Zhang and Jensen (2007) on the contribution of hotel occupancy (Attractiveness). We also agree with Croes (2010, 2011) on the importance of prices,

Services and Assessment. In sum, many authors confirmed the relevance of the indicators we obtained for measuring tourism competitiveness.

We show how our tourism destination competitiveness model, which we have adapted from Dwyer and Kim's (2003) integrated model, is adaptable to Spain's Mediterranean provinces, and now we can offer suggestions to managers to improve destination competitiveness. We can confirm that if destinations want to increase their competitiveness, managers should make improvements on the factors and variables that the model predicts. The final outcome of competitiveness will be prosperity at destinations (Crouch and Ritchie, 1999; Dwyer and Kim, 2003; Dwyer *et al.*, 2004; García Sánchez and Siles, 2014).

2.4.1   Innovation and tourism competitiveness

Innovation is a concept that initially appeared in the business world; companies engage in product innovation to attract new customers or maintain their market standings. Innovation also takes place in managing companies, such as when firms and managers add new concepts, incorporate technology into their production processes or seek ways to reduce costs and increase productivity.

For our purposes, the three initial, and basic, types of innovation (product, process and management) can be expanded to the services field, in which the same concepts are applied but focused on service processes, organization and human resources. Bulc (2011) states that innovation entails creating an idea, putting it on the market and managing it sustainably. Adapted to tourism, a service rather than a product, this definition entails applying innovation to tourism-related processes, human resources and technology (Meneses and Teixeira, 2011).

The literature is generally in agreement about how innovation is captured in tourism, relating it to tourism services and service processes; tourism industry management (including human resources); marketing and diffusion; and the institutional component. With regard to information and communication technologies (ICT) and tourism, a high degree of innovation has been introduced by adopting ICT to tourism work methods, which has constituted the majority of ICT investments in tourism (Sancho and Maset, 1999). Innovation aims to adapt current services or products to demand. Tourism demand has evolved and is more specialized, and as such, destinations must innovate to attract new tourists, who are now accustomed to using ICT daily and who now seek new types of tourism and different experiences.

Destinations wish to attract tourists, and innovation is one tool for reaching that objective. In Spain, the hotels that attract the most tourists are the most innovative (Sundbo *et al.*, 2007), and their innovations aim to expand supply in the coastal areas beyond the sun and sand product. Innovation is linked to competitiveness in that innovation is necessary for maintaining competitiveness in an industry, and competitiveness is a requirement for maintaining or improving market standing. By innovating offerings, destinations can gain a competitive advantage, with the aim of achieving increased benefits and sustainable growth (Pavia *et al.*, 2011). Innovation also improves competitiveness by increasing productivity with higher-quality products (Sundbo *et al.*, 2007). Moreover, as Sancho and Maset (1999) observe, innovation affects productivity, which improves competitiveness.

According to Porter (1990), specialization entails spreading innovation, and referring to Sancho (2008), Spain's coastal provinces are the most specialized in tourism; so specialized destinations are more innovative, therefore more competitive. It is also necessary for destinations to innovate to maintain their competitive positions with respect to other destinations; as Buhalis (1998) observes in regard to emphasizing ICT use in tourism innovation: 'destinations must use ICT and innovative organization procedures to maintain their competitive positions'.

Innovation helps destinations to become more competitive and thus attract more tourists than other destinations. Victorino *et al.* (2005) note that innovation gives companies a competitive advantage and customers priority. Destinations attempt to attract and satisfy the demands of more sophisticated tourists who are looking for new experiences (Hu *et al.*, 2009). Service innovation at individual destinations, particularly in transport, has been important because it brings destinations closer to each other.

An effective method for improving on this chapter's key competitiveness factors is through innovation. Innovation, in the variables that generate competitiveness, acts as a mediator to increase the estimator and independent variable values. Innovation could entail using ICT for flights and cruises, making destinations more accessible, and thus more competitive because they then attract more tourists. Cultural innovation could entail improving information access, such as in smart cities; better managing facilities; improving environmental sustainability to increase tourist satisfaction with the destination; improving hotel human resource management or expanding on local inhabitants' education about the destination; and improving the marketing and promotion of travel, sport events and other cultural factors. In sum, it is possible to innovate on each variable to increase productivity and, consequently, competitiveness.

We want to emphasize that destinations that wish to be more competitive must innovate, whether it entails improving social, management, technology and/or service processes. Our investigation of destination competitiveness factors identifies the variables that could be improved through innovation – 'innovation is the research output' (Sancho, 2008) – and from our research, destination managers can identify where they need to innovate and use our model as a new tool for competing with other destinations.

2.5   Conclusions

Tourism plays a relevant role in economies, and thus it must be enhanced and developed through increased government investments. Tourism must take competitiveness into account to improve its activity; tourism destinations must know their strengths and weaknesses, maintaining their strengths and improving their weaknesses. Thereby, destinations will improve their competitiveness, maintaining or improving their competitive position. Destination managers need advice regarding competing with other destinations, and in this chapter we have been able to suggest some recommendations for improving competitiveness using the presented model's tourism indicators. These recommendations could be applied to all destinations; our suggestions could help managers in these destinations identify the tourism competitiveness factors in which they are lacking and which they need to improve to increase competitiveness.

The most significant component that we identified was Specialization, and managers in these destinations should work to improve specialization, through public policies aimed at increasing the participation of foreign tourist arrivals or through promoting a better quality–price ratio. Next most important was destination Services, and managers could offer a wider range of infrastructure, transport, cleaning and other services to increase tourists' comfort in these destinations. To increase tourists' satisfaction, managers should improve aspects such as the appearance of beaches, care for the environment and food quality, all of which could, in turn, improve tourists' Assessment of the destination. Cultural activities must be promoted at destinations, by building new museums, educating inhabitants about local culture and pursuing other cultural activities. Destinations can also expand on their leisure options, taking into account our indicators to improve areas such as commercial centres, theme parks, golf courses and other indicators that represent leisure. Weather, of course, cannot be controlled, so we can only hypothesize about its effectiveness, but managers can take into account weather conditions and provide products that supplement the sun and sand offerings.

In sum, managers could improve on the factors we outline in this chapter, both the selected indicators and other indicators that represent the same concepts, and in this way they can improve their destinations' competitiveness, achieving prosperity and improving inhabitants' well-being as a result.

With regard to innovation's contribution to tourism competitiveness, we would like to comment that innovation is a determinant of tourism's evolution and adaptation to demand. Innovation has allowed for ICT development, improved human capital and improved the distribution of tourism products. These innovations result in improved productivity in the fields in which they are applied, and as such, innovation is necessary for increasing destination competitiveness. Using the competitiveness factors we have identified, destination managers can determine the areas where they need to innovate to improve their competitiveness.

Competitiveness is a very complicated concept to define, and its application to tourism destinations is a broad research subject. We used the most influential theories to apply a robust model to Spain's Mediterranean destinations. Our linear regression results confirm the effectiveness of our tourism competitiveness model and demonstrate that the model is effective in the Spanish context. However, it is necessary to identify additional indicators to build a more complete model. Meanwhile, our current results provide managers with guidance on how to improve tourism destination competitiveness.

Acknowledgements

The authors are grateful to Dr Francina Orfila-Sintes of Balearics University for the materials provided at the innovation investigation.

References

Buhalis, D. (1998) Strategic use of information technology in the tourism industry. *Tourism Management* 19(5), 409–421.

Buhalis, D. (2000) Marketing the competitive destinations of the future. *Tourism Management* 21, 97–116.

Bulc, V. (2011) Innovation ecosystem and tourism. *Academia Turística, Tourism and Innovation Journal* 1, 27–34.

Craigwell, R. (2007) Tourism competitiveness in small island developing states. Research Paper 2007/19 United Nations University, World Institute for Development Economics Research, Helsinki, Finland.

Croes, R. (2010) Small island tourism competitiveness: expanding your destination's slice of paradise. Paper presented at the Dies Natalis of the University of the Netherlands Antilles, Curacao, 12 January 2010.

Croes, R. (2011) Measuring and explaining competitiveness in the context of small islands destinations. *Journal of Travel Research* 50(4), 421–442.

Crouch, G.I. (2011) Destination competitiveness: an analysis of determinant attributes. *Journal of Travel Research* 50(1), 27–45.

Crouch, G.I. and Ritchie, J.R.B. (1999) Tourism, competitiveness, and societal prosperity. *Journal of Business Research* 44, 137–152.

Dwyer, L. and Kim, C. (2003) Destination competitiveness: determinants and indicators. *Current Issues in Tourism* 6(5), 369–414.

Dwyer, L., Mellor, R., Livaic, Z., Edwards, D. and Kim, C. (2004) Attributes of destination competitiveness: a factor analysis. *Tourism Analysis* 9(1–2), 91–101.

Enright, M.J. and Newton, J. (2004) Tourism destination competitiveness: a quantitative approach. *Tourism Management* 25(6), 777–788.

European Commission (2000–2013) Annual Macro-Economic Database. Available at: http://ec.europa.eu/economy_finance/db_indicators/ameco/index_en.htm (accessed 25 July 2014).

García Sánchez, A. and Siles, L.D. (2014) Tourism destination competitiveness: the Spanish Mediterranean case. *Tourism Economics Fast Track*, doi:10.5367/te.2014.0405.

Gooroochurn, N. and Sugiyarto, G. (2005) Competitiveness indicators in the travel and tourism industry. *Tourism Economics* 11(1), 25–43.

Hassan, S. (2000) Determinants of market competitiveness in an environmentally sustainable tourism industry. *Journal of Travel Research* 38(3), 239–245.

Hu, M.M., Horng, J. and Sun, Y.C. (2009) Hospitality teams: knowledge sharing and service innovation performance. *Tourism Management* 30, 41–50.

Kozak, M. and Rimmington, M. (1999) Measuring tourist destination competitiveness: conceptual considerations and empirical findings. *International Journal of Hospitality Management* 18, 273–283.

Meneses, O. and Teixeira, A. (2011) The innovative behaviour of tourism firms. *Economics and Management Research Projects: An International Journal* 1(1), 25–35.

Mihalic, T. (2000) Environmental management of a tourist destination: a factor of tourism competitiveness. *Tourism Management* 21(1), 65–78.

National Statistics Institute (INE) (2000–2012) Tourism statistics. Available at: http://www.ine.es/en/inebmenu/mnu_hosteleria_en.htm (accessed 2 December 2012).

Pavia, N., Stipanovic, C. and Mrnjavac, E. (2011) Innovation of business culture with the aim of developing Croatian tourism-case study of Valamar hotels and resorts. *Academia Turística, Tourism and Innovation Journal* 1, 95–102.

Pavlyuk, D. (2010) *Regional Tourism Competition in the Baltic States: A Spatial Stochastic Frontier Approach.* MPRA Paper 25052, University Library of Munich, Germany.

Porter, M.E. (1980) *Competitive Strategy: Techniques for Analyzing Industry and Competitors.* Free Press, New York.

Porter, M.E. (1990) *The Competitive Advantage of Nations.* Free Press, New York.

Ritchie, J.R.B. and Crouch, G.I. (2003) *The Competitive Destination: A Sustainable Tourism Perspective.* CAB International, Wallingford, UK.

Sánchez-Rivero, M. (2006) Elaboración de un ranking de competitividad de los destinos turísticos españoles: un análisis provincial mediante modelos de estructura latente. *Revista de Análisis Turístico* 1(1), 4–22.

Sancho, P.A. (2008) Innovación tecnológica, competitividad y productividad: una aproximación al sector hostelería y restauración de la Comunidad Valenciana. *Revista de Ocio y Turismo* 1, 153–164.

Sancho, P.A. and Maset, L.A. (1999) Sector turístico e innovación: un análisis a través de patentes. In: *I congreso nacional turismo y tecnologías de la información y las comunicaciones: Nuevas tecnologías y calidad TURITEC99.* Diputación de Málaga, Centro de Ediciones de la Diputación de Málaga (CEDMA), Málaga, Spain, pp. 249–261.

Sundbo, J., Orfila-Sintes, F. and Sorensen, F. (2007) The innovative behaviour of tourism firms-comparative studies of Denmark and Spain. *Research Policy* 36(1), 88–106.

TourSpain (2012–2015) National and Integral Tourism Plan (2012–2015). Available at: http://www.tourspain.es/en-us/vde/paginas/pnit.aspx (accessed 4 October 2014).

Victorino, L., Verma, R., Plaschka, F. and Dev, C. (2005) Service innovation and customer choices in the hospitality industry. *Managing Service Quality* 15(6), 555–576.

World Data Bank (2012) International tourism, number of arrivals. Available at: http://data.worldbank.org/indicator/ST.INT.ARVL (accessed 10 May 2014).

World Economic Forum (WEF) (2011) The Travel and Tourism Competitiveness Report 2011. Available at: http://www.weforum.org/reports/travel-tourism-competitiveness-report-2011 (accessed 15 October 2014).

World Economic Forum (WEF) (2013) The Global Competitiveness Report 2013–2014. Available at: http://www.weforum.org/reports/global-competitiveness-report-2013-2014 (accessed 25 June 2014).

World Travel and Tourism Council (WTTC) (nd.) Travel and Tourism Total Contribution to GDP. Available from: http://www.wttc.org/focus/research-for-action/economic-data-search-tool/ (accessed 14 July 2014).

Zhang, J. and Jensen, C. (2007) Comparative advantage explaining tourism flows. *Annals of Tourism Research* 34(1), 223–243.

3 Destination Evaluation through the Prioritization of Competitiveness Pillars: The Case of Brazil

Jose Manoel Gândara[1]* and Adriana Fumi Chim-Miki[2]

[1]Federal University of Paraná, Curitiba, Brazil; [2]CAPES Foundation, Brasilia-DF, Brazil, and University of Las Palmas de Gran Canaria, Spain

3.1 Introduction

The competitiveness of tourism destinations has been analysed according to different measurement models in recent decades (Crouch and Ritchie, 1999; Dwyer and Kim, 2003; Heath, 2003; Enright and Newton, 2004; Gooroochurn and Sugiyarto, 2005; Mazanec *et al.*, 2007; Barbosa, 2008; Gomezelj and Mihalic, 2008; Hong, 2009; Gandara *et al.*, 2013). In general, the models' determinants cover the main attributes to success in the tourism industry. The differences between them are the indicators used to compose the aggregate index that determines the degree of competitive against other competitors.

Noteworthy is the growing interest of academics and global organizations in the topic of competitiveness, leading them to create competitiveness measurement methods. Some of these methods have been developed for very specific areas, countries or regions. Some countries in particular, through those managing the tourism industry, have created internal competitiveness indices.

This growing interest of governments indicates a public awareness of the importance of tourism to the economy of a nation. Furthermore, the specific interest in monitoring competitiveness may indicate an understanding of this construct according to its key concept, which is explained by researchers when they say that 'tourism competitiveness is the ability of a destination to attract potential tourists, offering a satisfying tourism experience more than its competitors, and thus improving the national wealth in an economic model that generates improvements for local people' (Dwyer *et al.*, 2000; Ritchie and Crouch, 2000, 2003; Dwyer and Kim, 2003; Heath, 2003; Hong, 2009).

---

*E-mail: jmggandara@yahoo.com.br

According to Oral (1986), the competitiveness of a specific industry is the result of the convergence of management practices, modes of organization within the country and the sources of competitive advantage in the industry. Therefore, it is essential for governments of every level to maintain a monitor of the competitiveness determinants of the tourism industry and then, based on this information, prioritize actions to develop the industry.

Valls *et al.* (2004) consider this strategy of significant importance in the tourism development process, because it supports the process. It gathers together all the agents and their values, so that, through a public–private platform, a foundation is built for cooperation among all services of the destination. Thus, a consensus on the process of sustainable development is mobilized. In this sense, our analysis was based on reports and studies that used strategic/participatory methodology, creating data that reflected the reality of tourism in the region and the views of the local community.

This chapter analyses the tourism competitiveness of Curitiba-PR, Brazil, through the level of efficiency and the prioritization of competitiveness determinants, according to data obtained from previous research, in which a methodology of the GUT matrix was applied. This matrix identified the level or gravity of the attributes (G), the urgency of action for the improvement of the attributes (U) and the future tendency of the attribute, if nothing was done to improve it (T). The GUT matrix was subsidized by a previous analysis of the strengths and weaknesses of the city on tourism and its infrastructure.

The determinants used in this analysis were based on the competitiveness model developed by the Ministry of Tourism of Brazil (MTur). The Brazilian model was presented to Barbosa (2008), and it has been developed specifically to analyse the Brazilian scenario and its policy of 65 destination inductors of tourism development. Thus, according to the MTur Monitor, tourism competitiveness has 13 pillars, which were the basis of this analysis, allowing a comparison of the results obtained with the overall result, and with the average of Brazilian cities.

The qualitative data obtained from the GUT matrix of Curitiba were transformed in a 5-point Likert scale to compare with the results of the national survey. The level of competitiveness of the national model is measured from 0 to 100 points shared in five levels. The data were obtained through a structured questionnaire applied in 2010 to tourism stakeholders in the city of Curitiba. For a tune-up of knowledge and a good understanding of each one of the competitiveness pillars, prior to the implementation of the survey, three meetings with the group that composed the sample were conducted, in a focus group methodology. These results might contribute to the development of Curitiba's tourism competitiveness, since they could help in the planning of strategic action against domestic competitors.

In a secondary objective, this chapter develops and validates a methodology for verifying the competitive status of a city in Brazil through the use of qualitative data, enabling its use as a source of quantitative comparison. In the Brazilian scenario, there are many cases of cities with applications of qualitative methodologies in tourism similar to the data used in this research. Thus, the validation of a methodology to use these qualitative data contributes towards a new analytical front in the Brazilian tourism industry.

3.2   Literature Review

The quantitative analysis of tourism competitiveness using models in order to express this construct began to gain more attention after the Calgary model was presented by Crouch and Ritchie (1999). These two authors developed a conceptual model to analyse tourism competitiveness based on Porter's Diamond Model (Porter, 1980). In sequence, virtually all models that emerged had a conceptual basis in these two theories: Porter (1980) and Crouch and Ritchie (1999). However, despite a similar theoretical basis, various calculation methodologies and analyses have been presented in the scientific literature (Medina-Muñoz *et al.*, 2013).

Over the years, studies have shown maturity. They start on a purely economic basis, typical of the 1980s, to include new determinants, such as those related to sustainable development and quality of life, topics strongly present in the 1990s and the beginning of the 2000s. However, seeking to regain the convenience of calculations, the past few years have been focused on concepts of sustainable economy. The tourism competitiveness models presented by international agencies have adjusted the competitiveness pillars to encompass the multidimensionality of the concept, but with appropriate indicators to measure in tourism destinations (see the Global Competitiveness Index of the World Economic Forum).

The World Economic Forum (WEF) measures tourism competitiveness through a composite index of 14 determinants (the Travel and Tourism Competitiveness Index – TTCI), which are called the pillars of competitiveness, namely: (i) policy rules and regulations; (ii) environmental sustainability; (iii) safety and security; (iv) health and hygiene; (v) prioritization of travel and tourism; (vi) air transport infrastructure; (vii) ground transport infrastructure; (viii) tourism infrastructure; (ix) information and communications technology (ICT) infrastructure; (x) price competitiveness in the travel and tourism (T&T) industry; (xi) human resources; (xii) affinity for travel and tourism; (xiii) natural resources; and (xiv) cultural resources (Blanke and Chiesa, 2013).

Despite the fact that the methodology of the TTCI is criticized by many in the scientific community, it is one of the most used indexes in the management of countries, especially when they are looking for international competitiveness. Its easy access to comparative data across countries allows strategic decisions to be subsidized, and analyses the industry in terms of the macro economy, as well as analysing international competitors.

In the latest versions of the TTCI, competitiveness has been defined with a more economic focus than a social focus; despite this, the WEF highlights tourism as an industry that contributes to the minimization of social differences and is capable of generating a bottom-up development. In particular, in 2011, the annual WEF report defined competitiveness as a set of institutions, policies and factors that determined the productivity level of a country (WEF Report, 2013). It is, therefore, based on Porter (1980), who considers productivity to be very important to a country because it can establish the level of economic prosperity that can be attained by a nation.

In Porter's theories (1980), the success of a particular industry is explained by the theory of competitive advantage. So, the tourism industry monitors attributes and adds to them strategic management, innovation and other elements in an attempt to change comparative advantages to competitive advantages. According to Gandara *et al.* (2013), competitiveness should be seen as a process where differentiation of management is a factor of paramount importance. Several authors have suggested ways to transform a comparative advantage. For example, Go and Govers (2000) researched price as a competitiveness pillar. They defined that integrated quality management of a destination, together with promotions based on price, were a source of competitiveness. The World Tourism Organization (UNWTO) reinforces this idea, stating that a destination must be based on its competitive advantages, but it recognizes that, strategically, some comparative advantages can become competitive advantages (Eurostat *et al.*, 2001).

According to Rivero and Caldera (2004), a destination that convinces its citizens of the possibility of exploring its resources, where they understand their strengths and weaknesses, as well as developing an adequate marketing policy, can become more competitive than other destinations that still need to understand the role tourism plays in both economic and social development.

In this direction, many cities include social participation in their strategic planning and in public policy development. Hall (2001) recognizes that an important characteristic of planning is guidance for the future. That is, the planner must develop an action plan for tourism development with the goal of increasing features that make the destination and tourism product more attractive in the eyes of the consumer market in the medium and long term. Therefore, it is essential to define the successful determinants of the tourism industry and to monitor them.

Moreover, the prioritization of actions depends on the degree of urgency defined by the weight of importance versus the performance of the indicator established. Competitiveness analysis is based on two lines: the performance and the degree of importance of the indicator to destination competitiveness. This could be considered for the offer side, because it was executed based on the stakeholders, but with the effective participation of those directly interested in the success of the industry, and therefore more susceptible to the success of the strategic plans for improvement (Gandara *et al.*, 2013).

These models and theories, together with researchers' publications in similar methodologies, have guided the development of monitors in several countries, including Brazil. Following the global trend, in 2008, Barbosa introduced a tourism competitiveness monitor in Brazil. It was called the Model of Competitiveness of Tourism Destinations Inductors. The authors based their work on other studies, especially those of Dwyer and Kim (2003) and Ritchie and Crouch (2003), and some of Porter's (1980) theories.

Basically, the Brazilian model was similar to a TTCI of WEF, but it was adapted to Brazilian development policies, which used regionalization to induce tourism. The model has 13 pillars or determinants: (i) general infrastructure; (ii) accessibility; (iii) equipment and tourism services; (iv) tourism attractions; (v) marketing of the destination; (vi) public policy; (vii) regional cooperation; (viii) monitoring; (ix) local economy; (x) business capacity; (xi) social aspects; (xii) environmental aspects; and (xiii) cultural aspects (Barbosa, 2008).

The Brazilian policy declared 65 municipalities as inductor destinations of regional tourism development. These are cities that possess the basic core infrastructure and qualified tourism attractions and also receive and distribute tourism flows.

Therefore, political actions, analysis, monitoring and the development of federal plans focus on these destinations (Program of Regionalization of Tourism in Brazil, MTur, 2013).

3.3 Methodology

The empirical work was conducted in the city of Curitiba, in southern Brazil. Curitiba is the capital of the State of Paraná, with about 1,800,000 inhabitants, making it the eighth largest city in Brazil. Considered a model of urban planning and quality of life, it is one of the most influential cities in Brazil.

Curitiba is classified as an urban destination, and in 2010 received 3,410,219 visitors, with an average daily spend of US$91.15/day. The city has distinct infrastructure, and its historical and cultural formation is marked by the presence of various ethnic groups that influence the urban landscape, making it attractive (Horodyski et al., 2013).

Governments have attempted to overcome the restrictions of conventional planning, aiming to promote a more visionary city plan. The emergence of a strategic, participatory and specific plan reflects these changes in city planning, considering them as important tools to fuel the economic competitiveness of tourism destinations (Wu and Zhang, 2007).

This study used the data from an empirical work conducted by the Ministry of Tourism of Brazil in 2010. The aim was to subsidize the tourism competitiveness study conducted annually by this institution, so the work was divided into two phases: (i) developing a focus group with enough knowledge to understand the pillars of competitiveness and to analyse the strengths/weaknesses of Curitiba for tourism development; and (ii) to apply the GUT matrix GUT (gravity–urgency–trend). In addition, the methodology was carried out in the following stages:

- We conducted theoretical research on models of general competitiveness in the tourism industry, and on the current status of theories of tourism competitiveness.
- We analysed the data of the final report of the focus group called the 'Technical Group of Competitiveness Curitiba' and we analysed a GUT matrix applied to this group.
- We extracted the score imputed to 'gravity' in the GUT matrix for each pillar of competitiveness and we converted it in a 5-point Likert scale.
- We compared the weights of each pillar imputed by the focus group with the weights of each pillar of competitiveness present in the report published by the MTur.
- We verified the degree of importance of each pillar, based on the GUT analysis, to define the order of priority action for public–private actions in the tourism industry of the city of Curitiba.

Coordination of this work was provided by the Brazilian Ministry of Tourism (MTur). The sample of participants was not random; it followed an election process by rational selection. In this way, the participants invited to the focus group were chosen by direct actions in the local tourism industry, as entrepreneurs, leaders and participants of institutes linked with tourism researches, researchers from local universities and agencies of entrepreneurship. According to the records of the first meeting of the Technical Group of Competitiveness Curitiba (MTur, 2010), the real sample of experts (technical group/focal) consisted of 19 participants.

The participants were: four representatives of the Municipal Institute of Tourism (one Coordinator of CTUR and three employees of this public agency); two representatives of the Regional Governance in Tourism (two persons of the metropolitan forum of tourism); one representative of the core of receptive tour operators; two representatives of ABGTUR (participants of the Brazilian Association of Tour Guides); one representative of the Union of Tourism Industry of the State of Paraná, Curitiba; two representatives of the Convention and Visitors Bureau; two representatives of the state Paraná Secretary of Tourism; one representative of the Entertainment Association; one representative of SEBRAE-PR (Brazilian Support Service for SMEs); and one representative of ABOTTC (Brazilian Association of Tourism and Cultural Trains).

The first meeting was held on 13 August 2010, when the participants were informed of the objectives of the focus group, entitled 'Technical Group Competitiveness Curitiba', and of the methodology used for this work. With a goal to develop technical knowledge on the tourism industry in Curitiba at both the national and international level, and to deepen understanding of the concepts and indicators of tourism competitiveness among all participants, the meetings included studies of the following documents/reports:

- General Tourism Law.
- National Tourism Plan.
- Tourism Development Plan of Paraná.
- Strategic Plan for Development of Regional Tourism (2008–2011).
- Marketing Plan of the State of Paraná.
- Contract Management – Tourism Program of the Municipal Tourism Institute.
- Study of Competitiveness of the 65 Municipalities Inductors of Tourism Development by the MTur.

In the following group meetings, the MTur Monitor's 13 dimensions of tourism competitiveness were analysed, considering the strengths and weaknesses of the 62 variables used in this monitor for Curitiba city. This analysis was the basis for the focus group to run a GUT matrix.

3.4   Results

The first findings were to prioritize the list of variables that comprised the Brazilian Competitiveness Monitor, because the methodology of this governmental monitor did not present importance weights for each competitive pillar. The result of the analysis performed by the focus group through the GUT matrix is presented in Table 3.1.

Table 3.1 shows that the focus group considered some good competitiveness dimensions, namely: 'infrastructure' (capacity to treat tourists medically; power supply; tourist protection service and urban structure in tourism areas), 'services and tourism facilities' (qualification structure for tourism; capacity of restaurants). This assessment confirms the concept of Curitiba as being a model city in terms of differentiated infrastructure, a situation that is true in Brazil.

Table 3.1. GUT matrix – competitiveness study of the city inductor of tourism. (Organized by the authors, from reports of the Technical Group on Competitiveness of Curitiba, MTur, 2010.)

Dimension/variable	Gravity	Urgency	Tendency	Priority	Prioritization	Results
Infrastructure				**15.25**		
Capacity of medical service for tourists	1	1	1	1	3rd	Minimum priority
Power supply	1	1	1	1	3rd	Minimum priority
Tourist protection service	3	3	3	27	2nd	Low priority
Urban structure in tourism areas	2	4	4	32	1st	Low priority
Services and equipment				**26.57**		
Tourism signs	1	2	3	6	7th	Minimum priority
Attendance centre for tourists	2	3	3	18	2nd	Minimum priority
Venues for events	4	5	5	100	1st	High priority
Capacity hosting	2	3	3	18	2nd	Minimum priority
Receptive tourism capacity	2	3	3	18	2nd	Minimum priority
Qualification structure for tourism	2	3	3	18	2nd	Minimum priority
Capacity of restaurants	2	2	2	8	6th	Minimum priority
Access				**42.50**		
Air access	4	5	5	100	1st	High priority
Access by roads	4	4	4	64	2nd	Medium priority
Transport system in the destination	1	2	2	4	3rd	Minimum priority
Proximity to a large tourist centre	1	1	2	2	4th	Minimum priority
Tourism attractions				**10.00**		
Natural attractions	1	1	2	2	3rd	Minimum priority
Cultural attractions	2	3	3	18	1st	Minimum priority
Organized events	2	3	3	18	1st	Minimum priority

Continued

Table 3.1. Continued.

Dimension/variable	Gravity	Urgency	Tendency	Priority	Prioritization	Results
Technical scientific events or artistic events	1	1	2	2	3rd	Minimum priority
Marketing and promotion of tourism				**68.75**		
Marketing plan	4	5	5	100	1st	High priority
Participation in fairs and events	3	4	4	48	3rd	Low priority
Promotion of the destination	3	3	3	27	4th	Low priority
Destination has a website on the Internet	4	5	5	100	1st	High priority
Public policy				**43.40**		
Municipal support structure for tourists	2	3	3	18	4th	Minimum priority
Degree of cooperation with the state government	3	3	3	27	3rd	Low priority
Degree of cooperation with the federal government	2	3	2	12	5th	Minimum priority
Planning for the city and tourism	4	5	4	80	1st	High priority
Degree of public–private cooperation	4	5	4	80	1st	High priority
Regional cooperation				**42.40**		
Governance	3	4	4	48	3rd	Low priority
Projects of regional cooperation	4	4	4	64	1st	Medium priority
Planning of regional tourism	2	3	3	18	4th	Minimum priority
Development of tourism itineraries	2	3	3	18	4th	Minimum priority
Promotion and integrated marketing support	4	4	4	64	1st	Medium priority
Monitoring				**61.80**		
Research of demand	2	2	2	8	5th	Minimum priority

Continued

Table 3.1. Continued.

Dimension/variable	Gravity	Urgency	Tendency	Priority	Prioritization	Results
Research of offer	3	4	4	48	3rd	Low priority
System of statistics of tourism	4	5	4	80	2nd	High priority
Measuring tourism impacts	5	5	5	125	1st	Very high priority
Specific sector to research and studies	3	4	4	48	3rd	Low priority
Local economy				**12.00**		
Aspects of local economy	1	1	1	1	4th	Minimum priority
Communication infrastructure	2	3	3	18	2nd	Minimum priority
Infrastructure and business facilities	1	1	2	2	3rd	Minimum priority
Entrepreneurship or events to leverage tourism	3	3	3	27	1st	Low priority
Entrepreneurship				**2.75**		
Capacity of qualification and use of local staff	2	2	2	8	1st	Minimum priority
Presence of national or international groups in the tourism industry	1	1	1	1	2nd	Minimum priority
Competition and barrier to entry	1	1	1	1	2nd	Minimum priority
Presence of large companies, subsidiaries or branches	1	1	1	1	2nd	Minimum priority
Social aspects				**5.00**		
Access to education	1	1	1	1	3rd	Minimum priority
Jobs generated by tourism	2	2	1	4	2nd	Minimum priority
Policy to contain child sexual exploitation	1	1	1	1	3rd	Minimum priority
Use of attractions and tourism facilities by the population	1	1	1	1	3rd	Minimum priority

Continued

Table 3.1. Continued.

Dimension/variable	Gravity	Urgency	Tendency	Priority	Prioritization	Results
Citizenship, awareness and participation in tourism	2	3	3	18	1st	Minimum priority
Environmental aspects				**10.00**		
Structure and municipal environmental legislation	1	1	1	1	3rd	Minimum priority
Potentially polluting activities	2	2	2	8	2nd	Minimum priority
Public water supply network	1	1	1	1	3rd	Minimum priority
Public network for sewage treatment	1	1	1	1	3rd	Minimum priority
Destination of waste	3	4	4	48	1st	Low priority
Conservation units in the municipal territory	1	1	1	1	3rd	Minimum priority
Cultural aspects				**8.33**		
Cultural production associated with tourism	2	3	1	6	2nd	Minimum priority
Cultural heritage	2	3	3	18	1st	Minimum priority
Municipal structure to support culture	1	1	1	1	3rd	Minimum priority

The results are compatible with the Brazilian government policy that seeks to develop meeting tourism. 'Services and tourist facilities' was assessed as low priority, although the evaluation of urgency and tendency had medium priority. The group especially considered the maintenance variables of the ability to receive tourists in terms of the capacity/quality of accommodation and the conditions of receptive tourism. This assessment is compatible with the MTur data because Curitiba is one of the Brazilian cities with the best offer of hotels, but the group considered the lack of event spaces.

In turn, the dimension 'access' presented variations according to the mode of transport or according to the internal/external transport into the destination. The group recognized that the city needed better external connections, while internal transport in the destination performed well. On the other hand, the dimension 'tourism attractions' presented good efficiency in the GUT matrix.

The dimension 'marketing and tourism promotion' in the focus group analysis was assessed as high priority, because the group did not consider it efficient enough. Another dimension considered of high priority was 'public policy'.

The dimension 'regional cooperation' represents the capacity for public–private cooperation and for governance. This variable presented good performance. Meanwhile, the dimension 'monitoring' was one of the highest in the scale of priority, because there was no proper monitoring of the tourism industry, and especially of the environmental impacts of tourism.

The dimensions 'local economy' and 'entrepreneurship' presented a local efficiency of entrepreneurs and businesses, and was thus assessed as low priority. The dimensions 'social aspects', 'cultural aspects' and 'environmental aspects' were also considered low priority in the GUT matrix, indicating that they already had good efficiency.

According to the results, prioritization was focused more on variables related to destination management because the majority of other variables were considered to be performing well (see Fig. 3.1).

The use of the GUT methodology helped the group of experts to determine the future direction in terms of competitiveness pillars, considered by Hall (2001) to be an important feature of planning. It was observed that the variables related to resources had been evaluated efficiently. These variables form the basis of tourism development, as highlighted by many competitiveness authors (Crouch and Ritchie, 1999; Mihalič, 2000; Dwyer and Kim, 2003; Ritchie and Crouch, 2003; Enright and Newton, 2004). Meanwhile, the variables related to destination management presented low performance, according to the focal group. This other set of variables has the capacity to act on the comparative advantages and transform them to competitive advantages (Porter, 1980); thus, they can generate an improvement in competitiveness.

The second finding obtained from the GUT matrix conducted by the technical group was the level of competitiveness of the destination according to the view of

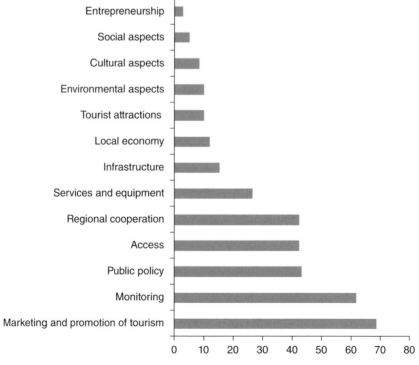

Fig. 3.1. Summarization of the GUT matrix – the prioritization level of the 13 competitiveness dimensions. (From authors' own elaboration.)

these experts. The competitiveness levels of the city of Curitiba were analysed considering the efficiency and potential evaluated by the focus group for each pillar (competitiveness determinant).

The 13 competitiveness pillars of the MTur were the elements of the GUT matrix and the variables, were the indicators to measure them (attributes). The MTur used a scale of 0–100 points split into five levels. Each level has a range of 20 points. We carried out a conversion of scales to provide a comparison; hence, the score attributed to the 'gravity' in the GUT matrix was considered by the focus group evaluating the competitive positioning of the pillars. This represented the level of performance in each attribute. It is important to note that the scales in the GUT matrix are used upside down. When an attribute is considered 'without gravity', the score is 1; thus, it is a very competitive attribute, corresponding to level 5 in the competitiveness score. This reversal was: without gravity (1) = extremely competitive (5); low gravity (2) = competitive (4); gravity (3) = medium competitiveness (3); high gravity (4) = low competitiveness (4); extreme gravity (5) = no competitiveness (1).

Table 3.2 presents the comparison between the evaluation by the focus group methodology and by the Monitor of the Tourism Ministry for each competitiveness pillar. The data used in this comparison are based on the Monitor competitiveness published in 2010 (FGV, MTUR, SEBRAE, 2010).

By comparing the degrees of prioritization presented in Table 3.2, we observed that the degree of importance for prioritizing actions, granted by the focus group, did not coincide fully with the competitive position of the dimension in the MTur data. The first and last dimension in terms of priority for competitiveness demonstrated a similar logical behaviour in both analyses. Lower competitiveness is associated with a higher priority for the improvement action. Thus, 'marketing and promotion of tourism' was considered the highest priority for Curitiba in this analysis, and coincided with the analysis of this dimension by the MTur, where the dimension occupies the 10th position between the 13 competitiveness indicators for Curitiba in 2010. 'Entrepreneurship capacity' stayed in the last position (13th) in the list of priorities of the focus group, coinciding with the MTur. Thus, this pillar occupied the first place in the indicators of competitiveness. However, the other dimensions have variations in this comparison.

On the other hand, when we reversed the scales of the focus group's levels of priority, where higher priority was less competition, we also applied a level considering the weight presented in the MTur index; because this scale was 0–100, we turned it into a Likert scale of 1–5. Then, differences can be seen in Fig. 3.2. The analysis by the focus group was more critical in five dimensions than the MTur analysis. The dimensions 'marketing and promotion of tourism', 'monitoring', 'public policy', 'access' and 'infrastructure' were considered less competitive in the evaluation by focal group than in the MTur evaluation.

To the contrary, in other dimensions the analysis by the MTur was more critical than the analysis by the focus group. In this way, 'services and tourism equipment', 'local economy', 'tourism attractions', 'environmental aspects', 'cultural aspects', 'social aspects' and 'entrepreneurship capacity' were considered more competitive by the focus group than when analysed by the MTur. The dimension 'regional cooperation' was valued the same by both.

It is noted that the city has a differentiation of resources and urban infrastructure, being well articulated in terms of regional cooperation for the development of tourism, although management still needs more contributions.

Table 3.2. Evaluation of the competitiveness pillars by the focus group. (From authors' own elaboration.)

Dimension	Gut index by focal group		MTur index of competitiveness		Variation	
	Priorization level	Reverse of scale (competitiveness index)	MTur score	MTur level	Level	Per cent
Marketing and promotion of tourism	3.50 (1)	2.5	59.4	3.0 (10)	−0.5	−16.7
Monitoring	3.40 (2)	2.6	54.3	2.7 (13)	−0.1	−3.7
Public policy	3.00 (3)	3	64.7	3.3 (9)	−0.3	−9.1
Access	2.50 (4)	3.5	77.5	3.9 (6)	−0.4	−10.3
Regional cooperation	3.00 (5)	3	58.6	3.0 (11)	0	0
Services and tourism equipment	2.14 (6)	3.9	67.6	3.4 (8)	0.5	14.7
Infrastructure	1.75 (7)	4.2	84.6	4.3 (3)	−0.1	−2.3
Local economy	1.75 (8)	4.2	80.9	4.1 (4)	0.1	2.4
Tourism attractions	1.50 (9)	4.5	72.9	3.7 (7)	0.8	21.6
Environmental aspects	1.50 (10)	4.5	86.1	4.3 (2)	0.2	4.7
Cultural aspects	1.67 (11)	4.3	57.7	2.9 (12)	1.4	48.3
Social aspects	1.40 (12)	4.6	80.0	4.0 (5)	0.6	15.0
Entrepreneurship capacity	1.25 (13)	4.7	90.0	4.5 (1)	0.2	4.4

3.5 Conclusion

One of the features of competitiveness studies is the comparison with other destinations, because competitiveness is a relative variable (Porter, 1980; Crouch and Ritchie, 1999; Ritchie and Crouch, 2003). The focus group considered Curitiba more competitive than the average presented by every capital city of all 26 States of Brazil, and more competitive than the global index of Brazil. This is coherent with the MTur analysis, because the MTur considers Curitiba to be better positioned in the scenario of Brazilian tourism. Practically, all dimensions of Curitiba are above the average of Brazilian capitals, and it is also above the country index. The only exception was the public policy dimension, which presented a slight drop compared with the average capitals, although it was above the country rate.

Tourism destination systems are difficult to manage. Management and promotion represent a great challenge due to the complex relationships among stakeholders and the variety of actors involved in the development and production of tourism products (Sautter and Leisen, 1999; Buhalis, 2000). In this sense, the merger of all stakeholders

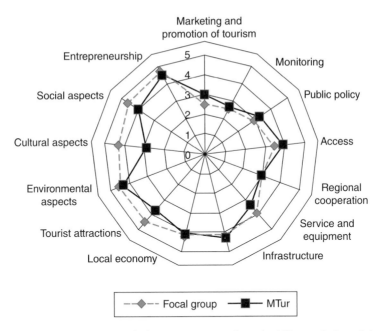

Fig. 3.2. Comparison of the level of competitiveness from the MTur analysis and the focal group analysis. (From authors' own elaboration.)

to develop strategic planning, like participatory planning, is essential to ensure the positioning, development and competitiveness of sustainable destinations (Gandara *et al.*, 2013). The work developed in the focus group to improve their knowledge on competitiveness, followed by an examination of the determinants of tourism competitiveness performed by them, represents a participatory and strategic way based on deep analysis of this thematic. The working knowledge of the focus group participants enriched the theoretical analysis, permeating it with realistic empiricism.

The analysis presented in this article has been developed from the work of a select group that acts directly on the local tourism industry, named the Technical Group of Curitiba Competitiveness. This process was part of a pilot work of the MTur to subsidize competitiveness studies in Brazil. The group was subjected to a series of conferences on competitiveness to improve the level of knowledge and its evaluation capacity. Therefore, the focus group methodology has been applied. From the strengths and weaknesses identified, considering 62 attributes of tourism competitiveness grouped in 13 pillars, the group evaluated competitiveness according to gravity (G), urgency of action to improve the attribute (U) and the future tendency of the attribute should nothing occur (T).

In simple logic, you can consider that the low competitive position of a pillar should correspond to the highest priority of action for effective improvement. However, the focus group, for its expertise in this economic sector, has applied different weights, generating a priority list of attributes that differ from the national competitive index. This was one of the most important findings of this study, because the MTur methodology does not define the degree of importance of each pillar, which makes management decisions very complicated. The managers need to know where to apply their efforts in the first place, especially because cities have limited resources and need to maximize them. The analysis matches a national reality, in which Curitiba really has a distinct urban infrastructure.

The analysis through the focus group has permitted a better and greater depth of understanding of the variables that represent each pillar of tourism competitiveness. The focus group's analysis has permitted a better and greater depth of understanding of the variables that represent each pillar of tourism competitiveness. The difference in the 'cultural aspects' pillar was as expected, because the group considered the cultural production associated with tourism to be good, and they also considered the municipality's public policies for culture to be appropriate. 'Tourist attractions' also presented a big difference between the assessments of the focus group and those of the MTur, possibly because the group knew the attractions and local events in depth. In this sample, the vast majority of the participants act as event organizers or are workers in institutions related with events. Similarly, the local knowledge of the focus group reality was reflected in the evaluation of the 'social aspects' and 'services and tourism facilities' pillars, which showed a better rating. On the other hand, the group considered negatively the pillars related to destination management, such as marketing, promotion, public policies and monitoring.

Overall, this work has contributed in two ways: it has developed a specific knowledge in the stakeholders, and this has contributed towards a better understanding of the tourism industry, so the results generated information that enabled the prioritization of management actions. This research validated a methodology to understand the data available from the MTur, and also developed a simple methodology to apply to cities. Its contribution can help to subsidize the decisions of public–private investors in the tourism industry. We recommend similar studies in other Brazilian cities, and also a nationwide standardization of the scales to measure competitiveness, as well its determinants. The limitation of this study was considered to be the number of participants in the focus group sample, despite the fact that the considerable knowledge between them minimized the margin of error.

Acknowledgements

This material is based on work supported by the Tourism Minister of Brazil and by the scholarship for Student PhDs, the CAPES Foundation, Ministry of Education of Brazil, Brasilia, DF.

References

Barbosa, L.G.M. (2008) *Estudo de competitividade dos 65 Destinos indutores do desenvolvimento turístico regional.* Relatório Brasil, Ministério do Turismo, Brasília.
Blanke, J. and Chiesa, T. (eds) (2013) The Travel & Tourism Competitiveness Report 2013. World Economic Forum within the framework of The Global Competitiveness and Benchmarking Network and the Industry Partnership Programme for Aviation, Travel & Tourism, Geneva, Switzerland, 478 pp.
Buhalis, D. (2000) Marketing the competitive destination of the future. *Tourism Research* 21(1), 97–116.
Crouch, G.I. and Ritchie, J.B. (1999) Tourism, competitiveness, and societal prosperity. *Journal of Business Research* 44(3), 137–152.
Dwyer, L. and Kim, C. (2003) Destination competitiveness: determinants and indicators. *Current Issues in Tourism* 6(5), 369–414.

Dwyer, L., Forsyth, P. and Rao, P. (2000) The price competitiveness of travel and tourism: a comparison of 19 destinations. *Tourism Management* 21(1), 9–22.

Enright, M.J. and Newton, J. (2004) Tourism destination competitiveness: a quantitative approach. *Tourism Management* 25(6), 777–788.

Eurostat, OECD, UN and UNWTO (2001) *Tourism Satellite Account: Recommended Methodological Framework*. Eurostat, OECD, UN and UNWTO, Madrid.

FGV, MTUR, SEBRAE (2010) Relatório Brasil: estudo de competitividade dos 65 destinos indutores do desenvolvimento turístico regional. MTur, Brasília.

Gandara, J.M., Chim-Miki, A.F., Domareski, T.C. and Biz, A.A. (2013) La Competitividad Turística de Foz do Iguaçu según los determinantes del 'Integrative Model' de Dwyer & Kim: analizando la estrategia de Construcción del Futuro. *Cuadernos de Turismo* 31, 105–128.

Go, F.M. and Govers, R. (2000) Integrated quality management for tourist destinations: a European perspective on achieving competitiveness. *Tourism Management* 21(1), 79–88.

Gomezelj, O.D. and Mihalic, T. (2008) Destination competitiveness – applying different models: the case of Slovenia. *Tourism Management* 29(2), 294–307.

Gooroochurn, N. and Sugiyarto, G. (2005) Competitiveness indicators in the travel and tourism industry. *Tourism Economics* 11(1), 25–43.

Hall, C.M. (2001) *Planejamento Turístico: políticas, processos e planejamentos*. Contexto, São Paulo.

Heath, E. (2003) Towards a model to enhance destination competitiveness: a South Africa perspective. *Journal of Hospitality and Tourism Management* 10(2), 124–141.

Hong, W.C. (2009) Global competitiveness measurement for the tourism sector. *Current Issues in Tourism* 12(2), 105–132.

Horodyski, G.S., Manosso, F.C. and Gândara, J.M. (2013) Conceitos e Abrangência do Souvenir na Dinâmica do Espaço Turístico: O Caso de Curitiba-PR. *Revista Turismo Visão e Ação* 15(1), 130–143.

Mazanec, J.A., Wöber, K. and Zins, A.H. (2007) Tourism destination competitiveness: from definition to explanation? *Journal of Travel Research* 46(1), 86–95.

Medina-Muñoz, D.R., Medina-Muñoz, R.D. and Chim-Miki, A.F. (2013) Tourism competitiveness assessment: the current status of research in Spain and China. *Tourism Economics* 19(2), 297–318.

Mihalič, T. (2000) Environmental management of a tourist destination: a factor of tourism competitiveness. *Tourism Management* 21(1), 65–78.

Ministério do Turismo (MTur) (2010) Ministério do Turismo. Disponível em. Available at: http://www.turismo.gov.br/turismo/home.html (accessed 10 April 2012).

MTur (2013) *Programa de Regionalização do Turismo – Diretrizes*. Brasília.

Oral, M. (1986) An industrial competitiveness model. *IIE Transactions* 18(2), 148–157.

Porter, M.E. (1980) *Competitive Strategy: Techniques for Analyzing Industry and Competitors*. The Free Press, New York.

Ritchie, J.R.B. and Crouch, G.I. (2000) The competitive destination: a sustainability perspective. *Tourism Management* 21(1), 1–7.

Ritchie, J.R.B. and Crouch, G.I. (2003) *The Competitive Destination: A Sustainable Tourism Perspective*. CAB International, Wallingford, UK.

Rivero, M.S. and Caldera, M.A.F. (2004) La Competitividad de los Destinos Turísticos: un Análisis Cuantitativo Mediante Modelos Logísticos. Aplicación a los Municipios Extremeños. I Jornadas de Economía del Turismo. Palma de Mallorca, Spain.

Sautter, E.T. and Leisen, B. (1999) Managing stakeholders a tourism planning model. *Annals of Tourism Research* 26(2), 312–328.

Valls, J.F., Bustamante, X., Guzmán, F. and Vila, M. (2004) *Gestión de destinos turísticos sostenibles*. Gestión 2000, Barcelona.

WEF (2013) The Global Competitiveness Report 2012–2013. World Economic Forum, Geneva, Switzerland.

World Travel and Tourism Council (nd.) World Travel and Tourism Council Annual Index 1990–2011. Available at: http://www.wttc.org/datagateway/ (accessed 20 July 2012).

Wu, F. and Zhang, J. (2007) Planning the competitive city-region – the emergence of strategic development plan in China. *Urban Affairs Review* 42(5), 714–740.

4 Creativity and City Tourism Repositioning: The Case of Valencia, Spain

José María Nácher Escriche* and Paula Simó Tomás

University of Valencia, Valencia, Spain

4.1 Introduction

Creative activities are important regional facilitators. The urban interaction of the professionals of art, communication, universities, science and R&D leads to an increase in productivity, quality of life and competitiveness. These creative clusters attract other creative professionals, generating leisure or professional visits, which in turn may generate the decision to reside in the visited destination. Urban positioning strategies show a growing interest in the creation or attraction of creative activities. This paper reviews the creativity and tourism literature, proposes a research method to detect creative flows and makes a first approach to the case of Valencia, Spain, a city with a long history of creativity and with a present that can make it a remarkable European creative destination.

4.2 Creative Industries and Cities

In a broader definition, creative industries include not only art, theatre and music, the publishing, audio-visual and video game industries, architecture and urban consulting, design and fashion, communication and marketing, but also science, universities, engineering, R&D and entrepreneurship, areas in which there is more method and planning and to which the concept of *innovation* is frequently applied. Generally speaking, these are intensive activities in knowledge, expertise and technology and they provide services to the final consumer experience. The theory that creativity-fostering cities are more competitive and politically stable has attracted extraordinary academic and institutional attention, including the existence of an EU strategy on this matter (Santagata, 2009; EU, 2010; UNCTAD, 2011; Florida, 2012; UNESCO, 2013).

*E-mail: jose.m.nacher@uv.es

It is assumed that the presence of clusters or concentration of creative inhabitants promotes more productive habitats and cities and a higher quality of life (Rindermann *et al.*, 2009; Lazzeretti *et al.*, 2012). Creative people have a higher education and obtain better qualifications and are often liberal and independent professionals, with self-governed rhythms and styles of life open to innovation, experimentation and interaction with urban areas (Florida, 2012). These people are the creative class or behave as *culturpreneurs* (Lange *et al.*, 2008; Florida, 2012). The relationship between educational level and GDP is well known and evidences externalities derived from human capital. People are more productive if they work with other educated people around them (Glaeser, 2011). As highly qualified people with middle and high incomes and a high degree of freedom, creative professionals have a greater mobility in both the performance of their professional activity and their leisure activities and private life.

There is a relationship between cities and territories that provide a culturally tolerant atmosphere towards unconventional people, such as gay people, 'bohemian' artists and musicians and the number of professionals belonging to the creative class who work, live or transit through the territory (Zukin, 1995; Florida, 2005). These high degrees of individualism and freedom involve a high participation in unconventional and experimental activities. We can speak of 'street cultural level' to define the attraction to creative people: at street-side cafes, buskers, nightlife galleries and bars, urban cycle routes, green zones, level of outdoor sports practice, etc. These are activities in which it is difficult to draw the line between participant and observer or between creator and creativity (Florida, 2012).

The conditions conducive to creative practice are linked to the configuration of urban public space – streets, squares and parks – and the commercial and leisure framework (UNHabitat, 2013). These containers are drivers of the named diversity and are capable of it, the breeding ground of creativity (Jacobs, 1973; Harvey, 2012). Creative classes emerge, consolidate and are also attracted by the vibrant quarters where public space encourages multiple uses and vitality throughout the day. People of different ages are stimulated by small blocks with access to stroll, which has a positive effect on the diversity of the commercial offer. These frames and networks arise in small-sized premises and are more favourable to the diversity of encounters, exchanges and complementary relationships between residents and visitors (Jacobs, 1973).

Evidence points to the historical or consolidated city – inner city – as the favourite area for professional activity and/or entertainment of creative professionals. More particularly, facilities for professional or leisure meetings are often located in older urban areas (Jacobs, 1973; Florida, 2005).

4.3   Tourism and Creative Cities

In this context, what can be called creative tourism? Early conceptualizations of creative tourism – first mentioned by Pearce and Butler (1993) – introduce it as a derivation of cultural tourism and, in contrast to the usual passive role of the second, creative tourism includes the active involvement of the visitor. Tourists, therefore, become co-producers or co-authors of their own experiences in applying and acquiring creative skills, and also in their relationships and connections with the residents (Richards and Raymond, 2000; UNESCO, 2006; Richards and Wilson, 2007; Richards, 2011; Whiting and Hannam, 2014). However, this literature hardly makes a distinction between the motives of the traveller. Any creative person can be attracted to and visit an area for business or leisure purposes. The decision to locate his or her business and/or residence in a potentially creative city will require previous analysis and visits (Richards and Wilson, 2007).

Fourteen per cent of international tourism is for professional reasons (UNWTO, 2014). For corporative strategies, professional tourism is a needed preliminary step to a possible commercial agreement between companies and organizations from different states and territories. Creative professionals travel more than average because the production processes involved in their activities are multidisciplinary and interactive with the environment and with other professional and creative markets that are more open to diversity and competition, with high degrees of internationalization from their origin. In business and professional tourism, many travellers practice leisure activities in their destination. Non-professional journeys for leisure reasons and the personal journeys of creative people occur according to specific guidelines, and the urban life that encourages creativity in potential destinations acts as one of the main attractions.

The literature on creative tourism is still limited, and the approaches to the idea of creative tourism do not have enough differentiation between creative trips for work or those for leisure or to satisfy relationship needs. Actually, if tourists exercise their creativity and travel within the context of a professional agenda, then we are dealing with business or professional tourism. If there are not pre-professional goals, the tourist is using his or her free time for leisure and personal relationships, practising their creativity in other destinations outside of their usual residence. It is plausible to hypothesize that, above all, creative professionals would be the protagonists of this creative tourism.

Currently, creativity in tourism is seen primarily as a mean of differentiation in offering experiences through the local identity within urban positioning strategies (Zukin, 2010). The growing demand for interactivity and experiential immersion, increasingly significant for consumer personal identity processes, and new professions that dilute the boundaries between work and leisure promote the restructuring and development of the cultural offer, especially the urban one, often led by entrepreneurs – *culturpreneurs*. These people's profession becomes their lifestyle, and introduces more experiential and interactive components of visitor participation in the production of their experience, as the evidence reflects (Richards and Raymond, 2000; Richards and Wilson, 2007; Richards, 2011; Florida, 2012).

A creative city's attractiveness to visitors and potential residents can only arise and consolidate if it locates creative people capable of proposing ideas and generating creative products, which also depends on the availability of technology, methods and an environment conducive to developing the required processes. From here, it is possible to develop a set of urban characteristics with the ability to attract creative visitors and associate certain objective indicators. In recent years, there have been various proposals for creativity indexes, which have come to recognize that creative people can be attracted to reside and have pointed out the importance in this attraction of urban capital quality – regulations, technology, facilities, education level – and public space as a scene conducive to the diversity of subcultures and relationships

(Landry, 1995; Hartley *et al.*, 2012; Landry and Hyams, 2012). Below, we present the current state of the research in progress on the development of Valencia, Spain, as a creative destination; then we proceed to the implementation of this methodology of evaluation in the first phase, finally reaching sufficiently robust conclusions on the method and the case.

4.4 Methodology

Our hypothesis is that the variables analysed by the creative professional in order to choose a city as a tourism destination or as a place of residence and/or for professional practice are the same. Indicators can show the features to tourists in their own creative selection process. But, as usual in local and urban analysis, it is not easy to develop these indicators because the sources are different and not always official or reliable. On the other hand, the creative status of the visit is produced by the active participation of *in situ* visitors, a fact that depends on the perception of tourists.

4.4.1 Creative destinations index

A creative destination needs to count on areas, places and public and private facilities with the capability to attract creative visitors and residents. According to the literature, creative professional reality, with its organizations and facilities, street life and leisure offer, accommodation and transport guided by the tolerant values of the creative collective, are the potential milestones, centres and living laboratories to investigate. Regardless of the information registered for this supply – number, temporal evolution, location – any index to be developed by the creative professional in his or her decision process, as well as the interested researcher, would have to consider the activities and attributes that are listed in Table 4.1.

Valencia is the third city and urban tourism destination in Spain, and the authors maintain the hypothesis that it is in the process of becoming a creative destination. To test this hypothesis, we have designed a research project from the University of Valencia. The empirical basis of this research is founded in the authors' observation of the participants, both members of the local tourism operations and the related leisure and foreign professional networks in Valencia, Spain, throughout the past 10 years. The authors' professional experiences have enabled them to organize in the past year two related meetings and in-depth interviews between the creative class and the related tourism professionals of Valencia. The meetings were designed and conducted by the authors in a useful manner to generate analytical notes.

The in-depth interviews were structured and explained beforehand to the local actors as a tool for the research in progress. The interviews were available and fulfilled online, in order to facilitate the collection of data and analysis, but were guided live or by telephone or e-mail. These 15 local actors were chosen as observers because of their creative profession or their central position in the local tourist system, which was linked to creative tourist preferences and motivations – lodging, gastronomy, alternative transport, corporate services, cultural leisure experiences, and nearly all of them located in the inner city and the ancient quarters. The aim first was to obtain

Table 4.1. Professional and leisure attractions and services for the creative class. (From authors' own elaboration.)

	Guides, leisure and tourism experience producers
Creative activities, creative tourism services	Science university, R&D, agencies in charge of promotion of companies and entrepreneurs
	Publishing sector, journalism
	Design, fashion, marketing and communication
	Arts and culture
	Information and communication technologies, video entertainment
	Architecture, engineering and urban planning
	Tourist accommodation
	Hospitality and restaurant industry
	Services and transport
	Halls, music halls and music programming, night leisure
	Sports organization
	Congress and event organizers
	Travel agencies, DMC, public agencies tourism, tourist information
	Local products and specialized shops and boutiques
	Guides, leisure and tourism experience producers
Urban attributes for creativity	Weather
	Security
	Accessibility and external connectivity
	Accessibility and internal connectivity
	Street life
	Creative industries
	Professional installations
	Professional networking ease
	Leisure and culture offer
	Gastronomy

Note: DMC = destination management companies.

empirical evidence of the existence and the main characteristics of the creative flow and the foreign residents. If the findings allowed the hypothesis to be maintained, the sample of interviewed actors and the investigation method would be expanded at a later stage in order to improve the reliability of the comparison.

4.4.2   Valencia as a creative city and destination

The Romans founded Valencia by the Mediterranean Sea in 138 BC. The city had a history of self-government during its Muslim era (711–1238) and as the capital of the Kingdom of Valencia inside the Crown of Aragon (1238–1715). Later, it was ruled from Madrid as part of centralized and absolutist Spain. Following the adoption of the new democratic constitution in 1978, the city regained its status as capital of the Autonomous Region of Valencia in 1982. Currently, it has a population of 787,301 inhabitants and ranks third in the Spanish urban hierarchy. It has a good location due to its relative accessibility to most Spanish cities, and it is well connected to the rest of the European Union by various airlines. Expert analyses place it as the third Spanish urban tourism destination for leisure and professional tourism, after Barcelona and Madrid (Exceltur, 2013).

Valencia and its metropolitan area has been the scene of some successful creative activities. In the past, European art history witnessed the presence of emerging players in Valencian schools – writers such as Vicente Blasco Ibáñez (1867–1928), painters like Joaquín Sorolla (1863–1923) and musicians such as Joaquin Rodrigo (1901–1999). This must have been due to the high density of musical organizations or 'bands' in the fields of training and interpretation, and the cluster of craftsmen sculptors of cardboard, wood and plastic around the local Fallas festival, a major tourist attraction with an estimated million visitors per year. More recently, the Valencian Institute of Modern Art, which was created in 1986, has become an important centre worldwide, with 1.13 million visitors annually (Turismo Valencia, 2014).

The city has two World Heritage sites – the 'Tribunal de las Aguas', an institution in charge of arranging agricultural irrigation since the Arab period (2009), and the 'Lonja de la Seda', a Gothic civil building from the 15th century (1996) – and Valencia and its surroundings were the birthplace of the Spanish paella, a famous dish included in the Mediterranean diet, with World Heritage recognition by 2010. In the scientific, technical and business sector, the competitiveness and international leadership achieved by the decorative ceramics industry excelled in the markets with its high added value through R&D and design.

Finally, the University of Valencia, founded in 1499 and with 58,000 students, is the fourth university in Spain in the international rankings and the second in the EU in receiving Erasmus students. In addition, the Polytechnic University of Valencia, founded in 1971, has 36,000 students. The city is the main European destination for university tourism and has scientific and technologic parks with their own emerging business networks and collaborative processes.

The Autonomous Region of Valencia was a major European tourism destination, with Benidorm as the centre of mass tourism looking for sun and beach, but when it recovered its capacity to self-govern, Valencia did not have a significant position as a destination. Since then, the city has spread to its outer limits and has lost the population in its oldest quarters in preference for the municipalities in the rest of the metropolitan area. There is great difficulty in preserving the urban vitality of the historical centre and the quarters known for their history and heritage – 'Russafa' and 'Cabanyal-Canyamelar', next to the coast – but the city has become a major tourism destination, due mainly to the creation of facilities for conferences, themed entertainment and major events by regional and local governments. The data provided by the local tourist board in Table 4.2 show the positive development of the city linked to its attractiveness as a tourism destination.

Of the total overnight stays, 2.2 million are foreign visitors, with a significant number from Italy and further afield, Britain, France, the Netherlands and Germany, as well as 113,000 visitors from the USA. Sixty-five per cent of visitors are motivated

Table 4.2. The evolution of tourism in Valencia over the past 20 years. (From Estadísticas Turísticas 2013 (Turismo Valencia, 2014).)

	1992	2000	2008	2013
Hotel overnights	805,875	1,557,819	3,453,723	3,982,410
Travellers	372,205	815,493	1,821,695	1,902,756

by leisure tourism, whereas the remainder is for professional purposes, with 11% for fairs and meetings. The 'Palacio de Congresos', proclaimed as the best venue in the world in 2010, has hosted 746 meetings, conferences and conventions, and receives 182,000 visitors annually. On the other hand, in the City of Arts and Sciences Complex, which was intended by the regional government to be Valencia's great icon of urban transformation, the Museum of Sciences Prince Felipe welcomes 1.41 million visitors, 'L'Oceanogràfic' receives 1.06 million visitors and 295,000 people visit 'L'Hemisfèric'. The latest evolution of the hosting offer shows a growth from 109 stores and 14,009 bed spaces in 2005 to 132 establishments and 17,786 bed spaces in 2013 (Turismo Valencia, 2014).

With the information available, this official positioning strategy has had the effect of improving knowledge of the city and its national and international reputation. Analyses of the major Spanish tourist business organizations have placed Valencia, with its main attractions in gastronomy, university education for foreigners, meetings and conferences, and high-quality catering and hotel industry, as the country's third city. The city is outstanding with regards to urban life, due to its accessibility and mobility – high-speed rail, public bicycle hire, bike lanes and intermodality – but it scores poorly on green spaces, security and air quality (Exceltur, 2013). These unquestionable positive developments in Valencia as a tourism destination have also been analysed by experts at the local university, who point out the high volume of public indebtedness required and the limited attention given to the attractiveness of the history, culture and local lifestyle of the city as the main mistakes (Nácher and García-Reche, 2009; Marrades and Rausell, 2014).

More recently, numerous relevant actions of local, regional and public policy are being investigated for alleged legal irregularities, with potential negative effects on the external reputation of the city. At the business, civil and institutional levels, the most notable events in the creative fields have been the setting up of the Berklee College of Music Graduate School, with 200 annual international students, and the first position as a university tourism destination in the EU through the Erasmus program. At the same time, there has been a gradual consolidation of new proposals for tourist lodgings (hotels, apartments, youth hostels) in the city centre and the main historical areas, as well as shopping, leisure, restoration and creative industries (design, urban consulting, teambuilding) often located in restored old buildings. These facts point to a significant growth of youth tourism, akin to creative tourism.

The flow of students professionally oriented to creativity shows the positive development of the city as a creative destination. Recent research suggests that the relative weight of tourists younger than 35 years has increased from 43% in 2007 to 63% in 2014. At this age, the main attractions are the climate, the value of life/price levels and an excellent location in the European context (Marrades and Rausell, 2014). Finally, the two most important variables in the current tourist image are

'Mediterranean' and 'history and culture', and the urban areas that exert major tourist attraction include, in a preferential way, the historical city (Turismo Valencia, 2014). In other words, Valencia has become a major urban destination following a conservative public policy strategy oriented to leisure and major professional events and facilities and a gradual recovery of culture and local lifestyle as a tourism attraction still produced in a disjointed way and scattered by local and foreign agents.

4.5 Results

Direct observation and analysis of the literature and available data on the urban and tourist development of Valencia and its surroundings offer favourable evidence to the hypothesis of its status as a creative destination. To test the hypothesis, 15 actors locally renowned in the fields of science, university and R&D, design, marketing and communication, music, lodging, gastronomy, leisure and cultural tourism were interviewed. Figure 4.1 maps the city, the main historical districts and where the local actors are located and have mainly observed local creative life. Undoubtedly, the final absence in the sample of local observers in certain urban areas may cause a bias in the result.

Open answers have been evaluated to find matching descriptions and ratings. Urban attributes underwent assessments in the Likert scale. Table 4.3 shows the

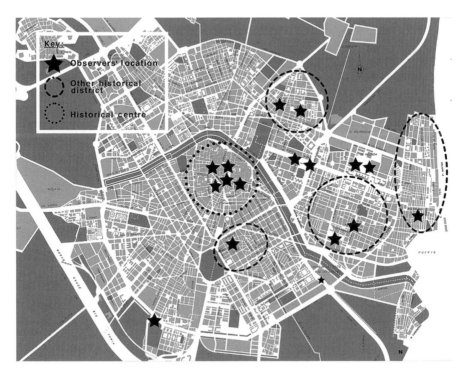

Fig. 4.1. Creative districts and the locations of observers in Valencia. (From authors' own elaboration.)

Table 4.3. Professional and leisure attractions and services for the creative class in Valencia. (From authors' own elaboration.)

Creative tourism	Relevant
Professions	Arts and culture; science, university and R&D; design, fashion, marketing and communication
Motivation	Leisure and professional
Origin	UK, the Netherlands, Germany, Italy, France (EU) Madrid, Barcelona
Attractive features	Weather, street life, urban accessibility and connectivity, dining
Urban areas	Inner city and historical quarters
Foreign creative residents	**Emerging**
Professions	Arts and culture; science, university and R&D; design, fashion, marketing and communication; leisure and tourism; gastronomy
Attractive features	Weather, safety, street life, cuisine, creative industries

characteristics of the visitor flow and the foreign creative collective most frequently observed and rated above average among the local actors.

The existence of a creative tourist flow and its positive evolution is clearly detected for both leisure and professional reasons. Leisure visits use weekends and bank holidays; professionals stay for 2–3 days for meetings and sometimes extend their stay for leisure up to 4–5 days. Students remain for longer stays, completing a semester or even a full year. The origin of the flow is located in the EU with the UK, the Netherlands, Germany, Italy and France as key visitor countries. Inside Spain, Madrid, Barcelona, the Valencian region, Albacete, Seville and Bilbao are the cities and regions of origin of visitors. They are relatively young visitors between 20 and 50 years, especially in the range between 30 and 40 years, with a medium-high purchasing power on average, travelling for leisure with their loved ones and as a group with other professionals.

The most frequently detected activities are arts and culture, university science and R&D, design, fashion, marketing and communication, and, at a lower level, architecture–engineering–urbanism, leisure, tourism and gastronomy. The observed personal style is informal and, to a much lower extent, modern. The most valued tourist attractions are considered to be the climate, street life, accessibility and urban connectivity, and gastronomy. Also, accessibility and external connectivity, security and cultural and leisure activities are valued positively. The preferred quarters and urban areas include the historical centre – 'L'Eixample' and 'Ciutat Vella' – and two historical districts whose original urban net survives – 'Benimaclet' and 'Poblats Marítims'. The most used means of transport are bicycle, subway, public bus and walking.

The presence of a resident creative collective coming from outside is detected too, but is still at an incipient stage. The professional reputation of an important part of the new residents against the emigration of young local creatives has been observed. There is much background diversity, although most originate from inside the EU, the British being the most detected. Again, the most noted professional areas are repeated: arts and culture, university science and R&D, design and communication, leisure, tourism and gastronomy. In regard to means of transport and the most visited urban districts, the tourist use pattern is also repeated, although a greater geographic dispersion seems to exist. Among the residential attractions, the main ones are the climate, security, street life and gastronomy. The creative sector, the facilities for professional contact and the external and internal accessibility and connectivity to the city are also outstanding.

To sum up, the observers interviewed agree on the existence of a flow of creative leisure and professional tourism in Valencia in the art and university fields, for which the Mediterranean lifestyle – weather, street life, urban size and gastronomy – and the location of the city in the Spanish and European urban networks are the main attractions. These visitors coexist with a flow of qualified professionals without a creative motivation, including university students, but quite matching their preferences and activities, a fact that may help to strengthen the final interactivity and the positive effects on urban competitiveness. The potential residential attraction is not so obvious and it would be applied to mature creative professionals.

The analysis of the case and the methodology used in this stage of the research has also confirmed, in Valencia, the normal behaviour of the creative class as visitors and residents. There is a clear preference for the historical urban areas, means of transport and activities – above all, gastronomy – that facilitate the social and relational interactions. The Mediterranean lifestyle of Valencia can be understood as the cultural expression of a territory historically prone to creativity.

4.6 Conclusion

Creative activities boost local development, and urban positioning strategies exist to promote the appearance and attraction of creative professionals. They travel, interact and are able to change their residence city more than the average. Tourism practised by creative professionals is characterized by their co-production of leisure or professional local activities carried out at the destination. Observing from within the local creative cluster provides proximity and improves the quality of information on the possible creative condition of the activity of tourists and residents. This is the creative city positioning strategies' previous stage.

Valencia, the third Spanish metropolis has a long and consolidated creative history. It is being evaluated as a possible creative destination through qualitative research among local professionals connected to creative visitors and residents. It has been noted that the city is attractive to creative people in their professional or leisure behaviour, both for tourists and, to a lesser extent, residents. Moreover, the use of qualitative research methods within the professional cluster facilitates an understanding of the factors involved, and helps to strength the creative cluster too.

References

EU (2010) EUROPE 2020. A strategy for smart, sustainable and inclusive growth. Available at: http://ec.europa.eu (accessed 21 November 2014).

Exceltur (2013) UrbanTur 2012. Monitor de Competitividad Turística de los Destinos Urbanos Españoles. Available at: http://exceltur.org (accessed 2 October 2014).

Florida, R. (2005) *The Flight of the Creative Class – The New Global Competition for Talent.* HarperCollins, New York.

Florida, R. (2012) *The Rise of the Creative Class – Revised and Expanded.* Basic Books, New York.

Glaeser, E. (2011) *Triumph of the City.* Penguin Books, New York.

Hartley, J., Potts, J. and MacDonald, T. (2012) The CCI creative city index 2012. *Cultural Science Journal* 5(1), 11–138.

Harvey, D. (2012) *Rebel Cities. From the Right to the City to the Urban Revolution.* Verso, London.

Jacobs, J. (1973) *Muerte y vida de las grandes ciudades.* Peninsula, Madrid.

Landry, C. and Hyams, J. (2012) *The Creative City Index: Measuring the Pulse of the City.* Comedia, London.

Landry, R. (1995) *The Creative City.* Demos, London.

Lange, B., Kalandides, A., Stöber, B. and Mieg, H.A. (2008) Berlin's creative industries: governing creativity? *Industry and Innovation* 15(5), 531–548.

Lazzeretti, L., Boix, R. and Capone, F. (2012) Why do creative industries cluster? In: Lazzeretti, L. (ed.) *Creative Industries and Innovation in Europe: Concepts, Measures and Comparative Case Studies.* Routledge, London, pp. 45–649.

Marrades, R. and Rausell, P. (2014) Turismo Low Cost para una ciudad más inteligente. Available at: http://www.valenciaplaza.com (accessed 5 October 2014).

Nácher, J. and García-Reche, A. (2009) El Sector Turístico. In: Soler, V. (ed.) *Economía Española y del País Valenciano.* Publicacions de la Universitat de Valencia, Valencia, Spain, pp. 319–344.

Pearce, D. and Butler, R. (1993) *Tourism Research: Critiques and Challenges.* Routledge, London.

Richards, G. (2011) Creativity and tourism: the state of art. *Annals of Tourism Research* 38, 1225–1253.

Richards, G. and Raymond, C. (2000) Creative tourism. *ATLAS News* 23, 16–20.

Richards, G. and Wilson, J. (2007) Creativities in tourism and development. In: Richards, G.Y. and Wilson, J. (eds) *Tourism, Creativity and Development.* Routledge, London, pp. 255–288.

Rindermann, H., Sailer, M. and Thompson, J. (2009) The impact of smart fractions, cognitive ability of politicians and average competence of peoples on social development. *Talent, Development & Excellence* 1(1), 3–25.

Santagata, W. (2009) *White Paper on Creativity: Towards an Italian Model of Development.* Bocconi University Ed, Milano.

Turismo Valencia (2014) Estadísticas de Turismo 2013. Available at: http://www.turisvalencia-guias.info (accessed 1 October 2014).

UNCTAD (2011) Economía creativa: Una opción factible de desarrollo, *Informe* 2010. Available at: http://unctad.org (accessed 12 October 2014).

UNESCO (2006) Towards sustainable strategies for creative tourism. Available at: http://unesdoc.unesco.org/ (accessed 12 October 2014).

UNESCO (2013) Creative economy report. Widening local development pathways. Available at: http://www.unesco.org (accessed 12 October 2014).

UNHabitat (2013) Streets as public spaces and drivers of urban prosperity. Available at: http://www.unhabitat.org (accessed 12 October 2014).

UNWTO (2014) Panorama OMT del Turismo Internacional. Available at: http://mkt.unwto.org (accessed 12 October 2014).

Whiting, J. and Hannam, K. (2014) Journeys of inspiration: working artists' reflections on tourism. *Annals of Tourism Research* 49, 65–75.

Zukin, S. (1995) *The Culture of Cities.* Blackwell Publishers, Oxford, UK.

Zukin, S. (2010) *Naked City: the Death and Life of Authentic Urban Places.* Oxford University Press, Oxford, UK.

5 Visual Semantics and Destination Competitiveness: The Case of Wedding Tourism in Mexico

GERARDO NOVO ESPINOSA DE LOS MONTEROS[1]* AND MARIBEL OSORIO GARCIA

[1]El Colegio Mexiquense, Zinacantepec, México; [2]Universidad Autónoma del Estado de México, Toluca, México

5.1 Introduction

While Mexico has not positioned itself explicitly as a wedding destination, it has in recent years begun to capitalize on those attributes that make it an attractive destination for such purposes and has begun to channel its efforts toward particular market segments, primarily the North American market. Its marketing efforts, particularly those using visual communication of destination weddings, have featured Mexican destinations that serve as ideal backdrops for such celebrations, while also highlighting the qualities that make them attractive for vacationing and tourism. For consumers, choosing a location for a destination wedding has become a complex task as more and more places attempt to incorporate into their offerings activities, amenities and integrated services for organizing a wedding.

Analysing tourism by the images used to depict it has become essential in order to study and understand it. This is because much of the information that tourists receive, and through which they create their own visual imagery, comes from such images as photographs, videos, advertisements and movies. It can be useful to examine publicity as a self-portrait of society, since it reflects tourist activities that lend themselves to studies of the images they depict and which connect intimately to the commercial communicative intentions of destinations and businesses. At the same time, from a visual semantics perspective, this foray into destination weddings illustrates a new phenomenon in the history of tourism as Mexico seeks to seize a true market opportunity at a time when the country has lost competitiveness.

In the framework of a larger project in which visual semantics used in tourism advertising from the system of the mass media has been studied (Novo *et al.*, 2012, 2013),

*E-mail: novogerardo@hotmail.com

the study of the wedding is viewed as a social interaction that belongs to one of the most important systems of modern society: the family (Luhmann, 2007). In this chapter, we are particularly interested in getting to know how the systematized use of schemas provides meaning to tourism communication and, in the current study case, how new iconic elements are added to the images used to represent tourism. To report on how these new visual semantics are added to the imagery of tourism, we analyse a relatively recent tourism product in Mexico: the destination wedding as an organized trip as sign of modern consumption.

5.2   Literature Review

The construction of positive images that motivate choosing the type of and place for a trip has been studied widely in recent years since it is considered a strategic factor for the competitiveness of destinations (Ashworth and Goodall, 1988; Woodside, 1990; Gartner, 1993; Day et al., 2002; Seddighi and Teocharaus, 2002; O'Leary and Deegan, 2005; Ryan and Cave, 2005; Iwashita, 2006; Tasci and Kozak, 2006; Govers et al., 2007; Paskaleva-Shapira, 2007; Tasci and Gartner, 2007; McCartney et al., 2008; Buzinde et al., 2010). Tourism advertising as a visual representation of travel has built itself a visual semantic based primarily on spaces, events, attributes and social interactions that deep down are satisfiers of needs. From this perspective, Mill and Morrison proposed to understand the trip and all the elements that structure it as satisfiers. In this regard, they propose that the key to understanding the motivation to travel is to view the trip as a satisfier, which represents, by itself, a chance to address different human needs: 'Tourists do not take vacations just to relax and have fun, to experience another culture, or to educate themselves and their children. They take vacations in the hope and belief that these vacations will satisfy, either wholly or partially, various needs and wants' (Mill and Morrison, 1985, p. 4).

On the other hand, John Urry's *The Tourist Gaze* doubtless raised a key direction for the study of images, and especially the way in which tourism places are looked at and consumed (Urry, 2004). Urry highlights that tourism arises from a binary relationship between the ordinary/daily life and the extraordinary one (Urry, 2004). From there, other proposals for research on visual semantics for tourism have been put forward. Haldrup and Larsen, inspired by the Urry's theory, constructed the notion of 'family gaze', referring to how family photography was socially organized and systematized in family tourism. This gaze is concerned with the 'extraordinary ordinariness' of intimate social worlds: '... places become scenes for acting out and active and route framing family life for the camera. Family members and their performance make experiences and places extraordinary and full of enjoyable life' (Haldrup and Larsen, 2012, p. 159).

For Crawshaw and Urry (1997), in a way, tourism is the appropriation of the memory of others, where the visual is the most important element for the construction of memories. In fact, the visual images of places are the ones that shape and provide a sense of anticipation, experience and memories regarding travelling. According to Caldas-Coulthard, in the construal of identities in tourism advertising, 'places and people are therefore recontextualized and resemiotized, mainly in tourism on the web, as setting and characters in visual narratives, where "characters" do "things" in specific "contexts"' (Caldas-Coulthard, 2008, p. 453). Therefore, destinations, and the creators of advertising messages should take advantage of the opportunities for social interactions that the places allow. Uzzel (1984) argues that, frequently, tourism promotion uses the wrong approach because the tourists look for destinations that meet their psychological needs; hence, attention should focus on the destinations that promote self-actualization, social interaction, sexual arousal and excitement.

The sociology of interaction developed by Erwin Goffman has been used as a reference in order to analyse the representations of interactions in the destination wedding product, particularly the theory of management of impressions. From this perspective, the behaviour of people is conditioned by the scenarios that provide the framework of their performance (Goffman, 2009). In this context, we argue that the representation of these frameworks of reference, made in the advertising of tourism, also condition the expectations of consumers regarding the interactions that will take place during the trip. Such interactions, roles and settings are chosen and taken advantage of, to be used as ideals in tourism advertising representations in the mass media. From this perspective, the projected image of tourism destinations leads the practice of tourism toward activities in which representations in the media are assumed in the framework of a staged background; in this case, schematized places and activities as scripts that will be proposed visually to consumers. Thus, we propose a distinction between a basic image, which is often used and is only supported by the attributes of the place, landscape and facilities, and a social image of the destination, in which multiple possibilities for leisure and relaxation are presented. This 'social' image is mainly made up of the representation of different interactions.

This study has been performed in the framework of such contributions, and we indeed believe that the images that represent opportunities for social interactions as motivation acquire greater expressive power, since they connote, in a broader sense, the possibilities offered by the destination and the trip. In other words, the presence of people triggers a universe of communication possibilities, unlike the transmission of images, where only locations or facilities are presented.

5.3   Methodology

To analyse the images aimed at this market segment, the web page of the Mexico Tourism Board (CPTM, 2014), in which destination weddings are promoted as a differentiated tourist product that aims to give a competitive advantage to Mexico as a country brand, was taken as a reference. This research is based on the assumption that destinations require positive and distinctive images that enable them to establish a competitive position in the mind of potential consumers. The schematized use of images in tourism advertising, rather than differentiating the destinations, homogenizes them, so that several destinations offer the same tourism products and the images used for promotion are very similar.

From a constructivist perspective, the speech of the photographs selected for the promotion of tourism in Mexican destinations as ideal places for weddings was analysed quantitatively and qualitatively. Different elements and functions that contribute to conveying a strategic message of positioning were identified. First, we appealed to the analysis of content as a systematic approach in order to outline and

classify the content of the photographs presented in the official website for the promotion of Mexico. The photo gallery of the section 'Tu boda en México' ('Your wedding in Mexico') was taken as a reference. This photo gallery is made up of 146
images taken by professional photographers. A first classification was used to locate
the images spatially. The setting, proposed by Goffman, was taken as a category of
analysis that encompassed the furniture, decorations, equipment and other elements
of a scenic background, which provided the stage and props for the flow of human
action that took place before, inside and on it (Goffman, 2009).

This first analysis made it possible to establish the type of destination expected,
and also served as the setting for making the actions represented in the advertising.
Beaches, urban sites/historical heritage, nature, churches, underwater scenarios and
finally tourist infrastructure (hotels, restaurants, theme parks, etc.) were considered
as categories. A second level of analysis was the identification and classification of
the actions, and particularly of the interactions, as a social system. We understand
interaction to be a social system formed in the presence of people who communicate
face-to-face and who are aware each other (Luhmann, 2007). Goffman (2009), for
his part, defines it as the reciprocal influence of one individual on another's actions
when they are both in close proximity to each other. Essentially, the representation
of these interactions led us to identify the schema present in the photographs, which
became constant and complied with specific functions for the production of meaning.

5.4   Results

The images analysed show that what is being sought is a distinction in relation to the
traditional ritual of a wedding ceremony performed in temples or enclosed spaces.
The organization of destination weddings offers the possibility to take advantage of
the great outdoors, which serve as a framework of great scenic beauty and constitutes
an experience far out of the ordinary. The photographs contained in the studied website represent marriage as a social event, but when the event takes place in a tourism
destination, especially one of sun and beach, it is associated with a series of satisfiers
where the pleasure that tourism produces is highlighted, with all the implications in
terms of resting, relaxation, aesthetic appreciation and social interactions. As a result,
some possibilities are derived: feasibility of intimacy, communication, romance, meetings, a sense of belonging, affection and esteem, according to Mill and Morrison's
proposal (1985). The images presented imply economic potential, which in turn is
associated with values related to the image of people, status and power. Hence, the
distinction of the wedding as an act of social prestige occurs when the event is taken
to an extraordinary setting, as a tourism destination.

According to Guiraud (1972), these images are framed in a code, as they respond
to a system of explicit and socialized conventions. As we look at them, we know, from
the very beginning, that we are witnessing a representation of the ritual act of marriage.
Another code is added to the cultural protocol of weddings; it is that of the tourism
industry, resulting in a third code, increasingly socialized and understandable, which
is the destination wedding. This construction can be seen under a creative technique
frequently used in advertising to give expressive power to a message; it is
known as symbolizing bisection, in which the advertisers or creative types present
two apparently strange worlds in which there is a common area, and it is precisely

from this unexpected common area where the impact and communication emerges (Joannis, 1990).

There has surely been a rigorous selection of pictures, and some of these are the product of careful editing and production, where aesthetics is emphasized. They intentionally contain a range of specific and symbolic elements placed on scene which comply with the functions of indicating, inducing and representing through specific means of communication, according to the terms proposed by Guiraud (1972). The selected photographs depict the ritual of the marriage through a series of interactions that show characters in specific situations collectively forming a sequence of events in an organized trip. The analysis of content of the CPTM's photo gallery enables us to observe, at first sight, that most of the images used for the promotion of destination weddings correspond to sun and beach destinations, positioned internationally.

The finding is not surprising since the offer and the development of tourism in Mexico has been focused on beach destinations such as Cancun, Los Cabos or Puerto Vallarta, whose infrastructure is oriented mainly to markets with a high purchasing power. In fact, the Riviera Maya on the Caribbean Mexican coast has become the favourite location of the US market for holding weddings, placing Mexico in a privileged place within the preferences of the North American market. Almost a third of the total pictures corresponds to urban or historic places and is much smaller in proportion to natural sites. The results from the scenarios are presented in Table 5.1.

The ceremony as a ritual practice was referred to in few cases, only 11 photographs, representing 7.5%; and the presence of elements of the local culture was noted in only two photographs. In these images, natural elements such as water, a sea snail or the ocean are considered as figurative performers, according to Vilches (1991). Despite being scarce, it should be highlighted that these photographs are also a sign that the wedding can acquire aspects of the traditional local culture and become a distinction compared to an ordinary ceremony in the place of origin of those who practice this type of tourism.

Photo settings typical of weddings are the most prevalent; in them, the referential emphasis as a communicative action focuses on couples posing for the next shot or on the bride with her attire and customary elements: the wedding gown, the bridal bouquet, the veil. A notable finding is that 64% of the photos belong to this category, in which the principal actors are placed in selected settings. Beyond them is the scenic beauty of the beach, blue skies, sunsets, golf courses, farms

Table 5.1. Scenarios of the tourism images of weddings.

Ambience or scenario	Appearance (%)
Beaches	51.7
Urban sites and historical heritage	31.97
Nature	5.44
Underwater scenarios	2.0
Religious temples	0.68
Tourist services (hotels, restaurants, bars, theme parks)	8.1
Total	100

and vernacular architecture, among others; the images fulfil the basic role of being the souvenir photos, which at the same time portray an image that projects status and prestige as a sign of purchasing power. Precisely in these photos, the emphasis is on the performance of the couples positioned at the centre of the image, surrounded by water, in unusual scenes in which the wedding gown replaces the bathing suit. Even in these cases, the images of tourism advertising do not stray far from conventional stereotypes. A woman's body appears again as part of the iconography of tourism, the image of the young woman on the beach, in the water, is repeated. The difference is that this time, instead of appearing half naked, she appears in a wedding gown.

Advertisers use similar images because they have been proven successful. This idea of theming in advertising is based on schematization, which facilitates communication towards the consumers and provides information for planning and carrying out activities during the trip as an itinerary. This is especially important for destination weddings, since the expectations of the trip focus on specific activities related to group social interactions such as the ceremony, the photo sessions, the celebration and other more personal interactions, or those of greater intimacy of the couple, such as walks or the dinner itself.

A variety of implications in tourism result from the use of such conventions from the variety of travel offers, because they give rise to classifications of standardized products like the honeymoon or destination wedding and produce codes of preference that fulfil the function of schematizing the attractive/not attractive, beach/indoors, exclusive/popular, accessible/inaccessible, or the ordinary/extraordinary. These distinctions determine the expectations and the decisions of the travellers and tend to be represented through different images that make up the specific semantics of each of the tourist products. In this case, destination wedding trips are a product that responds to a standardized expectation from the system of the family or the intimacy, according to the systems described by Luhmann (2007).

The paradox of consuming in order to be different, commonplace in advertising, and being just like everybody else at the end, is present in these representations (Berger, 2000; Osorio, 2010; Novo, et al., 2013). The different wedding ends up being the same as many others. Some activities or scenes are introduced to differentiate themselves from other destination weddings whose purpose is to contrast with ordinary ceremonies. With this intention in mind, characters are guided to represent atypical tasks of a wedding, but that are clearly aligned with the activities expected on the trips. So, the most often repeated script is the walks on the beach or simply posing for the camera in given scenarios. Releasing turtles on the beach, buying souvenirs or handicrafts are other activities portrayed, but to a lesser extent; these sound strange as part of the itinerary in the ritual of marriage, but for the purposes of communication they fill very well their role to distinguish between the ordinary and the extraordinary. The scripts that have nourished the visual semantics of product for honeymooners are now being used for those who are going to marry. The walks on the beach, horseback riding, hugging, kissing, romance or passion are also still present, but now in a wedding garment and not in a bathing suit.

Photographs of the destination wedding constitute pieces of communication that have left behind the old static study pictures. They are images that connote far more than the union of the couples. These photos by themselves constitute a universe of possibilities of communication because of their aesthetic beauty and the implications for consumption. In the case of Mexico, they represent an opportunity to attract domestic and foreign market segments with high economic possibilities. It is also a product that has given Mexico a competitive edge by taking advantage of its strengths as a destination with an extraordinary scenic beauty and cultural heritage, and the characteristic hospitality of the Mexican people.

In general, the images used on the CPTM website do not require any modification of proportions; there is no need to exaggerate. Actually, only one case was found in which the effect of superimposition was clear due to the fact that the couple was displayed in an underwater scene. In other cases, digital processing is the least that could be expected in advertising shots with regard to colour correction, contrast and light, among others. The pictures presented are clear and convincing and do not require further explanation.

5.5   Conclusion

The organization of wedding destinations as a relatively recent product in the history of tourism has incorporated new visual semantics, which are added to the iconography that has traditionally been used in tourism communication making up tourism imagery. These additions are the product of an evolutionary process of tourism that shows the changes and transformations in the design and marketing of different tourist products at destinations as complements of traditional supply. The images analysed refer the viewer to a series of visual promises in which the scenic beauty of the destination is taken as a frame of reference. The connotative functions of the images communicate the multiple concrete and symbolic possibilities of the destination. At the same time, the representation of social interactions provides expressive strength to the elements of communication, while also helping to generate a social image of the destination. The combination of this basic image with the social image is potentially useful because, in terms of production of meaning, the universe of possibilities about the creation of expectations increases considerably, depending on the satisfiers represented.

The visual semantics, which in the great majority contribute to the positioning of Mexico as a destination for weddings, are based on the traditional products of sun and sand, in which some attributes, such as the scenic beauty of the landscape, good weather and abundance of natural resources, stand out. Cultural heritage is given less prominence, and contact with local culture is even less of a priority. These representations of the 'different' experience are based on schematisms frequently used in advertising. The represented scripts in the trips, such as shopping, posing before monuments, admiring landscapes or walking, are still present in the construction of expectations of the trip, now in the framework of a different code.

Through the images presented on the website that promotes Mexico, the promise of a unique opportunity for social interaction is transmitted to the potential tourist, in which romance, fun, pleasure and social prestige are synthesized. As a distinctive element of Mexico, people can see in the pictures some elements linked with the Mexican style of life, highlighting the landscape, with its beaches, mountains or cities, with other objects added, many of them stereotyped, products that in the paradigm are bound to Mexican culture, such as handicrafts, traditional sweets or musical bands such as the Mariachis.

In recent years, Mexico has lost several positions in the world ranking of the country most visited by tourists, but it maintains good numbers for destination weddings. The climate, the competitive prices, the infrastructure and the idea of party and Mexican hospitality are positive attributes but, in order to maintain a competitive position, the quality of the tourism offer will have to be preserved and improved. At the same time, in terms of image, a differentiating product must be offered, one that really emphasizes the difference from other destinations in Latin America and the Caribbean. The risk is that other Latin American seaside destinations will be also become Mexico's main competitors by offering similar products.

References

Ashworth, G. and Goodall, B. (1988) Tourist images: marketing considerations. In: Goodall, B. and Ashworth, G. (eds) *Marketing in the Tourism Industry*. Routledge, London, pp. 213–238.

Berger, J. (2000) *Modos de ver*, 5ta ed. Gustavo Gili, Barcelona, Spain.

Buzinde, C., Manuel-Navarrete, D., Eunjung, Y.E. and Duarte, M. (2010) Tourists' perceptions in a climate of change. Eroding destinations. *Annals of Tourism Research* 7(2), 333–354.

Caldas-Coulthard, C. (2008) Body branded: multimodal identities in tourism advertising. *Journal of Language and Politics* 7(3), 451–470.

CPTM (2014) Mexico Tourism Board. Available at: www.visitmexico.com/es/bodas (accessed 30 November 2014).

Crawshaw, C. and Urry, J. (1997) Tourism and the photographic eye. In: Rojek, C. and Urry, J. (eds) *Touring Cultures*. Routledge, London, pp. 176–195.

Day, J., Skidmore, S. and Koller, T. (2002) Image selection in destination positioning: a new approach. *Journal of Vacation Marketing* 8(2), 177–186.

Gartner, W. (1993) *Image Formation Process*. In: Uysal, M. and Fesenmaier, D.F. (eds) *Communication and Channel Systems in Tourism Marketing*. The Haworth Press Inc, New York, pp. 191–215.

Goffman, E. (2009) *La presentación de la persona en la vida cotidiana*, 2da ed. Amorrourtu editores, Buenos Aires.

Govers, R., Go, F. and Kumar, K. (2007) Promoting tourism destination image. *Journal of Travel Research* 46, 15–23.

Guiraud, P. (1972) *La semiología*, 1a ed. Siglo XXI, Distrito Federal, México.

Haldrup, M. and Larsen, J. (2012) Readings of tourists photographs. In: Rakic, T. and Chambers, D. (eds) *An Introduction to Visual Search Methods in Tourism*. Routledge, New York, pp. 153–168.

Iwashita, C. (2006) Media representation of the UK as a destination for Japanese tourists. *Tourist Studies* 6(1), 59–77.

Joannis, H. (1990) *El proceso de creación publicitaria*, 1a ed. Deusto, Distrito Federal, México.

Luhmann, N. (2007) *La sociedad de la sociedad*, 1a ed. Herder-Universidad Iberoamericana, Distrito Federal, México.

McCartney, G., Butler, R. and Bennett, M. (2008) A strategic use of the communication mix in the destination image-formation process. *Journal of Travel Research* 47(2), 183–196.

Mill, R.C. and Morrison, A.M. (1985) *The Tourism System*, 1st edn. Prentice-Hall, London.

Novo, G., Osorio, M., Torres, J. and Esquivel, E. (2012) Imagen turística y medios de comunicación, una construcción social. *Perspectivas del Turismo* 21(6), 1409–1432.

Novo, G., Osorio, M., Torres, J. and Esquivel, E. (2013) Viajes, actuantes, escenarios e interacciones: un análisis de la publicidad turística de los destinos, a partir de sus semánticas visuales. *Investigaciones turísticas* 6, 27–46.

O'Leary, S. and Deegan, J. (2005) Ireland's image as a tourism destination in France: attribute importance and performance. *Journal of Travel Research* 43, 247–256.

Osorio, M. (2010) La comunicación social del turismo. Una propuesta teórica para su comprensión. In: Nechar, M. and Panosso, A. (eds) *Epistemología del turismo: Estudios críticos.* Trillas, Distrito Federal, México, pp. 83–97.

Paskaleva-Shapira, K.A. (2007) New paradigms in city tourism management: redefining destination promotion. *Journal of Travel Research* 46, 108–114.

Ryan, C. and Cave, J. (2005) Structuring destination image: a qualitative approach. *Journal of Travel Research* 44, 143–150.

Seddighi, H.R. and Teocharaus, A.L. (2002) A model of tourism destination choice: a theoretical and empirical analysis. *Tourism Management* 23, 475–487.

Tasci, A.D.A. and Gartner, W.G. (2007) Destination image and its functional relationships. *Journal of Travel Research* 45(4), 413–425.

Tasci, A.D.A. and Kozak, M. (2006) Destination brand vs. destination images: do we know what we mean? *Journal of Vacation Marketing* 12(4), 299–317.

Urry, J. (2004) *La mirada del Turista.* Universidad de San Martín de Porres, Lima.

Uzzel, D. (1984) An alternative structuralism approach to the psychology of tourism marketing. *Annals of Tourism Research* 11, 79–99.

Vilches, L. (1991) *La lectura de la imagen.* Prensa, cine, televisión, 1a ed. Paidós comunicación, Distrito Federal, México.

Woodside, A.G. (1990) Measuring advertising effectiveness in destination marketing strategies. *Journal of Travel Research* 29, 3–8.

Part II   Environmental and Climate Change Issues at Destinations

6 The Potential Effects of Climate Change on the Tourism Industry: A Study in Turkey

MUSA PINAR,[1]* IBRAHIM BIRKAN,[2] GAMZE TANIL[3] AND MUZAFFER UYSAL[4]

[1]*Valparaiso University, Valparaiso, USA; [2]Atilim University, Ankara, Turkey; [3]Dogus University, Istanbul, Turkey; [4]Virginia Polytechnic Institute and State University, Blacksburg, USA*

6.1 Introduction

Scientific research shows that the global climate has changed as a result of human activities that are increasing greenhouse gas concentrations in the atmosphere. The Intergovernmental Panel on Climate Change (IPCC) declared 'warming of the climate system is unequivocal'. Climate change includes an increase in continental average temperatures, temperature extremes and wind patterns, widespread decreases in glaciers and ice caps and warming ocean surface temperature that contributed to a sea level rise of 1.8 mm/year from 1961 to 2003 and approximately 3.1 mm/year from 1993 to 2003 (IPCC, 2007). These changes to the world's climate cause substantial concerns, for many reasons. For example, the rising sea level threatens the viability of many coastal zones and small islands; temperature rises are predicted to change precipitation patterns, which could exacerbate water supply problems and create a greater risk of both flooding and drought conditions in many parts of the world; and climate change also seems likely to increase the magnitude, frequency and risk of extreme climatic events, such as storms and sea surges. Moreover, recent research indicates that hot extremes, heatwaves and heavy precipitation events will become more frequent and tropical cyclones (typhoons and hurricanes) will become more intense (UNWTO, UNEP–WMO, 2008). Water scarcity and increased drought will also be serious problems for some regions.

There is a reciprocal relationship between tourism and climate change. On the one hand, tourism has an obligation to minimize its adverse impact on the environment, and thus on the emission of greenhouse gases, which in turn contribute to climate change. On the other hand, it is recognized that changes to the world's climate would have a direct impact on the use of resources, which could have far-reaching

*E-mail: musa.pinar@valpo.edu

implications for the tourism industry and destinations. Given the tourism industry's vulnerability to climate variability and change, UNWTO reports that climate change will affect global tourism in several broad ways (UNWTO, 2009, p. 5). They are: (i) climate defines the length and quality of tourism seasons and plays a major role in destination choice and tourist spending; (ii) it affects a wide range of the environmental resources that are critical to tourism, such as snow conditions, wildlife productivity and biodiversity, water levels and quality; (iii) it influences various facets of tourism operations (e.g. snow-making, irrigation needs, heating/cooling costs); (iv) it impacts environmental conditions that can deter tourists, including infectious diseases, wildfires and extreme events; and finally (v) weather is an intrinsic component of the travel experience and influences holiday satisfaction.

6.2   Literature Review

The literature is replete with studies, some of which are scenario-based, that demonstrate how climate change may affect the resources on which tourism is dependent both directly, through changing weather patterns (e.g. Gössling, 2002; Lise and Tol, 2002; Nicholls and Amelung, 2008; Jopp *et al.*, 2010), and indirectly, for example through altering the distributions and quality of natural resources (e.g. Nicholls and Amelung, 2008; UNWTO, 2008). It is also pointed out that not all the potential impacts of climate change are necessarily negative, and that new opportunities such as longer, more reliable and profitable tourism seasons in currently marginal destinations are projected as changing weather patterns attract more domestic and international visitors (Amelung *et al.*, 2007; Nicholls and Amelung, 2008; Shih *et al.*, 2009). Furthermore, it is also claimed that those tourism businesses that have lower potential for adaptation to climate change can be more vulnerable than tourists, who have a much wider range of options available (Wall, 1998; Lise and Tol, 2002; Amelung *et al.*, 2007). However, Nicholls (2004) points out that many policy makers and small- to medium-sized tourism businesses tend to work in short-term time frames focused on profitability, while most climate change scenarios are proposed for the next decade to century. However, these climate issues also beg for research that could include tourism business managers (e.g. hotel managers) and their perceptions of climate change and its anticipated impacts on their personal well-being and that of their business activities in general. Generating information involving hotel managers, as the key stakeholders, on how tourism may be affected by climate change and developing suitable adaptation and mitigation policies would be of immense value for the success and sustainability of business activities.

   A review of some studies also supports the notion that the effects of climate change are more relevant, especially in terms of tourism activities that may occur in fragile places such as coastal zones, mountain regions, ski destinations and beaches, where climate change puts tourism at risk (e.g. Hoque *et al.*, 2010; Richardson and Witkowski, 2010; Turton *et al.*, 2010). Therefore, it is essential to emphasize that regardless of the nature and magnitude of climate change impacts, all tourism businesses and destinations will need to adapt to climate change in order to minimize associated risks and to capitalize on new opportunities in an economically, socially and environmentally sustainable manner. All these recent global warming and climate changes and the potential impacts on personal life as well as business performance have become an important concern for all types of industries (Viner and Nicholls, 2005). Since the tourism industry as a whole could be impacted directly or indirectly, it is important to understand how managers in the hotel industry perceive the potential impact of global warming and climate change on the hotel industry. There is very limited, if any, work on understanding hotel managers' perceptions of climate change and its anticipated impact on personal well-being and firm performance, and whether these perceptions would also show variation by demographic and other organization-based variables.

Therefore, this study examines hotel managers' perceptions regarding the potential and/or expected impact of global warming and climate change on the tourism industry at both the personal and the industry level, as well as their commitments to actions to combat the effects of these changes during the next 10 years. The specific objectives are: (i) to examine hotel managers' perceptions regarding global warming and climate change regarding: (a) the potential or expected impact on the personal well-being of managers and on the tourism industry, and (b) a commitment to actions within the tourism industry to combat these potential impacts of global warming and climate change; (ii) to investigate the relationship between managers' perceptions regarding the impact of global warming and climate change and their demographic profiles of gender, age, education and managerial position; and (iii) to discuss the managerial implications of the findings

6.3 Methodology

In order to accomplish the study objectives, a survey instrument was developed. Based on a review of the literature (Uysal *et al.*, 1994; Kellstedt *et al.*, 2008) and interviews with experts on the topic, the survey included questions dealing with (i) the potential (negative) effects of global warming and climate change on the well-being of managers and the tourism industry, and (ii) the commitment to actions within the tourism industry to combat these potential negative consequences. More specifically, the survey questions (available from the lead author) measure the potential negative effects on the respondent's personal and financial well-being and on the environmental and financial aspects of the tourism industry, and the level of commitment or support for the activities to combat global warming and climate change. All these questions are measured on a five-point Likert-type scale, where 1 = strongly disagree and 5 = strongly agree. Finally, the survey included questions related to the respondent's demographic characteristics, such as gender, age, education, number of years worked in the current firm and in the industry and the position of the respondent.

Since the survey was originally developed in English, it was translated into Turkish and later back-translated into English by bilingual persons experienced in research, in order to avoid translation errors (Ball *et al.*, 2002) and to ensure that the intended meaning of the questions was maintained. The Turkish version of the survey was further pretested with respondents (hotel administrators) similar to the target population. These pretests of the English and Turkish versions of the questionnaire provided useful input for improving the survey questions and for establishing the face validity of the constructs (Churchill, 1979; Churchill and Iacobucci, 2005). The survey also included such demographic questions as gender, age, student classification and hometown size.

The survey was administered to hotel managers in Turkey. Since hotels and motels in Turkey have to be members of the Turkish Hotel Federation Association, their list was used to send the surveys to the managers of the member hotels. The association has a total of 2000 members in seven regions of Turkey. The General Secretary of the Association, who helped to distribute the surveys, was requested to send the survey instrument to upper managers. The survey was sent to all the member hotels, not to a subset or sample of hotels. In order to increase the credibility of the survey and the response rate, an endorsement letter from the Association President was included with the survey. Moreover, in order to eliminate any potential influence and biases in responding to the survey questions, the respondents were asked to fax or mail the completed survey directly. After several follow-ups, this process produced for analysis 154 useable surveys of the 2000 surveys sent out, with a response rate of 7.7%. This is a typical response rate in developing countries. The selected profiles of respondents indicate that the majority of them (69.3%) are male, most of them (68.6%) are between 30 and 50 years old, 63.8% have a college degree, 57.6% are top managers and 42.1% are department/division managers, 38.4% work at five-star hotels, and they have on average 17.1 years of experience in the industry and 8.5 years of experience in the current firm.

6.4   Results

In order to accomplish the study objectives, several statistical analyses were conducted. Initially, the survey questions 1 through 19 were submitted to factor analyses to determine the subscales or dimensions using principal component analysis with varimax rotation. As presented in Table 6.1, this procedure produced five distinct factors with eigenvalues in excess of 1.0 (Hair *et al.*, 2010, p. 111). These five factors collectively accounted for 65.68% of the common variance. The factor loadings for each factor in Table 6.1 are greater than 0.50, and therefore are very significant, according to the criteria for a sample size of 150 or more (Hair *et al.*, 2010, pp. 117–118). The results of the reliability analysis for internal consistency found that Cronbach's alpha coefficients for factors 1–4 were above the acceptable threshold level of 0.60 for exploratory research (Hair *et al.*, 2010). While the alpha of 0.52 is below the acceptable level of 0.60, it is included in the study because of having only two items with a high factor loading, and because this is an exploratory study. These alpha values indicate that the factor items show fairly high internal consistency. As shown in Table 6.1, we named these factors as perceived expected benefits, commitment to protecting, expected effect on the environment, consequences for firm/organizations and mental concerns.

In order to understand the concerns of the respondents about global warming and climate change issues, factor means are presented in Fig. 6.1. These factor means indicate that respondents perceive factor 4: consequences for hotels, as the most important concern (M = 4.35) of global warming and climate change, followed by factor 2: commitment to protecting the environment (M = 4.00), and by factor 1: perceived

Table 6.1. Factor analysis results, means, standard deviations and factor loadings.

Factor 1: Perceived negative effects (alpha = 0.84, % of variance extracted = 21.81)	Mean	Standard deviation	Factor loading
A noticeably negative impact on my physical health	3.80	0.90	0.813
A noticeably negative effect on my time for leisure and recreation	3.65	1.01	0.765
A noticeably negative impact on the general quality of life of personnel in the tourism industry	3.47	1.02	0.729
A noticeably negative impact on the environment where my employer operates tourism properties	3.68	0.92	0.725
A noticeably negative impact on the sustainability of the tourism industry	3.77	0.92	0.666
A noticeably negative impact on my economic and financial situation	3.45	1.03	0.620
Factor 2: Commitment to protecting (alpha = 0.72, % of variance extracted = 13.16)	**Mean**	**Standard deviation**	**Factor loading**
The equipment that is reusable should be preferred even if it is more expensive	4.15	0.80	0.815
I believe a person who consumes less is the most environment friendly	3.62	1.09	0.718
Renewable energy should be used even if it is more costly	4.22	0.77	0.665
Factor 3: Expected effect on the environment (alpha = 0.59, % of variance extracted = 10.83)	**Mean**	**Standard deviation**	**Factor loading**
Global warming and climate change will cause the sea level to rise significantly; as a result, some tourism resorts will be covered by water	3.41	1.01	0.689
There will be a noticeably positive impact on the economic and financial situation of the tourism industry (R)	3.44	1.19	0.664
There will be less snowfall, which will have a negative impact on skiing and on all winter sports	3.51	0.87	0.626
There will be a noticeably positive impact on the environment in which my family and I live (R)	3.53	1.43	0.555
Factor 4: Consequences for hotels (alpha = 0.65, % of variance extracted = 10.69)	**Mean**	**Standard deviation**	**Factor loading**
The firms/organizations that emit carbon dioxide to the environment should pay tax in proportion to their emission of carbon dioxide	4.22	0.95	0.795
In order to save energy, there should be stricter insulation regulations for buildings and equipment	4.47	0.76	0.621
Will **not** have a noticeably negative impact on my mental health and well-being (R)	3.33	1.09	0.812
Global warming and climate change will **not** have a noticeably negative impact on the satisfaction of tourism personnel (R)	2.53	1.02	0.753

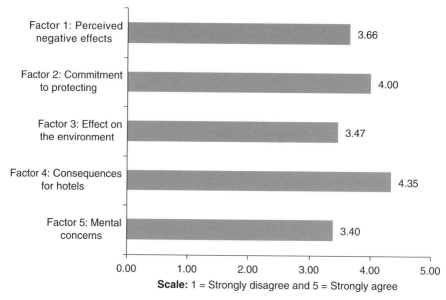

Fig. 6.1. Means for factor dimensions.

negative effects (M = 3.66). The other factors with mean values of 3.47 for factor 3 and 3.40 for factor 5 are not perceived to be as important as the other three factors.

In order to address the second objective of the study, the mean comparisons were conducted for each of the demographic variables and the results are presented in Table 6.2. The mean comparisons by gender found no significant difference between the perceptions of male and female respondents regarding each of the five factors. This indicates that both male and female managers have similar concerns about the potential effects of global warming and climate change. The one-way ANOVA analyses for age in Table 6.2 found no significant differences among the age groups for factors, except in factor 4. The results for factor 4: consequences for hotels, found significant differences among the age groups ($p < 0.05$). The pair-wise mean comparisons show significant differences between age groups of < 30 and 31–40, < 30 and 41–50, < 30 and > 50, and 31–40 and > 40. These findings indicate that as managers get older, it seems that they become more concerned about the potential consequences of global warming and climate change for hotels or their firms/organizations. For all other factors, the managers, regardless of their age, have similar concerns for the effects of global warming and climate change.

As for the education levels of the respondents, the results of one-way ANOVA in Table 6.2 found significant differences among education levels for factor 1 ($p < 0.10$) and factor 5 ($p < 0.05$), but no significant differences for other factors. The pair-wise mean comparisons for factor 1 show a significant difference between the perceptions of respondents with a junior college or less and graduate-level education ($p < 0.05$), where respondents with a graduate-level education have a significantly higher level of concern about the negative effects of global warming and climate change than those with a junior college or less education. Since other mean comparisons are not significant, these groups have similar perceptions for the negative effects of global warming

Table 6.2. Mean comparisons of climate change factors by demographic factors.

Gender	Factor 1: Perceived negative effects	Factor 2: Commitment to protecting	Factor 3: Effect on the environment	Factor 4: Consequences for hotels	Factor 5: Mental concerns
1. Female	3.78	4.01	3.58	4.29	3.32
2. Male	3.61	3.99	3.44	4.39	3.44
F-value	1.71	0.01	2.12	0.53	0.63
F-significance values	0.194	0.913	0.148	0.469	0.429
Mean comparisons	Not significant	Not significant	Not significant	Not significant	Not significant
Age	Factor 1: Perceived negative effects	Factor 2: Commitment to protecting	Factor 3: Effect on the environment	Factor 4: Consequences for hotels	Factor 5: Mental concerns
1. < 30	3.79	4.14	3.41	4.00	3.50
2. 31–40	3.64	3.89	3.51	4.30	3.38
3. 41–50	3.64	3.99	3.39	4.47	3.39
4. > 50	3.64	4.12	3.64	4.64	3.35
F-value	0.32	0.95	1.10	3.76	0.14
F-significance values	0.810	0.417	0.353	**0.012**	0.937
Mean comparisons	Not significant	Not significant	Not significant	1 < 2*; 1 < 3***; 1 < 4***; 2 < 4*	Not significant
Education	Factor 1: Perceived negative effects	Factor 2: Commitment to protecting	Factor 3: Effect on the environment	Factor 4: Consequences for hotels	Factor 5: Mental concerns
1. Junior college or less	3.46	3.79	3.44	4.31	3.04
2. College	3.65	3.99	3.42	4.31	3.53
3. Graduate	3.89	4.19	3.68	4.54	3.29
F-value	2.48	2.10	2.06	1.01	3.46
F-significance values	**0.087**	0.126	0.132	0.366	**0.034**
Mean comparisons	1 < 3**	Not significant	Not significant	Not significant	1 < 2*
Manager position	Factor 1: Perceived negative effects	Factor 2: Commitment to protecting	Factor 3: Effect on the environment	Factor 4: Consequences for hotels	Factor 5: Mental concerns
1. Supervisor	3.63	4.00	3.44	4.45	3.45
2. Department manager	3.68	4.05	3.53	4.28	3.34
Top manager	3.76	3.93	3.41	4.50	3.40

Continued

Table 6.2. Continued.

Manager position	Factor 1: Perceived negative effects	Factor 2: Commitment to protecting	Factor 3: Effect on the environment	Factor 4: Consequences for hotels	Factor 5: Mental concerns
F-value	0.20	0.21	0.40	1.05	0.20
F-significance values	0.817	0.910	0.674	0.352	0.823
Mean comparisons	Not significant	Not significant	Not significant	Not significant	Not significant

Note: **p-values** = *$p<0.10$; **$p<0.05$; ***$p<0.01$.

and climate change. Also, the pair-wise comparisons for factor 5 found a significant difference between the perceptions of respondents with a junior college or less education and college graduates ($p < 0.10$), indicating that the respondents with a college degree had significantly more concerns for mental issues caused by global warming and climate change than the respondents with a junior college or less education. Since other comparisons are not significant, there are no significant differences among these groups' perceptions of mental concerns caused by global warming and climate change. Finally, since the results of one-way ANOVA in Table 6.2 for manager positions are not significant for any of the factors, regardless of their positions, the managers have similar concerns for all factors resulting from global warming and climate change.

6.5 Conclusion

This study examined Turkish hotel managers' perceptions regarding the potential and/or expected impact of global warming and climate change on the tourism industry at personal and industry levels, as well as their commitments to action to combat the effects of these changes during the next 10 years. In order to accomplish this objective, a survey instrument was designed and administered to hotel managers in Turkey. The factor analyses identified five distinct factors, which were labelled as factor 1: potential negative effects, factor 2: commitment to protecting, factor 3: expected effect on the environment, factor 4: consequences for hotels and factor 5: mental concerns. These five factors collectively explained 65.68% of the variance, and Cronbach's alpha coefficients indicated high internal consistency among the factor items.

The factor means indicate that the respondents (hotel managers) are most concerned about the consequences of global warming and climate change for hotels. This is followed by commitment to protecting the environment and perceived negative effects. These results suggest that hotel managers have the highest concerns for protecting their hotels, and thus invest against the potential effects of global warming and climate change. Hotel managers have the second highest concerns for the potential negative effects that global warming and climate change could have on areas such as physical health, leisure and recreation, quality of life, work environment, sustainability of tourism and economic and financial situations. Since factor 2: commitment to protecting has the third highest rating, this may support the managers' concerns for the effects and consequences of global warming and climate change, which in turn may imply that they are willing and ready to deal with global warming and climate change issues.

The comparisons of factors by the respondent demographics indicate that, as for gender, both male and female managers have similar perceptions about the potential effects of global warming and climate change. Concerning their age, all age groups have the same perceptions for all factors, except factor 4: consequences for hotels, where it seems the older managers have significantly more concerns for the consequences of global warming and climate change for their hotels. This may imply that because of their age and experience, they might become more aware and concerned about the potential consequences of global warming and climate change. These experienced managers could serve as change agents and 'influencers' in promoting and dealing with global warming and climate change issues. Education level was not important for differentiating the hotel managers' perceptions about the climate change factors, except for factor 1 and factor 5. It seems that managers with more education are significantly more concerned with the perceived negative effects (factor 1) and mental concerns (factor 5) resulting from global warming and climate change. Finally, the results show that the managerial position of the respondents has no significant effects on their perceptions.

In summary, this exploratory study provided some insights on hotel managers' perceptions about the effects and consequences of global warming and climate change as it relates to various aspects of tourism. The findings show that hotel managers are collectively concerned about global warming and climate change, especially as it relates to consequences for hotels and potential negative effects, and are committed to protecting against the potential consequences. One major practical implication is that hotel employees are also as aware and sensitive as their managers about the possible impacts of climate change. Perhaps hotels can initiate mitigation and combat strategies that can be conveyed to employees and instil the importance of climate change on business practices and strategies. However, despite these insights, this exploratory study has some limitations; therefore, caution should be exercised in interpreting and generalizing the results. One limitation is that this is an exploratory study, and the survey instrument should be replicated in other studies. The second limitation is that the study included only hotel managers. Future research should include managers from other tourism-related fields, such as travel agencies, airline companies, etc. The third limitation was that the study was conducted in Turkey; thus, the results were limited to the perceptions of Turkish managers. We recommend that the same survey should be conducted with hotel managers in other countries.

References

Amelung, B., Nicholls, S. and Viner, D. (2007) Implications of global climate change for tourism flows and seasonality. *Journal of Travel Research* 45, 285–296.

Ball, D.A. Jr, Wendell, H., McCulloch, P.L., Frantz, J., Geringer, M., *et al.* (2002) *International Business: The Challenge of Global Competition*, 8th edn. McGraw-Hill Irwin, New York.

Churchill, G.A. Jr (1979) A paradigm for developing better measures of marketing constructs. *Journal of Marketing Research* 16(February), 64–73.

Churchill, G.A. Jr and Iacobucci, D. (2005) *Marketing Research: Methodological Foundations*, 9th edn. Thomson/South-western, Cincinnati, Ohio.

Gössling, S. (2002) Global environmental consequences of tourism. *Global Environmental Change* 12, 283–302.

Hair, J.F. Jr, Black, W.C., Babin, B.J. and Anderson, R.E. (2010) *Multivariate Data Analysis with Readings*. Prentice-Hall, New Jersey.

Hoque, S., Forsyth, P., Dwyer, L., Spurr, R., Ho, T.V., *et al.* (2010) *The Carbon Footprint of Queensland Tourism*. Sustainable Tourism CRC, Gold Coast, Australia.

IPCC (2007) Metz, B., Davidson, O.R., Bosch, P.R., Dave, R. and Meyer, L.A (eds) *Climate Change 2007: Mitigation. Contribution of Working Group III to the Fourth Assessment Report of the Intergovernmental Panel on Climate Change*. Cambridge University Press, Cambridge and New York. Available at: https://www.ipcc.ch/publications_and_data/ar4/wg1/en/ch5s5-es.html (accessed 10 March 2014).

Jopp, R., DeLacy, T. and Mair, J. (2010) Developing a framework for regional destination adaptation to climate change. *Current Issues in Tourism* 13(6), 591–605.

Kellstedt, P.M., Zahran, S. and Vedlitz, A. (2008) Personal efficacy, the information environment, and attitudes toward global warming. *Risk Analysis* 28(1), 113–126.

Lise, W. and Tol, S.J. (2002) Impact of climate on tourism demand. *Climatic Change* 55, 429–449.

Nicholls, S. (2004) Climate change and tourism. *Annals of Tourism Research* 31(1), 238–240.

Nicholls, S. and Amelung, B. (2008) Climate change and tourism in north-western Europe: impacts and adaptation. *Tourism Analysis* 13(1), 21–31.

Richardson, R.B. and Witkowski, K. (2010) Economic vulnerability to climate change for tourism-dependent nations. *Tourism Analysis* 15(3), 315–330.

Shih, S., Nicholls, S. and Holecek, D. (2009) Impact of weather on downhill ski lift ticket sales. *Journal of Travel Research* 47(3), 359–372.

Turton, S., Dickson, T., Hadwen, H., Jorgensen, B., Pham, T., *et al.* (2010) Developing an approach for tourism climate change assessment: evidence from four contrasting Australian case studies. *Journal of Sustainable Tourism* 18(3), 429–447.

UNWTO (2009) Live the deal – new travel and tourism climate initiative launched in Copenhagen. Available at: http://www.forimmediaterelease.net/pm/3137.html (accessed 10 March 2014).

UNWTO, UNEP–WMO (2008) Davos declaration. Climate change and tourism: responding to global challenges. Available at: http://www.unwto.org/pdf/pr071046.pdf (accessed 10 March 2014).

Uysal, M., Jurowski, C., Noe, F.P. and McDonald, C.D. (1994) Environmental attitude by trip and visitor characteristics. *Tourism Management* 15(4), 284–294.

Viner, D. and Nicholls, S. (2005) Climate change and its implications for international tourism. In: Buhallis, D. and Costa, C. (eds) *Dynamics: Trends, Management and Tools*. Elsevier, Oxford, UK, pp. 156–169.

Wall, G. (1998) Implications of global climate change for tourism and recreation in wetland areas. *Climate Change* 40(2), 371–389.

7 Using Tourism to Mitigate Against Climate Change: The Case of the Caribbean

Kimberley Blackwood,[1]* Juley Wynter-Robertson[2] and Nadine Valentine[1]

[1]University of the West Indies, Kingston, Jamaica; [2]University of the West Indies, Cobbla, Jamaica

7.1 Introduction

To facilitate tourism, there must be movement wherein an individual has to travel from one location to another using a form of transportation. Travel in Caribbean tourism is mainly by airplanes and cruise ships. Tourists travel to the region mainly for sun, sand and sea, and most Caribbean islands have not cultivated a tourism industry based on much beyond that (Pattullo, 2005). Mass tourism began in the Caribbean in the 1960s with the advent of low-cost air travel. Jamaica, Barbados and the Bahamas were among the first places to develop a resort-based tourism programme. Within 20 years, these locations began to experience the problems that are now typically associated with unplanned growth (Cameron and Gatewood, 2008).

Tourism is considered one of the most highly climate-sensitive economic sectors. Many tourism destinations are dependent on climate as their principal attraction, sun and sea, or on environmental resources such as wildlife and biodiversity. Given that these resources are extremely sensitive to climate variability, a changing climate will have profound consequences on tourism flows, and subsequently on the important contribution of tourism to poverty reduction and economic development, especially in developing countries. At the same time, tourism also contributes to global warming. It is estimated that tourism accounts for approximately 5% of global carbon emissions, although the tourism industry has pledged to bring down this figure progressively through partnerships, awareness raising and new technologies.

Tourism is a contributor to climate change; however, its contribution is insignificant in comparison to the large industrial countries that account for a large percentage of greenhouse gas (GHG) emissions. Due to the significance of tourism on

---

*E-mail: kimberleyvblackwood@gmail.com

economic development, the Caribbean governments can use tourism as a mitigating measure against climate change. This paper gives some views on how Caribbean governments could use tourism as a mitigating measure against climate change. It provides insights on how to motivate responsible tourism initiatives which can minimize the impact of tourism on its surroundings. As one of the biggest sectors worldwide, the tourism industry has a major contribution to global development.

Therefore, the tourism industry can influence other sectors by inspiring them and sending signals to industries, governments, communities and tourists that measures to adapt and mitigate climate change are not only vital to the future but also make economic sense. It is a good time for the region to expand its responsible practices, because the target market is growing and people have become more aware and interested in this topic. Tourists are prepared to pay a little bit more money for responsible services because they feel satisfied in contributing to a sustainable environment. The primary objective of this paper, however, is to provide suggestions regarding strategies that the Caribbean governments might adopt and promote in tourism in order to mitigate the effects of climate change.

7.2   Literature Review

Tourism is defined by McIntosh *et al.* (1995) as the sum of the phenomena and relationships arising from the interaction of tourists, business suppliers, host government and host communities in the process of attracting and hosting tourists and other visitors. This definition identifies four important elements of tourism, namely the tourists, businesses providing travel-related services, governments that exert policy control over tourism, and the community members who live in the areas visited by tourists. These elements all come together to create a tourism industry and work as a cycle where one cannot survive without the other.

The Caribbean is recognized as one of the most tourism-dependent regions in the world, highly dependent on tourism as a source of foreign exchange (Bloommestein, 1995). Tourism is the single largest earner of foreign exchange in 16 of the 28 countries in the Caribbean (Bryan, 2001). The great importance that tourism plays in the Caribbean economy is reflected in the number of people employed and the income generated from the industry; it is also estimated that the tourism industry directly and indirectly employs one in four people in the Caribbean, and generates approximately US$2 bn a year in income for the region (Bryan, 2001).

The Caribbean is facing intimidating challenges to achieving sustainable tourism development. High population density, a changing world climate, environmental degradation and sector imbalances for available resources (Watts, 1998) all contribute to the growing developmental challenges. It is therefore particularly important for Caribbean policy makers to be aware of the perverse effects of economies and to formulate policies that address these perverse effects, such as climate change (Grandoit, 2005).

The United Nations International Strategy for Disaster Reduction (2008) defines climate change as the alteration of the world's climate that we humans are causing, through fossil fuel burning, clearing forests and other practices that increase the concentration of GHGs in the atmosphere. The main source of global climate change is human-induced changes in atmospheric composition. These trepidations primarily result from emissions associated with energy use, but on local and regional scales urbanization and land-use changes are also important (Thomas and Trenberth, 2003).

Although there has been progress in understanding climate change, there are many scientific and technical disablements to plan accurately for, adapt to and mitigate against the effects of climate change. There is still considerable uncertainty about the rates of change that can be expected, but it is clear that these changes increasingly will manifest themselves in tangible ways (Thomas and Trenberth, 2003). Among the negative impacts of climate change on the tourism industry are: warmer temperatures; sea level rise; saline intrusion into freshwater aquifers; coastal flooding and erosion; heat stress; coral bleaching; biodiversity loss; increased emergence of vector-borne diseases, namely dengue and malaria, etc.; changes in rainfall patterns resulting in droughts or floods; decreased fresh water availability; and increased intensity of storm activity.

Being cognizant of the need to ensure that climate change does not destroy the tourism product, the Caribbean governments began looking at how best tourism might mitigate against the impact of climate change. One such initiative was at the 2nd International Conference on Climate Change and Tourism, convened by the World Tourism Organization (UNWTO), the United Nations Environment Programme (UNEP) and the World Meteorological Organization (WMO) in Davos, Switzerland, in October 2007. There were numerous requests from participants, many from developing countries, for assistance in building capacity for the management of issues relating to tourism developments and climate change impacts.

There are two major activities that may be applied in utilizing tourism as a moderating factor against climate change adaptation and mitigation (Rogner *et al.*, 2007). Adaptation and mitigation are interchangeable up to a point, but mitigation will always be required to avoid irreversible changes to the climate system, and adaptation will still be necessary due to the irreversible climate change resulting from current and historic rises in GHGs. Unabated climate change would increase the risks and costs substantially (IPCC, 2007), as both mitigation and adaptation strategies are required immediately to limit the impact of climate change.

Studies are showing that more and more international visitors are gravitating to higher altitudes and latitudes (Bigano *et al.*, 2007). Ultimately, this will affect the Caribbean negatively. Tourists now have many choices of new and unexplored destinations, and so many competitors, including China, have simulated the tropical concept of sand, sun and sea (McBain, 2007) to survive this inevitable situation. The Caribbean will therefore need to find creative ways of marketing its destinations and to create sustainability for the environment and the modified tourism product.

7.2.1   Sustainable tourism

In 2004, the UNWTO defined sustainable tourism as 'tourism that takes full account of its current and future economic, social and environmental impact, addressing the needs of visitors, the industry, and the environment and host communities'.

The triple P of sustainable development tourism

The triple P model is used worldwide as a tool to take the three elements, People (social), Planet (environmental) and Profit (economic), into account when working on a project or in an organization. It is being proposed that this model be adopted at the regional level if Caribbean governments are to mitigate the effects of climate change successfully and sustainably. The following outline the areas to be included by governments, using tourism as the driver:

PEOPLE. Tourism must respect the social and cultural identity of the host communities, their cultural heritage and traditional values. This refers to people inside and outside the Caribbean tourism industry, who can work together to mitigate the effects of climate change through social, economic and political participation. Health, art, culture, living environment and safety are all other aspects that must be taken into consideration.

PLANET. Tourism can make use of the natural resources of a country, but it must maintain the ecological processes and help conserve the natural heritage and biodiversity. This is the environment, which includes the soil, air, nature, surface water, groundwater and landscape. Notably, the Caribbean has had many inimical implications on its coral reefs, wetlands and forests.

PROFIT. Tourism must establish long-term economic relations and share fairly the social and economic benefits between all stakeholders. For host communities, this means stable employment and income, which contribute to poverty reduction.

PLEASURE. There is a fourth P – *pleasure*, not in a limited sense of the word, but with a broad range of possible reactions such as joy, emotion, surprise, which is how you create added value. *Pleasure* for the traveller in the sense of the experience, *pleasure* for the local host in the sense of being respected and having decent work – just consider the fourth P as a check for the other Ps.

Trends in sustainable tourism development

According to the UNWTO, the tourism industry is one of the largest global employers in the world, with a yearly growth rate of business turnover of 20–34% since the 1990s. In 1970, there was a revolution in the field of responsible tourism. Globally, a new environmental movement was emerging as a consequence of significant dissatisfaction and concerns about mass tourism. Responsible tourism particularly developed during the last years of the 20th century. To a varying extent, almost every country that is involved in tourism is now involved in ecotourism (UNWTO website: https://pub.unwto.org/WebRoot/Store/Shops/Infoshop/Products/1269/1269-1.pdf). A few trends and developments in the field of sustainable tourism are outlined below and are being proposed as approaches to be endorsed and incentivized by Caribbean governments.

CERTIFICATION. The use of green labels and certification has increased tremendously. The main reason for companies in the tourism industry to seek and attain green certification is to demonstrate to the market and its community their commitment to employing best practices that protect the environment and the community in which they operate.

AWARDS. Many organizations in the tourism and travel industry have started to hand out awards to companies that work in a responsible way. They do this to encourage corporate social responsibility among operators and organizations in the tourism industry.

CONSUMER DEMAND. Consumers want more and more travel that offers authenticity, connections with nature, environmental stewardship and personal growth. Partly because of this increase in consumer demand, sustainable tourism has become a key focus of many tourism-related companies.

TRAVELLERS' PHILANTHROPY. Travellers' philanthropy is about travellers giving back. Worldwide, travellers, as well as travel organizations, are giving financial resources, time and talent to stimulate the well-being of local communities. This emerging movement helps to support and empower local communities by expanding their skills, providing jobs and making long-lasting improvements in health care, education and environmental stewardship.

7.3   Methodology

A qualitative methodology is utilized that is mainly exploratory in approach and appropriate in areas such as climate change, where there is sufficient knowledge; however, the issues of the Caribbean tourism industry, how it is being impacted by climate change and the measures needed to alleviate these challenges, are not yet fully defined. Several articles and studies on Caribbean tourism and climate change were examined and incorporated in the compilation of this research. This approach provides a number of advantages, being a far more sensitive form of research; it affords an opportunity to probe and explore existing studies and make a compelling case.

7.4   Results

A strategic approach to mitigation and adaption would be to revisit all the sectors in tourism. These include the sectors of accommodation, food and beverage, transportation, attractions, tour services, events and adventure tourism as well as recreation. Going forward, diversification of the tourism product should be on the basis of travel motivators, as the product leans heavily towards mass tourism, with the hypothesis that sun, sand, sea and sex will appeal to every tourist.

In nations and destinations where the nature of climate change risks are well established, the implementation of a formal planning process to engage tourism stakeholders and to allocate responsibilities would be more appropriate. Figure 7.1 could be utilized in the framework for adaptation and implementation.

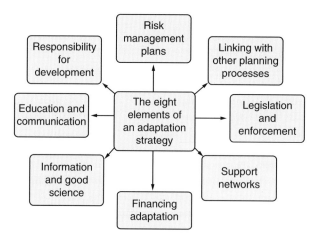

Fig. 7.1. Essential elements of an adaptation strategy.

7.4.1 Information and good science

Mitigation against climate change will require greater efforts in marketing. Tourists are generally self-directed and so the Caribbean will need to make the best use of its assets. A business model approach to marketing will be needed, with a careful analysis of the customer segments. Product differentiation could include marketable packages for these segments. These could include business and recreational packages, weekend vacations instead of long vacations, as well as recreational packages with clusters of attractions. India has already engaged in the aggressive marketing of spiritual wellness, and the Internet has become more critical for advertising. Adapting an e-mail marketing programme can improve business-to-business communication, as well as communication with guests. The effective application of market intelligence will be useful in identifying the types and purposes of travel, as well as information on tourist arrivals. Travel services may be improved by studying the preferences of tourists and their levels of satisfaction having received the service. Information technology may be improved by updating the online portals for reservations and making them user-friendly for enhanced customer feedback.

Targeting nearer destinations has been seen as a mitigation strategy against climate change (ECLAC, 2011). In this regard, visitors from North America would be encouraged to travel to the Caribbean instead of going to Europe and the Far East, so as to reduce greenhouse emissions from travel. Studies have shown that preserving environmental resources (Zhang *et al.*, 2009, p. 352) and developing international standards for competitiveness will also enhance the environmental link. The Caribbean still serves as a pristine location for European tourists and so nature-based tourism is a product that will make use of this supply component. The region's natural resources, though affected by climate change, may be highlighted as a unique ecotourism product for adventurers and nature lovers. Sun, sand and sea are still unique resources for most destinations, but diversification in niche markets will showcase natural resources and improve competitiveness on the global market. Among these resources are the natural mineral baths in places such as St Thomas and Clarendon, Jamaica; the Duns River Falls, among the seven rivers in the world that run directly to the sea; Somerset Falls, the rich rural landscape of Portland; and the indigenous plants and animals, for example the iguana lizard, the Jamaican doctor bird and the coney, all have unique potential.

Jungles, mountains, forest, rivers, beaches and coastlines are among the attraction potential of destinations (Gössling and Hall, 2006, p. 1). Among our most popular attractions so far are the Rainforest Adventurers, by Mystic Mountain, and Adventure Park in Negril, Jamaica. Similar attractions may be incorporated in Portland and the Blue Mountains.

Attractions will need to be more scientifically appropriate and appealing. Excursion trips may also include visits to heritage farms, agricultural museums (IICA, 2010) and rural tours complemented by opportunities for rest and relaxation. Community tourism also will benefit from coordinated tours, and both products could be merged.

7.4.2 Responsibility for development

The types of accommodation available increasingly should be inland, as weather patterns resulting from climate change will affect shorelines. In a study by Buzinde *et al.* (2010), the findings showed that climate change would see a shift from focusing on the beachfront to one of focusing on inland accommodation, with the hope that the tourist would still have an interest in the destination. More of these inland destinations would benefit from added features, so that interest is preserved even in the event of natural disasters. These additions or features may include animals, swimming pools, water features, gardens and the unique positioning of buildings so that the natural surroundings are accessorized. In light of this, legislature should be in place to prevent deforestation. Currently, building codes for hotels are not being adhered to, even though it is mandatory that buildings should be 100 m from the coast. Unpredictability in the earth's movement is a manifestation of climate change, and so the heights of many of our hotels are already a risk. A demonstration of this is the collapse of a section of the Bahia Principe Hotel in Runaway Bay, Jamaica. Hotel designs will become critical. Effective designs should facilitate energy efficiency and better ventilation and illumination (ECLAC, 2011), while incorporating natural and artificial shade.

Additionally, the upgrade of existing structures, especially those of historical significance, could go towards improving heritage tourism. The character of buildings in areas such as Spanish Town and downtown Kingston, Jamaica, could form part of the offering of heritage tours.

Attractions may also be simulated in strategic locations. Dubai has done this by building a man-made beach and receiving the award for best beach. The island could also increase the number of marine parks. The Sandals group has partnered with the Government of Jamaica through the Ministry of Agriculture and Fisheries (http://jis.gov.jm/dr-tufton-promises-laws-to-protect-fishing-industry/) in this regard, and so the Sandals Group now has a fish sanctuary as part of a public–private sector effort.

7.4.3   Linking with the planning process

Energy efficiency will be a mitigating factor against the impact of climate change. The rise in temperatures will generate more heat and so hotels will be using more energy for cooling and air conditioning. A study done at the University of the West Indies, Mona Campus, has proved that it makes economic sense to use solar energy as an efficient energy source and that wind and water power may be used in areas where it exists in abundance. Electrical fixtures and fittings should also be incorporated, so that hotel operations are more efficient and the energy bill reduced. The use of renewable energy will save a lot of foreign exchange and so occupancy sensors can provide savings of 35–45% of lighting costs. Most hotel rooms have individual air-conditioning units that emit significant amounts of carbon emissions. This will further exacerbate the degeneration of the ozone layer and so absorption chillers may be an alternative (ECLAC, 2011).

In the event of a hurricane, waste management will become more critical for the preservation of health and the maintenance of sanitary practices. Waste water as well as sewage could be harnessed and processed by way of biodigesters. Biodigesters are alternatives to pits and collect waste in a controlled environment, somewhat like a pressure cooker; the sewage and waste water breaks down anaerobically and emits water and methane as a by-product. This may be concealed in the landscape creatively without odour, while the water is used for drip irrigation and the methane used as an energy source instead of liquid petroleum gas.

Foreign direct investment has been relatively high in tourism and so a reduction in the hotel's operating cost may enhance its competitiveness in an uncertain natural environment. In this regard, the government is obliged to provide more social services for hotel workers, as well as pension benefits. Contingencies should be created in the hotel's budget for insurance in the event of bush fires and other eventualities (ECLAC, 2011).

The enhancement of cultural tourism could be another mitigation strategy, as it would add to the diversified product line. Our cultural heritage has not been making as much of an impact as it could; however, there is a rich history behind our racial diversity and cultural practices and this may improve our heritage tourism product. There once was a rustic Arawak/Taino museum displaying artefacts and information on the history of the Tainos. This has been revised as an attraction called the Outa Meni Experience; however, the history of the Maroons, Indians and Chinese, once highlighted, can provide a better appreciation of our national diversity for curious 'tourist gazers'. Jamaica has many historic milestones and so Port Royal and Trench Town are also possibilities for national highlighting.

Increased marketing of tour services could also help in mitigating against climate change. Tour operations will complement the attractions and provide word-of-mouth advertising. Tours also provide a controlled environment for leisure and an opportunity to see the countryside. Tour operators are strategic partners in the supply chain and, like travel agencies, improvements should be made in the areas of coordination and scheduling.

Entertainment activities are also a potential diversified product for tourism. Effective marketing will improve visitor arrival and so another mitigation strategy is to promote events along with package deals. Among some events are Jamaica

Lifestyle and Wellness Fest, Trelawny Yam Festival, Montego Bay Yacht Club Easter Regatta, Jamaica International Ocho Rios Jazz Festival, Portland Jerk Festival and the National Theatre Company (NDTC) Season of Dance Improvement.

Health and wellness tourism have become niche markets that have generated significant income for countries including Austria, the nations of the Caribbean, Cuba, Hungary, Israel, Italy, Romania, Switzerland and the USA (Smith and Puczko, 2009; Voigt, *et al.*, 2010). The demand for wellness vacations is gaining worldwide popularity as the Baby Boomers have now retired and are desirous of a better quality of life. This trendsetting group of Americans have more disposable income, education and time (Steiner and Reisinger, 2006), and so many are looking increasingly at spa treatments and other experiences to reduce their stress and to improve their health and wellbeing (Voigt *et al.*, 2010). This segment may benefit from personal care, guidance on health-related matters, therapies and professional competence, as well as wellness amenities in the island's lush landscape. Health and wellness tourism will help with mitigation by integrating and matching all the strengths of the tourism product and adding the strengths of the leading spa destinations.

7.4.4   Support networks

The changes in rainfall patterns will challenge the island's food security. Presently, there is a high propensity to import. Mitigation in food production should be pursued with the object of self-sufficiency. Agricultural production should therefore be improved in areas of high rainfall. The use of technology including plant tissue culture should be engaged to increase disease-free planting material and to improve crop production. Farmers in the resort areas should stand to benefit from linkages in the Tourist Linkages Hub, but the channels of distribution to hotels should be monitored more closely by the state so that the demands of the hotel are consistently met. Efforts should be made to produce foods that are normally imported. Among these are fruit and herbs.

Additionally, food production may be improved by increasing support to small farmers and the systems of distribution. Of worthy note is the establishment of community tourism, Agro Parks and the Tourism Linkages Hub. These partnerships are expected to enhance competitive advantages, and may increase the number of farmers supplying the hotels. In Trinidad and Tobago, the tourism industry has an 'Adopt a Farmer' programme wherein farmers have a ready market and are partners with schools in the creation of school gardens. These schools produce herbs for the hotels and the income helps with the development of the schools.

Restaurants are part of the value chain, and in Jamaica tourists and chefs enjoy the unique flavours of local produce; however, exposure is limited and tourists do not have much Jamaican food experience. Consistency in the supply of produce needs to be improved, but there is a non-punitive import policy, leading to the demise of the tourism leakage rate. Additionally, improvements will be needed in the timeliness with which accounts with agroproducers are settled (Reid, 2009). Strategic food production can develop culinary tourism with the use of indigenous foods and traditional methods (IICA, 2010). Tourists are also gravitating towards traditional dishes, and opportunities exist to showcase Jamaican foods by introducing, for example, coconut water instead of cranberry juice and guava and cherries instead of American apples. There could also be an increase in the usage of herbal teas and sauces in the dining experience. Partnerships could also be established with food processors and the Scientific Research Council so that chefs would be made aware of the diversity of Jamaican foods.

7.4.5   Legislature and enforcement

Policies to address emissions from aviation and shipping have made little progress at the international level. However, in a unique policy to be applied at a regional level, the European Union emission trading scheme (ETS) will, under current proposals, include aviation and shipping in its allocation of emissions permits from 2012. The rapid introduction of biofuels may be one of the few options for cutting aviation emissions, but it still faces technical, social, economic and environmental difficulties and should be subject to independently monitored sustainability criteria (OECD and UNEP).

Vehicles that are used for tours and transporting guests are encouraged to conform to National Energy policy (Ministry of Transport and Works, 2009); however, this policy should also apply to the general transportation industry. To reduce emissions further, one researcher has suggested the possibility of an underwater transit railway system.

Climate change will manifest seasons of drought and low rainfall. This is the experience of many Jamaican communities and so hotels should be encouraged to practice water conservation with the incorporation of specialized faucets and the creation of catchment areas for specific housekeeping chores. In some hotels, guests are asked to indicate when they wish to have their linen laundered (ECLAC, 2011); however, this should be made standard practice for all hotels.

Import policies are no longer stringent, but hotels could be encouraged to introduce seasonal local fruit and foods. The Caribbean has a Climate Change Centre and so the government could also partner with other countries as well as with stakeholders in banking and the private sector (ECLAC, 2011). In Barbados, there is a coastal zone management programme, while in Belize there has been a decrease in the number of beach properties. Efforts may also be engaged to facilitate tourists who wish to be philanthropic. This will encourage committed partnerships and goodwill.

7.4.6   Risk management plans

Risk management will become more critical in an environment of climate change. The Offices of Disaster Preparation and Emergency Management should have an iterative emergency programme. Efforts should therefore be made to address infrastructure that supports the residents not only in resort areas but also the general populace. In this regard, there should be proper drainage, water disposal, water supply in areas without, and roads should be more inland away from the eroding coastlines (ECLAC, 2011). The coastal and marine services, as well as the military, should be on high alert, with standards in place for marina piers and bulkheads in the event of storm surges and sea level rise. Areas prone to bush fires, especially those in resort areas, should be monitored for early detection of spontaneous combustion (ECLAC, 2011).

Urban planning is a mitigation strategy for tourism so that less people become vulnerable to climate change. The working hours of those employed in the sector may also be reduced so that commute time and emissions are also reduced. Additionally, hotels in tourist areas could partner with the locals for goods and services and so reduce the risk of social hazards and criminal activity. Hotels could practice and so market their facilities as eco-friendly and as a green destination.

Many of our newer hotels have erected walls as a demarcation, but these have blocked out many scenic views. Efforts should be made to erect conservation areas, and these should be monitored by the National Environmental Protection Agency (NEPA). Beach erosion has been described as one of the most pressing and dramatic manifestations of climate change (Phillips and Jones, 2006; Schleupner, 2008) and so, like many of our Caribbean partners, efforts should be made to maintain the coastline and preserve the deteriorating reefs. In Belize, there is a thrust to restore mangroves and protect the shorelines. In St Lucia, the fisherfolk have formed a divers association, a collaborative group to showcase the island's natural flora and fauna.

7.4.7   Education and communication

In integrating all strategies for mitigation against climate change, the government would need to play a key role by supporting all the strategies and educating the public of the implications of climate change and the role they would be required to play. Employees should also be engaged so they might understand the implications to their jobs. Efforts should also be made to build public awareness in the media, as well as among students. In the Kingston metropolitan region, some public buses may be seen with advertising slogans sensitizing the public to climate change. Health ministries will need to be proactive in the event of outbreaks of diseases related to water shortages and flooding (Chen et al., 2008). Additional efforts should be made to improve social services so that nationals, business travellers and investors would not be frustrated with the bureaucracy of conducting business. Staff at all levels of the tourism industry will need to be trained to appreciate this paradigm shift.

7.4.8   Financing adaptation

Going forward, financing will be needed in the form of a climate change adaptation fund so that changes might be implemented and funds raised for more vulnerable hotels. In Guyana, President Jagdio secured funds to conserve the island's forestry. Policies will be needed for physical planning wherein building lines are mandated to move back from eroding coasts (ECLAC, 2011). Emerging measures relating to climate change should be incorporated into tourism policies. Existing policies will need to be reinforced regarding environmental laws; building and construction codes and non-compliance should be more punitive.

7.5   Conclusion

The effects of climate change in the Caribbean are not events in the distant future. The tourism industry and economies and livelihoods of the region are already being affected by sea level rise and erosion, and also by extreme impacts such as coral bleaching, flooding and drought. Effective responses are necessary from all stakeholders – government, communities and tourism industry players. In integrating all the strategies for alleviating climate change, the government will need to play a key role by supporting the strategies and educating the public of the implications of climate change and the importance of their contribution. Employees in the industry should also be engaged, so they may understand the importance of their contribution. Efforts must be made to build public awareness, implement new strategies and reinforce regulations and relevant policies that will address the reduction of GHGs.

This paper is important because it provides new insights into how Caribbean governments can use tourism to mitigate against climate change. This qualitative approach allows for a proactive strategy, as most research in the past highlights the impacts of tourism on climate change. Researchers have taken a more positive approach to the issue and, based on these insights, recommendations have been made and measures are to be adopted by Caribbean regional governments.

The following adaptation measures can be undertaken by the Caribbean governments:

- Development of a risk management framework, including guidelines and an early warning system.
- Awareness raising and the implementation of training programmes.
- Integration of climate change issues in tourism policies and development of preventive regulations.
- Detailed analysis of risk management and business plan development at two destinations.
- Establishment of a network and a website for the dissemination of practical experience and background information.
- The incorporation of tourism aspects in the national climate change framework.

There is an urgent need in the region for technical and financial resource assistance, enhanced capacity and evidence-based adaptation strategies that are practical and effective in reducing vulnerability and increasing resilience for sustainable development.

A critical need exists for sustainable tourism development that incorporates climate change mitigation strategies and these include the following:

- Regional petition of the governments of developed countries to reduce GHG emission.
- Promotion of green tourism.
- Development of renewable energy plants.
- Energy savings by the tourism industry.
- Private and public partnership to formulate and implement a tourism plan that takes climate change into consideration.

- Future promotions should be based primarily on increasing tourists' spending and their average length of stay.
- Destinations should assess the origin of their emissions and understand the areas where the most economical reductions could be made.
- Focus on three sectors – transport, accommodation and activities.
- Establishing a meaningful boundary system for transport has been suggested in order to incorporate all the energy used in the destination, including fuel bunkered for all transport systems.

Climate change presents an opportunity for the Caribbean tourism industry to position itself as one of the greenest tourism destinations in the world. In this regard, the industry should build capacity in adaptation and mitigation, implementing the principles for 'carbon neutral' destinations, incorporating into packages, with some urgency, voluntary or 'opt-out' carbon offsetting of flights and encouraging airlines to reduce CO_2 emissions by 4000–5000 t. Additionally, there should be a combination of voluntary and mandatory measures to ensure that the tourism industry supports the goals by retrofitting their properties with an energy efficient and eco-friendly system. Of utmost importance in reversing the trend of growing GHG emissions in tourism is the need for tourists to change their behaviour and for structural changes to be made in the tourism industry. Governments should also look at providing incentives to tourism entities that engage in the process of eliminating, reducing, substituting or offsetting their climate change footprint. There should be serious consideration given to the introduction, or revamping where necessary, of railway trains as a mode of ground transportation in the tourism industry, thus reducing the emission of carbon compounds.

Ultimately, cross-sectorial, interministerial and cross-ministerial cooperation and collaboration is required to ensure tourism is utilized as a mitigating force against climate change. Tourism can play a significant role in addressing climate change. It must show leadership as an agent of change for both adaptation and mitigation – the time for action is now.

References

Bigano, A.J., Hamilton, M. and Tull, R. (2007) The impact of climate change on domestic and international tourism: a simulation study. *The Integrated Assessment Journal* 7(1), 25–49.

Bloommestein, E. (1995) Sustainable tourism in the Caribbean: an enigma. In: Griffth, M.D. and Persaud, B. (eds) *Economic Policy and the Environment: The Caribbean Experience.* Centre for Environment and Development, Kingston, Jamaica, pp. 167–190.

Bryan, A.T. (2001) Caribbean tourism: igniting the engines of sustainable growth. *The North–South Agenda, 52.* North South Center, University of Miami, Miami, Florida.

Buzinde, C.N., Manuel-Navarrete, D., Yoo, E.E. and Morais, D. (2010) Tourists' perceptions in a climate of change: eroding destinations. *Annals of Tourism Research* 37(2), 333–354.

Cameron, C.M. and Gatewood, J.B. (2008) Beyond sun, sand and sea: the emergent tourism programme in the Turks and Caicos Islands. *Journal of Heritage Tourism* 3(1), 55, doi:10.2167/jht036.0.

Chen, A.A., Bailey, W. and Taylor, M.A. (2008) Enabling activities for the preparation of Jamaica's Second National communication to the UNFCCC : vulnerability and adaptation in human health prepared by in association with the climate studies group. Mona University of the West Indies, Kingston.

Economic Commission for Latin America and the Caribbean (ECLAC) (2011) An Assessment of the
    Economic Impact of Climate Change on the Tourism Sector in Jamaica, LIMITED LC/CAR/L.313,
    22 October 2011, pp. 54–61. Available at: http://www.cepal.org/portofspain/noticias/paginas/0/44160/
    Grenadalcarl329.pdf (accessed 26 June 2015).
Gössling, S. and Hall, C.M. (2006) An introduction to tourism and global environmental change.
    In: Gössling, S. and Hall, C.M. (eds) *Tourism and Global Environmental Change. Ecological, Social,
    Economic and Political Interrelationships*. Routledge, London, pp. 1–34.
Grandoit, J. (2005) Tourism as a development tool in the Caribbean and the environmental by-products:
    the stresses on small island resources and viable remedies. *Journal of Development and Social
    Transformation* 2(2), 89–97.
Inter-American Institute for Cooperation on Agriculture (IICA) (2010) Promoting Sustainable and
    Cometitive Agriculture in the Americas. An Annual Report. Available at: http://www.summit-
    americas.org/jswg/iica_rep_2010.pdf (accessed 26 June 2015).
IPCC (2007) *Climate Change 2007: Synthesis Report*. IPCC, Geneva, Switzerland.
McBain, H. (2007) Caribbean tourism and agriculture: linking to enhance development and competi-
    tiveness. ECLAC – Studies and Perspectives series. *The Caribbean*, N 2.
McIntosh, R.N., Goeldner, C.R. and Ritchie, J.R. (1995) *Tourism, Principles, Practices, Philosophies*.
    John Wiley and Sons, Inc, Toronto, pp. 734.
Ministry of Transport and Works (2009) National Transport Policy. Hon. L. Michael Henry, CD, MP,
    Minister of Transport and Works, 15 September 2009. Available at: http://www.mhtww.gov.jm/
    general_information/reports/hm-sectoral20092010.pdf (accessed 26 June 2015).
Pattullo, P. (2005) *Last Resorts: The Cost of Tourism in the Caribbean*. Monthly Review Press, New York.
Phillips, M.R. and Jones, A.L. (2006) Erosion and tourism infrastructure in the coastal zone: problems,
    consequences and management. *Tourism Management* 27(3), 517–524.
Reid, R. (2009) Agri-food Value Chains – the Bigger Picture. ICCA Regional Agribusiness Specialist.
    Available at: http://www.iica.int/Eng/regiones/caribe/trinidadytobago/Documents/Agrifood_
    value_chains.pdf (accessed 23 April 2014).
Rogner, H.H., Zhou, D., Bradley, R., Crabbé, P., Edenhofer, O., *et al.* (2007) Intensities. Introduction.
    In: Metz, B., Davidson, O.R., Bosch, P.R., Dave, R. and Meyer, L.A. (eds) *Climate Change 2007:
    Mitigation. Contribution of Working Group III to the Fourth Assessment Report of the Intergovernmental
    Panel on Climate Change*. Cambridge University Press, Cambridge, UK and New York.
Schleupner, C. (2008) Evaluation of coastal squeeze and its consequences for the Caribbean island
    Martinique. *Ocean and Coastal Management* 51(5), 383–390.
Smith, M. and Puczko, L. (2009) *Health and Wellness Tourism*. Butterworth-Heinemann, London.
Steiner, C.J., and Reisinger, Y. (2006) Ringing the fourfold: a philosophical framework for thinking
    about wellness tourism. *Tourism Recreation Research* 31(1), 5–14.
Thomas R. and Trenberth, E.K. (2003) Modern global climate change. *The Science Journal* 302(5651),
    1719–1723, doi:10.1126/science.1090228.
United Nations, International Strategy for Disaster Reduction (2008) *Climate Change and Disaster
    Reduction*. International Environment, Geneva. Available at: http://www.unisdr.org/files/4146_
    ClimateChangeDRR.pdf (accessed 26 June 2015).
Voigt, C., Brown, G. and Howat, G. (2010) In search for transformation: an examination of the benefits
    sought by wellness tourists. *Tourism Review* 66(1/2), 16–30.
Watts, D. (1998) The water balance and soil erosion in the Eastern Caribbean. In: Barker, D., Newby, C. and
    Morrissey, M. (eds) *A Reader in Caribbean Geography*. Ian Randle Publishers, Kingston, Jamaica,
    pp. 17–24.
Zhang, X., Song, H. and Huang, G.Q. (2009) Tourism supply chain management: a new research
    agenda. *Tourism Management* 30(3), 345–358.

8 Green Economy Practices in the Tourism Industry: The Case of Limpopo Province, South Africa

Charles Nhemachena,[1]* Siyanda Jonas[2] and Selma Karuaihe[2]

[1]*International Water Management Institute, Pretoria, South Africa; [2]Human Sciences Research Council, Pretoria, South Africa*

8.1 Introduction

Tourism as an industry contributes significantly to the national and provincial economies of South Africa, accounting for over 5% of gross domestic product (GDP). In recent years, the focus on the green economy initiatives across the various sectors is gaining momentum. In its 2013 World Tourism Barometer, the United Nations World Tourism Organization (UNWTO, 2013) showed that the contribution of tourism to the global economy was estimated at around 9% of GDP, through direct and induced impact. Moreover, the sector's contribution to employment was estimated at an average of 1 in 11 jobs generated globally. The contribution of the tourism industry in South Africa has led the government to recognize the sector as, *inter alia*, a key sector that can precipitate addressing the challenges of inequality, poverty and unemployment. For instance, the *State of Travel and Tourism in South Africa* posits that the government identifies tourism as one of the key contributing sectors to the medium-term strategic priorities of growing the economy and creating decent work (Republic of South Africa, 2013).

The focus on green economy is supported by the Environmental Pillar (2012), which argues for the need to plan a clear pathway to a greener economy to help correct and rebalance our environmental, social and economic systems to produce a sustainable, dynamic equilibrium. This requires society to recognize that the environmental system we have has finite resources and there is a need to adjust production and consumption patterns given rapid population growth, depleted resources and the slow rate of regeneration of the biosphere and atmosphere. Strategic planning in green economy interventions is important to help create sustainable green jobs and capitalization on innovative green economy opportunities to develop local economies.

* E-mail: cnhemachena@gmail.com; c.nhemachena@cgiar.org

A green economy seeks to drive growth, jobs, environmental improvement, poverty eradication and social equity by shifting investments towards clean technologies and natural capital, as well as human resources and social institutions (UNEP-IMF-GIZ, 2012; UNEP, 2013).

With growing global attention on green economy and growth, there is a need for research efforts to understand current green practices, as well as the opportunities and challenges presented by the green economy in the tourism industry. Strategic opportunities in tourism identified by the United Nations Environment Programme (UNEP) 2011 include: water consumption, waste management, protection of biodiversity, energy efficiency in hotels and improvement of linkages with the local economy. The South African green economy report identified nine key focus areas: (i) green buildings and the built environment; (ii) sustainable transport and infrastructure; (iii) clean energy and energy efficiency; (iv) resource conservation and management; (v) sustainable waste management practices; (vi) agriculture, food production and forestry; (vii) water management; (viii) sustainable consumption and production; and (ix) environmental sustainability (Department of Environmental Affairs, 2010; Development Bank of Southern Africa, 2011). Clearly, tourism can play a critical role in contributing to driving the green economy initiatives in South Africa.

The tourism industry presents opportunities for making significant contributions to promoting economic growth, creating jobs and addressing the challenges of poverty, inequality and unemployment. For example, the South African tourism industry has been identified as one of the main contributing sectors to the medium-term strategic priorities of growing the economy and creating decent work (including green jobs) (Republic of South Africa, 2013). The objective of this chapter is to explore the understanding of the green economy concepts and practices currently implemented in the tourism industry in the Limpopo Province. There is no empirical evidence of a baseline study on green economy concepts and practices in South Africa, and this chapter addresses that gap using the Limpopo Province as a case study. The analysis was based on baseline survey data collected across randomly selected tourism businesses and key informants from 23 municipalities in the Limpopo Province to help shed light on the understanding of and different green economy practices undertaken in the province by industry stakeholders and government.

8.2   Literature Review

The future of tourism is linked inextricably to good and quality environment, which means that tourism is also linked with the wider shift from conventional economic practices towards an increasingly green economy. Tourism in the green economy refers to tourism activities that can be maintained, or sustained, indefinitely in their social, economic, cultural and environmental contexts: 'sustainable tourism'. Sustainable tourism is tourism that takes full account of current and future economic, social and environmental impacts, addressing the needs of visitors, the industry, the environment and host communities (UNEP, 2011).

Many countries across the world have experienced varying impacts of the several concurrent crises that have unfolded during the last decade (e.g. climate, biodiversity, fuel, food, global financial system). The collective impacts of these crises affect progress and opportunities to sustain prosperity and achieve the Millennium Development Goals (MDGs) – e.g. MDG1 on reducing extreme poverty in addition to compounding persistent social problems (e.g. job losses, socio-economic insecurity, disease and social instability) (UNEP, 2011). These factors led to the recent traction of the green economy concept as an important tool for sustainable development and poverty eradication. In addition, there is growing evidence of 'a new economic paradigm – one in which material wealth is not delivered perforce at the expense of growing environmental risks, ecological scarcities and social disparities' (UNEP, 2011, p. 14). The UNEP 2011 report 'Towards a Green Economy' states that transitioning to a green economy has the potential to become the new engine of growth, net generator of decent jobs and a vital strategy to eliminate persistent poverty. Therefore, there is growing evidence globally to suggest that transitioning to a green economy has sound economic and social justification.

UNEP (2011) also argued strongly for investment of 2% of global GDP in greening ten central sectors of the economy (agriculture, buildings, energy supply, fisheries, forestry, industry, tourism, transport, water and waste). This would shift development and unleash public and private capital flows towards a low-carbon, resource-efficient pathway. The central sectors identified by UNEP are: (i) investments in natural capital (agriculture, fisheries, water and forests); (ii) investments in energy and resource efficiency (renewable energy, manufacturing, waste, buildings, transport, tourism, cities); and (iii) support required for maintaining the transition to a global green economy (modelling global green economy investment scenarios, enabling conditions and financing).

8.2.1   South Africa green economy landscape

South Africa, like many other developing and African countries, faces current and persistent challenges of poverty and unemployment. Additional challenges that the country faces include threats to environmental degradation, loss of biodiversity and the effects of climate change. The challenges of inequality and poverty facing South Africa also present opportunities for the transition towards a green economy. South Africa views a green economy 'as a sustainable development path based on addressing the interdependence between economic growth, social protection and natural ecosystem' (Department of Environmental Affairs, 2010, p. 5). In addition, the South African government regards a shift to a green economy (including a low-carbon economy) as more sustainable in the long term (National Planning Commission, 2012). According to the 2010 Green Economy Summit report, the green economy refers to two interrelated developmental outcomes for the South African economy: (i) growing economic activity (which leads to investment, jobs and competitiveness) in the green industry sector; and (ii) a shift in the economy as a whole towards cleaner industries and sectors with a low environmental impact compared to its socio-economic impact.

The South African government has prioritized the tourism industry through various policies and development initiatives, with green economy initiatives gaining momentum. The nine provinces including the Limpopo Province are expected to align their policies and frameworks to the national strategies. The Limpopo provincial strategy on tourism is aligned to the national policies and frameworks and the Limpopo Tourism Growth Strategy (TGS 2009–2014), which states that the tourism vision of the Limpopo Province is 'making Limpopo Province the preferred ecotourism destination in Southern Africa' (Limpopo Provincial Government, 2013). The strategic focus of Limpopo as an ecotourism destination is centred on its competitive advantage in mainly three areas: (i) its resource base; (ii) Limpopo's culture and heritage; and (iii) its location within the Southern African Development Community (SADC), with emphasis on expanding Limpopo's tourism offering into Mozambique to enhance the 'bush to beach experience' (Limpopo Provincial Government, 2009, 2013).

Evidence shows that transition to a green economy is already under way in South Africa, a point underscored by this chapter and a growing wealth of literature by various organizations (e.g. government departments, universities, research institutions, civil society). For example, South Africa has put in place policies and plans to promote green growth as a new source of growth for addressing the environmental and socioeconomic challenges facing the country. Examples include the South African framework for responding to the economic crisis and UNEP's Global Green New Deal, National Development Plan (NDP) Vision 2030, New Growth Path (NGP), Green Economy Accord and National Strategy for Sustainable Development (NSSD). A number of key programmes and interventions from these policies and initiatives are being implemented in various sectors, such as energy and environment. These are discussed in more detail below.

The 1996 South African Constitution

Section 24(b) of South Africa's new Constitution commits the state to 'secure ecologically sustainable development and use of natural resources while promoting justifiable economic and social development'.

South Africa's 2009 framework response to the international economic crisis

The South African framework for responding to the economic crisis and UNEP's Global Green New Deal recognizes the opportunities in the development of industries that combat the negative effects of climate change and urges South Africa to develop strong capacity in green technologies and industries. The framework, together with many other national policy documents and plans (e.g. NDP, Vision 2030, NGP, NSSD), emphasizes the need to implement pro-employment programmes that promote sustainable and inclusive growth. The transformation of businesses and the adoption of sustainable consumption and production processes is expected to ensure growth in green sectors, more green and decent jobs, reduced energy and material intensities in production processes, less waste and pollution and significantly reduced greenhouse gas emissions (Department of Environmental Affairs, 2010).

2009–2014 Medium Term Strategic Framework (MTSF)

The MTSF 2009–2014 priority 9 highlights the implementation of the 2008 Cabinet approved National Framework for Sustainable Development (NFSD) to ensure that the country follows a sustainable development trajectory. South Africa has since finalized the National Strategy for Sustainable Development (NSSD) and Action

Plan, which was approved by the Cabinet in 2011. The NSSD and Action Plan defines key sustainable development principles for the country, while being mindful of global challenges and growth ideals. Creating sustainable jobs is one of the South African government's top five priorities in the MTSF 2009–2014. Implementing pro-employment green economy programmes offers opportunities to contribute to this national priority, as well as to that of combating the negative effects of climate change.

Green Economy Summit

The Green Economy Summit of 2010 was convened under the overarching theme, 'Towards a resource efficient, low-carbon and pro-employment growth path'. The summit, made up of a broad multi-stakeholder base, broadly committed to ensuring that the country's growth path was resource efficient, far less carbon intensive and more labour absorbing, and also mobilized and further developed the significant scientific and technological capacities of society at large. The Green Economy Summit identified nine priority sectors and areas for promoting a low-carbon, resource-efficient and employment-intensive green economy. In his opening address, President Zuma stated that:

> In the midst of the global economic crisis, the United Nations Environment Programme called for a Global Green New Deal. Today, at this summit, we are responding to that call. We are certain that out of this summit will emerge a national green economy plan, informed by valuable insights on key areas of focus and on issues requiring our national attention in the short, medium and long term.

The summit summarized the green economy as 'a sustainable development path based on addressing the inter-dependence between economic growth, social protection and natural ecosystem' (Department of Environmental Affairs, 2010).

New Growth Path

The 2010 New Growth Path (NGP) sets out critical drivers for employment creation and growth, implying fundamental changes in the structure and character of production to generate a more inclusive and greener economy over the medium to long run, through macro- and microeconomic interventions. The NGP sets a target of 5 million new jobs to be created by 2020, based on strong and sustained inclusive economic growth and rebuilding of the productive sectors (e.g. infrastructure development) of the economy. The NGP places job creation and decent work at the centre of economic policy (Economic Development Department (EDD), 2010).

Green Economy Accord

In November 2011, South Africa unveiled a Green Economy Accord (GEA) to launch a partnership between the South African government, the business community, trade unions and civil society. The GEA is one of a series of accords agreed under the NGP. The GEA set goals to create 300,000 jobs in contribution to the NGP's objective of creating 5 million new jobs by 2020, with 80,000 jobs in manufacturing and the rest in the construction, operations and maintenance of new environmentally friendly infrastructure, and to double the country's clean energy generation.

The potential for job creation rises to well over 400,000 by 2030. Additional jobs will be created by expanding the existing public employment schemes to protect the environment, as well as in the production of biofuels. Job creation potentials are expected in natural resource management and construction in the short to medium term, and in renewable energy construction and manufacture of inputs in the medium to long term.

The Industrial Policy Action Plan (IPAP2)

The Industrial Policy Action Plan (IPAP2) builds on the National Industrial Policy Framework (NIPF) and the 2007/08 IPAP. It is a significant step forward in scaling up the government's efforts to promote long-term industrialization and industrial diversification beyond the current reliance on traditional commodities and non-tradable services, with the aim of expanding production in value-added sectors with high employment and growth multipliers that compete in export markets, as well as those that compete in the domestic market against imports. The IPAP is also an integral component of the NGP. The IPAP2 emphasizes the manufacturing aspects of the green economy, i.e. green industries and industrial energy efficiency. In addition, IPAP2 champions the South African Renewables Initiative (SARI), aimed at funding initiatives to achieve greater critical mass of renewable energy generation, hand-in-hand with the localization of manufacturing related to renewables.

Integrated Resource Plan 2010 and Integrated Energy Plan

The key objectives of these plans include averting the risk of power shortages in the near term while increasing energy supply and efficiency to support the needs of a growing economy in the longer term; ensuring affordable energy to support inclusive development; addressing local environmental threats related to energy use, notably those related to air pollution and human health; and shouldering an appropriate share of future responsibility for the long-term global challenge of restricting emissions of CO_2 and other greenhouse gases. The country plans to generate about 15% of its electricity from renewable sources by 2020 and to enhance energy efficiency.

National Strategy for Sustainable Development (NSSD) and Action Plan

The NFSD defines key sustainable development principles for the country, while being mindful of global challenges and growth ideals. The NSSD recognizes the insufficiency of a simple 'triple bottom line' approach to sustainable development in South Africa, due to complex development considerations such as high inequalities. The South African approach to sustainable development, therefore, regards social, economic and ecosystem factors as embedded within each other and underpinned by the systems of governance (Department of Environmental Affairs, 2011). The 2011 NSSD identifies five main sustainable development priorities and objectives: (i) enhancing systems for integrated planning and implementation; (ii) sustaining our ecosystems and using natural resources efficiently; (iii) towards a green economy; (iv) building sustainable communities; and (v) responding effectively to climate change. Strategic objective number three focuses on a just transition towards a resource-efficient, low-carbon and pro-employment growth path. This, together with the other objectives, provides a broader commitment from the government to steer the economy into an inclusive growth path.

National Development Plan (NDP) Vision 2030

The National Development Plan (NDP) Vision 2030 approved by the Cabinet in September 2012 argues that to address the socio-economic and environmental challenges, South Africa needs to achieve rapid, inclusive economic growth while at the same time making the transition to a low-carbon economy. The central objectives of the NDP Vision 2030 are to eradicate poverty and sharply reduce inequality by 2030. Creating 11 million jobs and achieving an average annual real GDP growth of 5.7% are among the series of targets set by the NDP to be met over the next two decades.

National Climate Change Response Policy

South Africa announced in March 2009 that it would put in place a binding climate change policy in 3 years to cap emission growth by 2025. The measures contained in the plan included regulatory, fiscal and legislative framework that would make tracking and reporting of emissions mandatory. The country has since developed a climate change response policy that was accepted by the Cabinet in 2011.

The policies presented above provide the overarching national framework and enabling environment for advancing the concept of green economy and sustainable growth in South Africa. Furthermore, the policies and plans acknowledge that the country's economic growth and development path is too resource intensive, and that this needs to change. Generally, policy developments have witnessed an emerging trend in South Africa's national policy discourse, which calls for more responsible use of natural resources. The South African government recognizes the current natural resource constraints and ecosystem pressures and the need to transition into sustainable consumption and production patterns and greener economic growth trajectories (Development Bank of Southern Africa, 2011). However, addressing the trade-offs associated with the transition to a greener and more environmentally sustainable economy requires the careful design and sequencing of decisions to ensure that the decline of legacy sectors (e.g. coal-fired electricity generation) is balanced by a concurrent growth in green economy sectors (National Planning Commission, 2012).

In view of the above discussion, the challenge for the Limpopo Province is to identify and profile various green economy activities being implemented in the various sectors of the province, including tourism. It is therefore necessary for a study of this nature not only to help policy makers and industry participants understand the concepts of green economy but also to utilize the findings to guide future policy interventions nationally and locally.

8.3   Methodology

The analysis is based on baseline survey data collected across the Limpopo Province to help understand the knowledge of the green economy concept and the different green economy practices being implemented. A sample of 41 tourism businesses and key informants from 23 municipalities in Limpopo Province was selected purposefully from the province to explore the understanding and implementation of green economy activities in the province. Descriptive statistics were used to characterize the understanding of the different green economy practices being implemented in the tourism industry in the Limpopo Province. A secondary document review helped to provide a broader conceptual understanding of the green economy concept from international and national perspectives. In addition, key green economy sectors and interventions were explored from a review of the published literature, both internationally and in South Africa.

8.4   Results

Tourism establishment owners and managers were asked to provide their understanding of the green economy concept. The responses reported showed that about 30% viewed it as saving water and energy, which impacted directly on their net profits as businesses. Some reported that it involved the recycling of waste material (18%) and saving electricity (13%) (see Fig. 8.1). About one-quarter of the respondents reported that they did not know anything about the green economy concept. Respondents were also asked what they thought the transition to a green economy meant for the Limpopo Province. Twenty-nine per cent of the respondents reported that they did not know and 24% reported that it had to do with environmental conservation.

Furthermore, Fig. 8.2 shows that some respondents reported that transitioning to a green economy for the province meant saving water and energy (14%). The views and perceptions of tourism business establishments on the green economy shows that for businesses such as those in tourism, the implementation of green economy activities should provide some direct or indirect positive returns to the business. For example, savings in water and electricity reduce operating expenses and contribute to

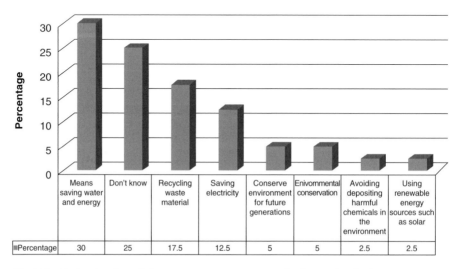

Fig. 8.1. Understanding of the green economy concept in the tourism industry.

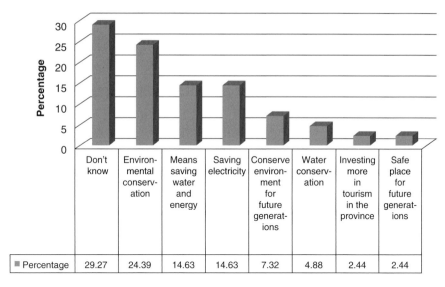

Fig. 8.2. Understanding of what transitioning to a green economy in the tourism industry means for the Limpopo Province.

increasing net revenues and profits. Therefore, promotion of green economy activities in businesses such as tourism establishments should consider, among other factors, the implications of such activities on businesses returns.

8.4.1   Green economy activities being implemented by tourism establishments

Some of the current green economy activities being implemented by tourism establishments include energy efficient product distribution, installation and maintenance; recycling of waste materials; and education, compliance and awareness.

The energy efficient product distribution, installation and maintenance activities reported include using energy efficient bulbs (24%); switching off lights, water heaters and taps in unoccupied rooms (21%); water-saving practices; and using gas stoves for cooking and heating. Only about 7% reported that they were not doing anything. As discussed above, the current activities are mainly energy- and water-saving practices.

Although the respondents identified the recycling of waste material as one of the green economy activities being implemented by tourism business establishments, further discussions showed that current activities mainly included the separation of waste material before it was taken up by recycling companies. Only 10% reported that they recycled some of their waste materials. About 45% of the respondents reported that they were not involved in any waste-recycling activities in their establishments.

The education, compliance and awareness activities reported were mainly for staff members (56%) to ensure that they adhered to the implementation of various activities that the establishments would have identified for implementation.

For example, staff would be trained and made aware of the need to switch off electricity and air conditioning, as well as to ensure that all water taps were closed properly. Although the respondents reported that the training and awareness was mainly for their staff members, some reported through further discussions that they also made efforts to raise awareness among their clients to use water and electricity responsibly. For instance, some reported that they displayed information in the rooms on water and electricity conservation, such as encouraging clients to reuse their towels and to switch off appliances and lights when moving out of the rooms. About 44% of the respondents reported that they did not have any education and awareness programmes in their business.

8.4.2   Main green practices, services or products currently being used by tourism establishments

Figure 8.3 presents the main green practices, services or products, currently being used by tourism establishments. The results show that the main practices include energy efficiency (53%) and water preservation (33%). Again, much of the green practices by the tourism establishments interviewed focused on energy and water savings. Furthermore, from a business perspective, green economy practices that can be taken up widely in the sector need to demonstrate the benefits to the businesses to increase uptake and implementation. In addition, there is a need for awareness campaigns to promote green economy activities that can be taken by tourism establishments and other businesses.

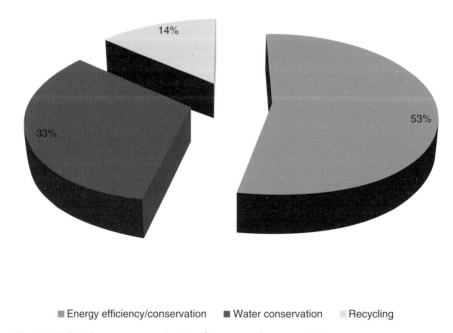

■ Energy efficiency/conservation   ■ Water conservation   ▨ Recycling

Fig. 8.3. What does your organization/firm currently use on site?

8.4.3   Opportunities and challenges in implementing green economy activities for tourism establishments

Opportunities available to promote green economy activities in the Limpopo Province

In terms of opportunities available to promote green economy activities in the Limpopo Province, the respondents from tourism establishments identified clean energy and energy efficiency programmes (see Fig. 8.4). The main activities identified include using alternative energy, mainly for heating and cooking – especially shifting to gas (31%) and installing solar water-heating systems to cut down costs on electricity (19%). However, 44% reported that they did not know of any opportunities for clean energy and energy efficiency in the province.

Barriers limiting the implementation of green economy activities in tourism establishments

Lack of information (39%), costs of implementation (27%) and shortage of workers with knowledge of and skills in green economy (22%) were reported as the main barriers limiting the implementation of green economy activities in tourism establishments (see Fig. 8.5). Efforts to increase green economy activities in the tourism industry should aim to address some of these factors. For example, more efforts need to be invested in educating tourism businesses on the opportunities that they can derive from implementing various green economy activities. Where possible, funding opportunities can be made available from the government and the private sector to

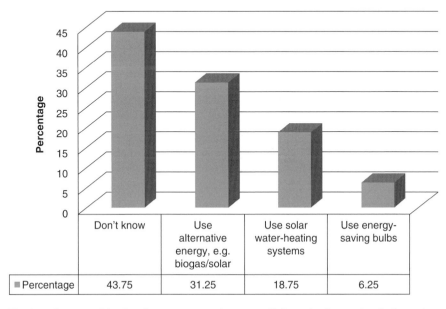

Fig. 8.4. Opportunities for clean energy and energy efficiency in the tourism industry in Limpopo.

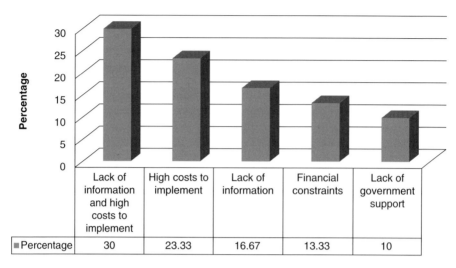

	Lack of information and high costs to implement	High costs to implement	Lack of information	Financial constraints	Lack of government support
■ Percentage	30	23.33	16.67	13.33	10

Fig. 8.5. Barriers limiting the implementation of green economy activities in tourism establishments.

promote some of the green economy activities in the tourism industry. Furthermore, more resources should be put into investing in the training of workers and owners on how to implement and maintain the green economy technologies that can be implemented in the tourism industry, as discussed above.

New skills or knowledge requirements for future employees

The main new skills or knowledge requirements for future employees that would be required to implement green economy activities/practices in tourism establishments include the principles of energy efficiency and conservation (54%), waste minimization (43%) and recycling (34%). The support that would contribute to help reduce greenhouse gas emissions in the municipalities include information about the specific actions to take to reduce greenhouse gas emissions cost-effectively (43%); success stories showing how similar municipalities reduce their greenhouse gas emissions cost-effectively (34%); technical support, for example training and online questions and answers (32%); and financing options to reduce greenhouse gas emissions (24%). The results show the importance of information and evidence of success stories and financing options in promoting the implementation of green economy activities that would contribute to reducing greenhouse gas emissions.

8.5   Conclusion

The main objective of the chapter was to shed light on the understanding of the green economy concept and the practices being implemented in the tourism industry in the Limpopo Province. The analysis was based on baseline survey data collected across tourism businesses in the Limpopo Province to help understand the knowledge of the green economy concept and the different green economy practices being implemented. The empirical analyses were based on a sample of 41 tourism businesses selected randomly from the province to explore the understanding and implementation of green economy activities in the province. Descriptive statistics were used to characterize an understanding of the different green economy practices being implemented in the tourism industry in Limpopo Province.

The findings from the analysis show that there is generally a lack of understanding of the green economy concept among the tourism businesses sampled. Further, the main green economy practices being implemented include water- and electricity-/energy-saving initiatives driven mainly by the need to cut operating costs and increase net profits. Most of the tourism businesses interviewed showed a lack of knowledge of any government policies and/or incentives to promote green economy investments in the tourism industry besides the provision of energy-saving bulbs. The results also show the need for increased awareness raising on the green economy concept, both its meaning and how it will benefit the businesses, including skills development in green economy practices to encourage implementation. Among the constraints, the lack of information on the green economy and the high costs of implementation were identified as the key constraints in implementing green economy initiatives in the province. Policy measures that address these constraints, in addition to other limitations, would contribute towards enhancing the implementation of green economy activities in the province.

Acknowledgements

This work was funded by a grant from Limpopo Economic Development, Environment and Tourism. We also thank members of the tourism establishments in the Limpopo Province for participating in this study.

References

Department of Environmental Affairs (2010) *Green Economy Summit Report.* Green Economy Summit, 2010. Department of Environmental Affairs, Pretoria, South Africa.

Department of Environmental Affairs (2011) *National Strategy for Sustainable Development and Action Plan (NSSD 1) 2011–2014.* Department of Environmental Affairs, Pretoria, South Africa.

Development Bank of Southern Africa (2011) *Programmes in Support of Transitioning South Africa to a Green Economy.* Development Planning Division Working Paper Series No 24. Development Bank of Southern Africa, South Africa.

Economic Development Department (EDD) (2010) *The New Growth Path Framework.* EDD, Pretoria, South Africa.

Environmental Pillar (2012) *Greening the Economy and Creating Sustainable Employment.* Environmental Pillar, Knockvicar, Boyle, Co Roscommon, Ireland.

Limpopo Provincial Government (2009) *Towards a Revised Provincial Tourism Growth Strategy, 2009–2014: Strategic Focus and Framework.* Limpopo Provincial Government, Limpopo Province, Republic of South Africa.

Limpopo Provincial Government (2013) *Tourism Strategy 2013/2014: Focus Areas and Specific Targets.* Limpopo Provincial Government, Limpopo Province, Republic of South Africa.

National Planning Commission (2012) *National Development Plan 2030: Our Future – Make It Work.* The Presidency, Republic of South Africa.

Republic of South Africa (2013) *The State of Travel and Tourism in South Africa*. Department of Tourism, Pretoria, Republic of South Africa.

UNEP (United Nations Environment Programme) (2011) *Towards a Green Economy – Pathways to Sustainable Development and Poverty Eradication*. United Nations Environment Programme, Geneva, Switzerland.

UNEP (2013) *Fiscal policy briefing paper*. United Nations Environment Programme, Geneva, Switzerland.

UNEP-IMF-GIZ (2012) *Fiscal Policies: Towards an Inclusive Green Economy*. Summary Report of the UNEP-IMF-GIZ Workshop, 2012, Geneva, Switzerland.

UNWTO (2013) *UNWTO Tourism Highlights*. Madrid.

9 Environmental Resources and the Hotel Industry: The Case of Slovenia

Tanja Mihalič*

University of Ljubljana, Ljubljana, Slovenia

9.1 Introduction

Tourism products and experience encompass a multidimensional concept that includes not only purposely produced tourism services but also environmental resources, such as 'not produced for tourism' climate, traditions, the friendliness of locals, or traditional architecture. Research has shown that tourists have become increasingly demanding in regard to the natural and sociocultural surroundings and their quality (Aguiló *et al.*, 2005).

The role of environmental resources in tourism supply, demand and competitiveness has been debated for almost a century (Mariotti, 1938; Planina, 1966; Mihalič, 2000; Ritchie and Crouch, 2003). The tourism demand potential of a destination's environmental resources and how they trigger that demand and bring value to tourism firms has been studied and become an integral part of tourism economics. Following the sustainable tourism development paradigm, environmental resources entered the competitiveness and destination management debate (Mihalič, 2000; Dwyer and Kim, 2003). However, much more research is needed to understand how tourism firms strategically refer to the quality of environmental resources and how they manage them.

In the above context, this paper surveys the role of environmental resources in the framework of competitive advantage resource theory and surveys the competitiveness potential of environmental management. The purpose is to study whether tourism firms see environmental management as a strategic resource and if they differentiate between the strategic importance of environmental quality (EQM) and impacts management (EIM). The research hypothesis is tested using explanatory factor analyses and statistical tests, with the support of the Statistical Package for the Social Sciences (SPSS).

---

*E-mail: tanja.mihalic@ef.uni-lj.si

9.2   Literature Review

Initially, the interest in tourism environmental resources was merely theoretical; however, given the rise of the tourism sustainability debate, the topic gained managerial and policy relevance. More ecologically and environmentally aware tourists demand more environmental resource-based tourism experiences. From this aspect of tourism, theories distinguish among natural, cultural and social environments or resources. According to some tourism researchers (Inskeep, 1991; Mihalič and Kaspar, 1996; Ritchie and Crouch, 2000, 2003; Dwyer and Kim, 2003; UNWTO, 2004), natural resources refer to a destination's general topography, scenery, nature, flora, fauna, biodiversity, beaches, mountains, rivers, lakes, seas, oceans and waterfalls, climate, sun, snow and wind, as well as cleanliness and sanitation and space. In addition, the elements of the cultural environment can include music, traditions, gastronomy, traditional arts and handiwork, history, architectural attractions, clothing, language, the hospitality of locals and their friendliness and openness, cooperation, religion and safety. In the context of sustainable and responsible tourism, other elements become relevant in creating an attractive image of an environmentally responsible destination. These include sharing tourism benefits with the local population, or cooperation among tourism stakeholders that includes the local inhabitants and their quality of life. Many researchers and international organizations see responsible tourism as a means to exercise global civic responsibility based on a moral commitment to reduce the negative impact of tourism (Bianchi and Stephenson, 2014). Repressive states or local communities have often threatened the rights of their citizens, such as land, economic, human or cultural rights. Some such destinations might become unattractive destinations for potential travellers.

Tourists are becoming sensitive to the actual environmental quality of their destinations (Poon, 1989). More and more visitors expect tourism destinations and firms to be managed in a sustainable or environmentally responsible manner. This relatively new sensitivity, following the uncritical mass tourism development model, brought attention to the environmental responsibility and sustainability of places and firms. More specifically, firms are expected to follow the new business model that extends their traditional responsibility for economic results towards their responsibility for their own impact on the natural and sociocultural environment. For tourism destinations and firms, environmental management issues are now an integral part of daily concerns. 'Indeed, in the late 20th century, it becomes evident that environmental tourist attractions must be maintained and offered to visitors in the quantity and quality that they demand…' (Mihalič, 2013, p. 1). No doubt, for tourism firms, the quality of environmental resources and their environmental management has become critical to tourism markets.

Furthermore, the tourism literature distinguishes between two different, yet interrelated aspects of tourism – environmental resources relationship (Table 9.1). First, destination environmental competitiveness can be based on the existing attractive environmental quality of the destination and, second, maintained and increased by appropriate managerial efforts related to environmental impacts (Mihalič, 2000). In this context, the environmental management of tourism refers to two different aspects: first, to the aspect of environmental impact management (EIM) and, second, to the aspect of environmental quality management (EQM).

Table 9.1. Key elements of destination environmental impact (EIM) and environmental quality management (EQM).

No	Name	Aspects of destination management	Refers to	Environmental image regarding destination	Environmental image regarding tourism firm
1	2	3	4	5	6
1	EIM	Environmental impact actions: recycling, SO$_2$ reduction, resource saving, pollution reduction, sharing tourism benefits with local population, environmental education, etc.	Environmental impact management of: product/service, company (hotels, tour operators, travel agents, facility operators, carriers, etc.)	Environmentally responsible (concerned) tourism destination	Environmentally responsible (concerned) tourism firm (hotel, tour operator, event organizer, etc.)
2	EQM	Environmental quality such as: water quality, air quality, noise levels, visual quality, friendliness of locals, authenticity of culture, tourism-influenced standard of life of the locals, etc.	Environmental quality characteristics of the destination: place, city, beach, resort, etc.	Environmentally sound (attractive) tourism destination (unspoiled, authentic, etc.)	In an environmentally sound (attractive) tourism destination (unspoiled, authentic, etc.)

Notes: EIM = environmental impact management; EQM = environmental quality management, referring to the management of the environmental quality of a destination; E = environment, referring to natural, cultural and social environment at the destination.

The first aspect refers to environmental management and recognizes the (negative) impacts of tourism on the environment. Environmental pollution, degradation of the landscape or cultural authenticity, tourism development on the account of local inhabitants, or even tourism development without integrating the local inhabitants into the tourism benefits, are becoming *non grata*, and are sometimes not tolerable. Therefore, many environmental management practices that minimize negative impacts and/or emphasize and fairly distribute tourism benefits have been developed, generally marketed using terms such as 'sustainability', 'ecotourism', 'responsible tourism', 'community-based tourism' and similar. Environmental management, relating to the impacts of tourism, travel and other industries on the environment, as well as that of visitors and the domestic population, is the basis for the creation of the image of an environmentally concerned or responsible destination.

The second aspect relates to the given environmental quality of the destination. This can be illustrated by the cleanliness of the beaches, the quality of the bathing water, the authenticity of the culture and place, the attractiveness of the landscape, clean air, and so on. The environmental quality of a destination is a prevailing issue in making a travel-related decision; it is a competitiveness factor among different tourism destinations with varying environmental quality. Management of the environmental quality of the destination is the basis for creating the image of an environmentally sound destination and may include the reinstating of an already degraded environment.

From the point of view of a tourism destination or firm, the two aspects of environmental management are codependent. On the one hand, the negative environmental impacts of travel and tourism influence the environmental quality of the destination, yet on the other hand, managing the environmental quality requires lowering the negative environmental impacts of tourism (and other) activities. At the same time, there is an essential difference between the two, from the standpoint of the consumer. It is very often presupposed that an environmentally aware tourist acts in an environmentally responsible manner. In such a case, the information on environmental impacts would be essential for his or her choice of an environmentally concerned destination. However, according to the research findings, there is a gap between tourists' environmental awareness and their corresponding actions. Indeed, the destination choice is influenced by the (environmental) attractiveness of the destination in the first place. Thus, an environmental manager can increase destination competitiveness by managing environmental quality. Environmental management by simply managing (lowering) the environmental impacts of tourism is not sufficient.

Nevertheless, environmental resources have become an integral part of modern destination competitiveness models. One destination competitiveness study (Crouch, 2011) suggests that a destination's physiography and climate, both of which are environmental resources, form the most important competitiveness determinant. In another tourism competitiveness meta-study, authors (Tsai *et al.*, 2009) studied 16 different models of destination competitiveness. Six of these models considered the environment as a major determinant of tourism destination competitiveness (Ritchie and Crouch, 1993; Kozak and Rimmington, 1999; Dwyer and Kim, 2003; Heath, 2003; Enright and Newton, 2005; Gooroochurn and Sugiyarto, 2005).

However, the above models study the competitiveness of tourism destinations. It is evident that the role of tourism's natural, cultural and social environment has been well established in a theory of the destination's competitiveness. However, competitiveness studies in the hotel industry that focus on the competitiveness of hotel firms have paid much less attention to environmental resources. The latter are seen as a characteristic and responsibility of a destination management organization, and the hotel industry benefits from the destination's environmental image and characteristics. The available hotel industry competitiveness factors examine a limited number of factors but fail to develop a model (Tsai *et al.*, 2009). They apply methodological tools (such as DEA – data envelopment analysis; LISREL – linear structural relations; SERVQUAL – service quality; and SEM – structural equation modelling) or conceptual models (such as Porter's diamond and hotel performance measurement framework). In regard to environmental resources, some authors partially discuss environmental costs, in particular energy costs and the costs of waste in relation to hotel competitiveness (Trung and Kumar, 2005; Karagiorgas *et al.*, 2007). They stated that the increasing costs of resources could affect the income, environmental performance and public image of hotel firms.

It should be mentioned that the environmental debate in the hotel sector is much better developed in the field of eco-labelling, corporate social responsibility (CSR) and the triple bottom line sustainability concept, yet not in a context of overall resource-based competitiveness theory. To our knowledge, no research to date has explored the strategic value of environmental resources, such as environmental management, for hotel firm competitiveness advantage in such a context. This is what this survey will do.

Tourism firms therefore have to create the appropriate sources of competitive advantage that will enable them to respond to the markets and create their own competitive position. While environmental resources represent an important factor for tourism competitiveness, other sources are also important. As suggested by resource-advantage theory (Hunt and Morgan, 1996; Hunt, 1997), sustainable competitive advantages can only be created through intangible sources such as responsiveness to consumer needs and preferences. Porter (1998) defines the concept of a firm's competitive advantage as the ability of the firm to add value to its products.

The literature suggests three different views on creating competitive advantage (Bilgihan *et al.*, 2011). The first, the positioning view (Porter, 1985), differentiates among three competitive positions in the marketplace, which are cost leadership, differentiation and focus strategy. A firm should choose one of the three competitive positions in the marketplace in order to achieve and maintain competitive advantage. In this context, this paper is interested in whether a kind of environmentally focused differentiation strategy could create and maintain competitive advantage. Second, the resource-based view looks at the firm's resources and competences when evaluating the competitive advantage of the firm. In order to create competitive advantage, these resources and capabilities should contribute to the performance of the firm or destination. Theory argues that these resources need to be rare, inimitable or non-substitutable (Bilgihan *et al.*, 2011). More specifically, sustainable competitive advantage is achieved by using these resources to offer a unique, positive tourism experience. In the context of this paper, we argue that some competitive advantage resources might refer to a firm's capabilities to create and offer a unique environment-related experience. Third, the dynamic capabilities view combines the previous two views: the positioning and resource-based view. Dynamic capabilities are defined as a 'firm's ability to integrate, build, and reconfigure internal and external competences to address rapidly changing environments' (Teece *et al.*, 1997, p. 516). This view suggests that firms have to develop dynamic capabilities to be able to offer competitive products in response to new marketplace trends and requirements. It also suggests that firms should have the capacity to react to the changing business environment; making appropriate and timely responses to market trends and demands is critical (Teece *et al.*, 1997). In this context, the primary interest of this paper relates to environmental market trends and requirements and whether environment-related actions are associated with competitive advantage.

9.3   Methodology

Slovenia is an alpine and Mediterranean country, located in central-east Europe at the north-eastern corner of the Adriatic Sea. In 1991, Slovenia became an independent country. The country is small, with a population of 2 million. This member state of the European Union (since 2004) shares a border with Italy, Austria, Hungary, Croatia and the Adriatic coast. Slovenia spans alpine, continental and Mediterranean climate zones, and its tourism includes mountain, sea, city, spa, gambling and farm destinations. The country receives about 2.7 million visitors/year and 9 million overnight stays, with more than 60% of tourists coming from outside Slovenia (SURS, 2012).

In 2010, tourists (62% foreign) stayed for a total of 8.9 million nights (SURS, 2012). Inbound visitor numbers totalled 3 million in 2010 (SURS, 2012). Foreign tourism earnings were €1.9 bn, representing 42% of the total export of services (BS, 2012). In 2010, Slovenia had around 160 hotels, with a capacity of around 28,000 beds. About 80% of hotel businesses could be classified as small and medium-sized businesses in terms of their size. The hotel structure is quite homogeneous in terms of management structure, mixed (state, private) ownership and medium in size, and the share of family owned and run hotel businesses is low. International foreign direct investment and management contracting in Slovenia is low. Only a few international chains were present (for example, two hotels belonged to Best Western and one to Relais Châteaux).

The quality of more than 50% of all hotel capacities is at the four-star level, while approximately 40% of capacity is at the three-star level. Accommodation capacities are divided among different types of destinations: the majority is in mountain destinations (28%) and sea resorts (26%), followed by spa resorts (21%). The accommodation sector in the capital, Ljubljana, then accounts for around 10% of all hotel capacity in the country, with other places 13% (SURS, 2012).

Slovenia is marketed as a green area of Europe through such slogans as 'Slovenia is green', 'Slovenia goes green' and 'Slovenia promotes green' (ITEF and STO, 2011). Environmental resources are seen as important competitive advantages for Slovenian tourism, and the country is currently focusing on sustainable development issues (Dwyer *et al.*, 2012). Previous research on competitive advantage factors in the Slovene hotel industry have studied factors of quality, contacts, image, pricing and information and communication technology and their potential for competitiveness (Mihalič and Dmitrović, 2000; Mihalic and Buhalis, 2013). This paper expands the previous research by adding environmental management as a possible competitiveness factor.

In the context of the competitive advantage theory, as explained in one of the previous sections of this chapter, the main purpose of this survey is to study environmental resources as competitive advantage resources (CAR) in a framework of a resource-based competitiveness view for tourism firms. In this context, two main research questions have been explored.

First, taking into account increasing environmental awareness and environmental trends in the tourism market, we explored whether hotel managers see environmental management as a competitiveness factor of its own.

Second, taking into account the theoretical and practical discourses between the two aspects of environmental management, we explored whether managers distinguished between the two aspects of environmental management, namely environmental quality (EQM) and environmental impact management (EIM).

Further, informed by the dynamic capabilities view and a survey of the ability of hotel firms to react to new market conditions, the third research question was explored. In line with the increasing importance of environmental trends, we asked if tourism managers prioritized environmental management in comparison to other managerial topics.

Figure 9.1 presents our theoretical construct and hypothesis. Hypothesis one (H1) claims that tourism managers see environmental management as a competitive advantage factor. The second hypothesis tests whether tourism managers distinguish

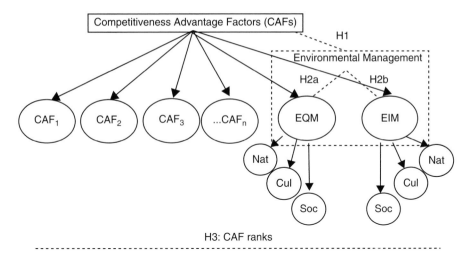

Fig. 9.1. Proposed model.

Notes: CAF = competitive advantage factors; Cul = cultural environment; EIM = environmental impact management; EQM = environmental quality management; Nat = natural environment; Soc = social environment.

between the two aspects of environmental management and claims that managers see environmental quality management (H2a) and environmental impact management (H2b) as a competitive advantage factor of its own. In Fig. 9.1, these hypotheses are represented by dotted lines that present the tested connections.

In line with our third research question, we claim that tourism managers put environmental management on top of their competitive advantage factors list. Figure 9.1 illustrates the third hypothesis by a dotted line under all factors, questioning their importance ranking.

9.4   Results

Data were collected in 2010 via a questionnaire of competitive advantage resources. Hotel managers in 160 Slovenian hotel firms that existed at the time were asked to assess the importance of specified resources of competitive advantage regarding their company on a five-point Likert scale (1 = not important and 5 = very important). The response rate and population coverage was 57%. An explanatory factor analyses based on the principal component method and Promax rotation to allow factors to correlate was used. The first factor, environmental resources, includes both aspects, e.g. both EIM and EQM aspects, of variables of the natural, cultural and social environments. The result confirmed our first hypothesis, namely that environmental management constituted a competitive advantage factor of its own (Table 9.2).

Unfortunately, both components of environmental management (that is, both EQM and EIM aspects) constitute the same factor. Thus, the analysis did not confirm our second hypothesis. We were not able to confirm that managers distinguished

Table 9.2. Factor analysis of competitive advantage resources, Slovene hotel firms.

Competitive advantage resources	Competitive advantage factors			
	Environmental management	Image	Sales	Quality
1	2	3	4	5
Care for cultural environment	**0.912**	0.412	0.432	0.357
Quality of cultural environment	**0.911**	0.290	0.371	0.252
Quality of social environment (local inhabitants)	**0.776**	0.146	0.562	0.412
Quality of natural environment	**0.774**	0.275	0.078	0.161
Cooperation with local environment	**0.755**	0.528	0.308	0.551
Care for natural environment	**0.748**	0.607	0.256	0.534
Service/product diversity regarding competition	0.189	**0.773**	0.172	0.115
Innovativeness	0.402	**0.767**	0.305	0.234
Corporate image/reputation	0.524	**0.76**	0.331	0.501
Brand recognition	0.279	**0.736**	0.344	0.454
PR and promotion quality	0.252	**0.618**	0.332	0.443
CRS	0.128	0.225	**0.813**	0.296
R&D expenditure	0.451	0.564	**0.753**	0.568
Favourable terms of payment	0.430	0.173	**0.723**	0.194
Sales channels	0.296	0.452	**0.723**	0.469
High market share	0.329	0.34	**0.705**	0.341
High service/product quality	0.223	0.379	0.355	**0.800**
Quality of HR	0.283	0.322	0.179	**0.780**
Responsiveness and reliability of the services	0.275	0.112	0.431	**0.723**
Summated scale – factor mean	4.109	4.365	3.747	4.710
Standard deviation	0.684	0.546	0.703	0.448
Rank	3	2	4	1

Notes: PR = public relations; CRS = corporate social responsibility; R&D = research and development; HR = human resources. Bold represents the factor's corresponding resources.

between the two aspects of environmental management. Although both aspects are logically interrelated, they hold different attractiveness potential for visitors and we expected that hotel managers would have a different attitude towards these aspects. Further, the environmental impact management issues are mainly the competency of hotel managers, yet the environmental quality of the destination is more external and they have less, or almost no, power to manage it, although as one of the destination stakeholders, they do contribute to it.

Further, in addition to the environmental management factor, our factor model has revealed three more factors that refer to more traditional management of the firm. These were named image, sales and quality (see Table 9.1 for competitive advantage factors) and represent the remaining factors connected to the firm's traditional operations. The factor ranks (Table 9.2) showed that the environmental management factor was ranked after quality and image, as it got a statistically significant lower grade on its importance for competitiveness. Thus, our third hypothesis that environmental resources are becoming increasingly important and thus stand high on the firm's priority list has not been confirmed. More specifically, the mean value of the importance of environmental management (4.109) is statistically significantly lower compared to the mean values of factors quality (4.710) and image (4.365), as presented in Table 9.3 (t-values −8.393 and −4.024 correspondingly).

In the context of environmental tourism demand trends and previously discussed 'new tourism', we expected that Slovene hotel managers would prioritize the environmental management issues in their competitiveness strategies. Nevertheless, the competitive advantage factors are interdependent and correlated (see Table 9.3, column 7), meaning that managerial efforts in the framework of other competitiveness factors impact environmental resource positioning and performance, and vice versa. In order to understand the real competitiveness potential of environmental management for hotel firms, indirect connections among the factors need to be tested empirically.

9.5   Conclusion

This research benefits the literature on tourism, as it originally addresses the role of environmental resources on the list of firms' competitive advantage resources and distinguishes between the two dimensions of environmental management. It argues that firms should strategically address the issue of a (given) environmental quality of a destination and the issue of minimizing a firm's negative impact on its environment. The empirical research in the Slovene hotel sector has confirmed that environmental management is becoming a competitiveness factor. In reality, hotel managers see environmental management as a competitiveness factor, though as less important than the factors quality and image. However, more in-depth, empirical research into the correlation among factors and the indirect impacts of environmental management on competitiveness via other factors, such as image and quality, is needed, to justify a higher rank for environmental management on managerial lists.

Table 9.3. Paired samples test competitive advantage factors and correlation coefficients, Slovene hotel firms.

Pair	Factors	Paired sample test				Bivariate corr. coeff.
		Mean	t	df	Sig. (2-tailed)	
1	2	3	4	5	6	7
1	Environmental management – image	−0.266	−4.024	91	0.000	0.486**
2	Environmental management – sales	0.357	4.767	89	0.000	0.478**
3	Environmental management – quality	−0.584	−8.393	90	0.000	0.378**

Note: ** = statistically significant coefficients.

This research benefits the Slovene hotel industry by complementing existing hotel competitiveness research (Mihalič and Dmitrović, 2000; Mihalic and Buhalis, 2013) and by providing actual information for hotel managers in deciding how to relate to environmental resources and how to design their new competitiveness strategy and policy. The model can be used to study the actual importance of environmental resources in any hotel sector. A limitation of the present research presents itself with respect to the generalization of the importance of environmental resources and management for all types of destinations, such as city or beach destinations. This should be overcome by more segmented research in the future.

References

Aguiló, E., Alegre, J. and Sard, M. (2005) The persistence of the sun and sand tourism model. *Tourism Management* 26(2), 219–231.

Bank of Slovenia (BS) (2012) Bilten Banka Slovenije. Vol. April. Bank of Slovenia, Ljubljana.

Bianchi, R.V. and Stephenson, M.L. (2014) *Tourism and Citizenship. Rights, Freedoms and Responsibilities in the Global Order.* Routledge, London.

Bilgihan, A., Okumus, F., Nusair, K.K. and Kwun, D.J.-W. (2011) Information technology applications and competitive advantage in hotel companies. *Journal of Hospitality and Tourism Technology* 2(2), 139–153.

BS (2012) Bilten Banka Slovenije. Vol. April. Bank of Slovenia, Ljubljana.

Crouch, G.I. (2011) Destination competitiveness: an analysis of determinant attributes. *Journal of Travel Research* 50(1), 27–45.

Dwyer, L. and Kim, C. (2003) Destination conmpetitiveness: determinants and indicators. *Current Issues in Tourism* 6(5), 369–413.

Dwyer, L., Cvelbar, L.K., Edwards, D. and Mihalič, T. (2012) Fashioning a destination tourism future: the case of Slovenia. *Tourism Management* 33(2), 305–316.

Enright, M.J. and Newton, J. (2005) Determinants of tourism destination competitiveness in Asia Pacific: comprehensiveness and universality. *Journal of Travel Research* 43(4), 339–350.

Gooroochurn, N. and Sugiyarto, G. (2005) Competitiveness indicators in the travel and tourism industry. *Tourism Economics* 28(4), 1771–1707.

Heath, E. (2003) Towards a model to enhance destination competitiveness: a southern African perspective. *Journal of Hospitality and Tourism Management* 10(2), 124–141.

Hunt, S.D. (1997) Resource-advantage theory: an evolutionary theory of competitive firm behavior? *Journal of Economic Issues* 31(1), 59–77.

Hunt, S.D. and Morgan, R.M. (1996) The resource-advantage theory of competition: dynamics, path dependencies, and evolutionary dimensions. *Journal of Marketing* 60(4), 107–114.

Inskeep, E. (1991) *Tourism Planning: An Integrated and Sustainable Development Approach.* John Wiley, New York.

ITEF and STO (2011) Partnerstvo za trajnostni razvoj slovenskega turizma. Podlage za Strategijo razvoja in trženja slovenskega turizma 2012–2016. (Partnership for sustainable tourism development in Slovenia 2012–2016. Materials for Slovenian development and marketing tourism strategy 201–2016.) Institut for Tourism, Economic Faculty and Slovenian Tourism Board, Ljubljana.

Karagiorgas, M., Tsoutsos, T. and Moiá-Pol, A. (2007) A simulation of the energy consumption monitoring in Mediterranean hotels: application in Greece. *Energy and Buildings* 39(4), 416–426.

Kozak, M. and Rimmington, M. (1999) Measuring tourist destination competitiveness: conceptual considerations and empirical findings. *International Journal of Hospitality Management* 18(3), 273–283.

Mariotti, A. (1938) Corso di economia turistica. De Agostini, Novara, Italy.

Mihalič, T. (2000) Environmental management of a tourist destination: a factor of tourism competitiveness. *Tourism Management* 21(1), 65–78.

Mihalič, T. (2013) Performance of environmental resources of a tourist destination: concept and application. *Journal of Travel Research* 52(5), 614–630.

Mihalic, T. and Buhalis, D. (2013) ICT as a new competitive advantage factor – case of small transitional hotel sector. *Economic and Business Review* 15(1), 33–56.

Mihalič, T. and Dmitrović, T. (2000) The competitiveness of the Slovenian hotel and travel industry before and after EU entry. Paper presented at the Tourism and transition: proceedings of the International Conference held in Dubrovnik, Faculty of Tourism and Foreign Trade, Dubrovnik.

Mihalič, T. and Kaspar, C. (1996) *Umweltökonomie im Tourismus* (St Galler Beiträge zum Tourismus und zur Verkehrswirtschaft, 27). Paul Haupt, Bern.

Planina, J. (1966) Primarna in sekundarna turistična ponudba ter njuje posebnosti). [Primary and Secondary Tourism Demand and their Specifics]. *Turistični vestnik* 1966(4), 161–164.

Poon, A. (1989) Consumer strategies for a new tourism. In: Cooper, C. (ed.) *Progress in Tourism, Recreation and Hospitality Management*. Bellhaven Press, London, Vol 1, pp. 91–102.

Porter, M.E. (1985) *Competitive Advantage: Creating and Sustaining Superior Performance*. Free Press–Collier Macmillan, New York and London.

Porter, M.E. (1998) *The Competitive Advantage of Nations*. Free Press, New York and London.

Ritchie, J.R.B. and Crouch, G.I. (1993) Competitiveness in international tourism – a framework for understanding and analysis. Proceedings of the 43rd Congress of the International Association of Scientific Experts in Tourism, 17–23 October, San Carlos de Bariloche, Argentina, pp. 23–71.

Ritchie, J.R.B. and Crouch, G.I. (2000) The competitive destination: a sustainable perspective. *Tourism Management* 21(1), 1–7.

Ritchie, J.R.B. and Crouch, G.I. (2003) *The Competitive Destination: A Sustainable Tourism Perspective*. CAB International, Wallingford, UK.

SURS (2012) *Statistical Yearbook 2012*. Statistical Office of the Republic of Slovenia, Ljubljana.

Teece, G.J., Pisano, G. and Shuen, A. (1997) Dynamic capabilities and strategic management. *Strategic Management Journal* 18(7), 509–633.

Trung, D.N. and Kumar, S. (2005) Resource use and waste management in Vietnam hotel industry. *Journal of Cleaner Production* 13(2), 109–116.

Tsai, H., Song, H.Y. and Wong, K.K.F. (2009) Tourism and hotel competitiveness research. *Journal of Travel and Tourism Marketing* 26(5–6), 522–546.

UNWTO (2004) *Indicators of Sustainable Development for Tourism Destinations: A Guidebook*. United Nations World Tourism Organisation, Madrid.

10 Ecological Modernization and Environmental Education: The Case of Turkey

Habib Alipour* and Hossein G.T. Olya

Eastern Mediterranean University, Gazimagusa/KKTC, Turkey

10.1 Introduction

Educational institutions are recognized as suitable venues to provide environmental awareness through their various programmes (Shin, 2000). Based on the Tbilisi Conference on Environmental Education in 1977, the main objectives of environmental education are awareness, knowledge, attitudes, skills and participation (http://www.gdrc.org/uem/ee/tbilisi.html). Overall, environmental education provides valid information for understanding the biophysical environment, creating motivation and guiding the discovery of suitable solutions to biophysical environmental problems. It is also involved, and plays an effective role, in environmental movements as a social and political culture (Hajer, 1996; Potter, 2010). Eventually,

> Those now being educated will have to do what the present generation has been unable or unwilling to do: stabilize world population, reduce the emission of greenhouse gases that threaten to change the climate … protect biological diversity, reverse the destruction of forests everywhere, and conserve soils.
>
> (Orr, 1996, p. 7)

An environmental issue, as a challenge for the 21st century, is a foregone conclusion; therefore, its inclusion in the curriculum of tourism education has been stressed and recognized as an essential part of the tourism curriculum (Fidgeon, 2010). It has been realized that training and education enhances environmental awareness regarding the negative and positive impacts of tourism, which leads to a pro-environmental attitude and behaviour among stakeholders, i.e. tourists, the host community, the commercial sector and the government (Ballantyne *et al.*, 2011).

In keeping with the above narrative, which discursively outlines the role of education, this study focuses on the role of the university as an institutional platform for environmental

---

*E-mail: habib.alipour@emu.edu.tr

education and which has obvious components that legitimize institutional transformation (Mol, 2002; Choy and Lau, 2013).

However, overcoming these challenges cannot be perceived as a magic wand. In order to achieve environmentally and socially acceptable tourism models, it is essential for educational institutions to embark upon transforming market value led behaviour and environmentally laissez-faire attitudes towards more environmentally – and social value driven – responsible tourism (Mihalic, 2014). Therefore, education will play a catalytic role in embedding environmental values among students, who will be apt to take strategic actions in implementing environmental policies for the betterment of their firms and local population.

10.2   Literature Review

As a backdrop to this study, the theory of ecological modernization (TEM) is initiated as a discourse in response to ecological problems; this is because sustainable development, notwithstanding its grand goals, is perceived as vague and difficult to operationalize (Eder, 1996). This is not, however, meant to undermine the credibility of the sustainable development paradigm. In fact, it has been a major force in the transformation of environmentalism into the ecological discourse that is TEM (Hajer, 1996; Giddens, 1998). Such a transformation, Giddens (1998) noted, is reflected in the fact that the 'countries most influenced by the idea of ecological modernization are the cleanest and greenest of the industrial nations'. In Eder's (1996, p. 210) words, 'Its transformation into a new ideological master frame provides the possibility of a way out, legitimating social institutions by means of environment-related ethical frames.'

The paradigmatic structure of TEM is rooted in a process of production and consumption (i.e. the decoupling or delinking of material flows from economic flows) and institutional transformation, especially in the public sphere (Eder, 1996; Mol, 2002). The crux of the theory was initially established when:

> The social dynamics behind these changes that are the emergence of actual environment-induced transformations of institutions and social practices in industrialized societies are encapsulated in the ecological modernization theory. This theory tries to understand, interpret and conceptualize the nature, extent and dynamics of this transformation process.
>
> (Mol, 2002, p. 93)

However, TEM is not employed solely to justify shifting the institutional structures of solid waste management and improving its system in Malaysia (Saat, 2013), or reforming the planning system in Australia's island state (Castles and Stratford, 2014); the focus of our study is the institutional transformation of the educational entities, universities, in the context of TEM. Four constructs of transformation are targeted by the TEM school of thought through environmental education and green education policy.

The core hypothesis of TEM is that 'production processes are increasingly designed and conducted using ecological criteria' (Mol and Sonnenfeld, 2000, p. 9). Therefore, we can also assume that *universities, as the bastion of educational institutions, have the potential to transform the attitude and behavior of the students (i.e. consumers) towards ecocentricism knowing the fact that they are fixated on anthropocentricism.*

Therefore, as institutions of science and knowledge, universities need to move towards greening the curriculum on the one hand and encouraging environmentally oriented extracurricular activities on the other. In the context of TEM, educational institutions need to revise the politics of knowledge and its dissemination to their consumers (students). In Grove-White's words, 'If we are to produce accounts of environmental problems that are sensitive to culture and indeterminacy, we will need different institutions, and different knowledge cultures' (as cited in Beck, 1996, p. 26). Such a culture is nothing other than environmentalism, and it will not become a mediator of environmental attitude/behaviour unless there is a clear institutional policy change towards long-term, policy-useful knowledge regarding environmental issues. Focusing on tourism education, the above argument is converging with a 'knowledge-based platform' 'which is characterized by a preference for objective, scientific methods to obtain knowledge about the tourism industry, and by the concomitant rejection of simplistic judgments regarding the nature of mass and alternative tourism' (Weaver and Lawton, 1999, p. 15).

Nevertheless, this school of thought has transcended Western economies and has grown into an intellectual stock that becomes more heterodox as its scope and influence expands. In Giddens's words, 'Ecological modernization implies a partnership in which governments, businesses, moderate environmentalists, and scientists cooperate in the restructuring of the capitalist political economy along more environmentally defensible lines' (Giddens, 1998, p. 57). This is clearly reflected and realized by Beck (1996) within the context of the *risk society*.

10.2.1 Environmental attitude/behaviour and education nexus

Numerous theoretical frameworks have been used in an effort to elaborate and explain the factors that result in the development of an attitude that will eventually generate the behaviour required for certain environmental actions. Among those factors, education, knowledge and awareness have been discussed extensively as influential variables in displaying pro-environmental behaviour (Ivy *et al.*, 1998; Kollmuss and Agyeman, 2002; Thapa, 2010; Kuo and Jackson, 2014). As Lozano *et al.* (2013) emphasize on the role of the university as a better leader in the initiation of sustainable development, the university system needs to restructure through: including environment and development issues in the curricula; research; physical plant operations; outreach and engagement with stakeholders; and in assessment and reporting.

In this study, an attempt has been made to place the aforementioned factors and the role of the university within the context of TEM by emphasizing the university's curriculum and students' environmental awareness. The overarching concept is that the aforementioned independent factors will eventually lead to the development of a responsible attitude and behaviour towards the environment. TEM's call for institutional transformation (i.e. the greening of universities) is considered a shift away from and revision of the traditional curriculum; environmental education becomes a transformation from rhetoric to reality. As Beck stated, 'The constellations of risk society are created because the self-evident truths of industrial society (the consensus on progress, the abstraction from ecological consequences and hazards) dominate the thinking and behavior of human beings and institutions' (Beck, 1996, p. 28).

In this study, efforts were made to examine the case of the Eastern Mediterranean University (EMU) and its quest to disseminate environmentalism among its consumers in the context of what Stevenson eloquently explained:

> The need for students to engage in ideological and critical inquiry is indicated by an examination of the different ideologies which underlie proposals for environmental reform. Such educational ideals, however, conflict with the dominant practices in schools, which emphasize the passive assimilation and reproduction of simplistic factual knowledge and an unproblematic 'truth'.
>
> (Stevenson, 2007, pp. 139–140)

This is the first study in which TEM has been used to justify the role of the university as an institution in the process of transformation and to monitor its performance in the context of the theory of planned behaviour (TPB) through the measurement of the knowledge, attitude and behaviour of students in different fields of study and at varying educational levels. This means that we provide a mechanism that demonstrates how educational institutions should function parallel to ecological modernization (EM) principles and assess the operation of encouraging pro-environmental behaviour based on internal (knowledge, value, conscience) and external (non-educational institutions) factors. In other words, while EM sets the context, TPB becomes instrumental in the validation of the environmental knowledge/attitude/behaviour nexus (Fig. 10.1).

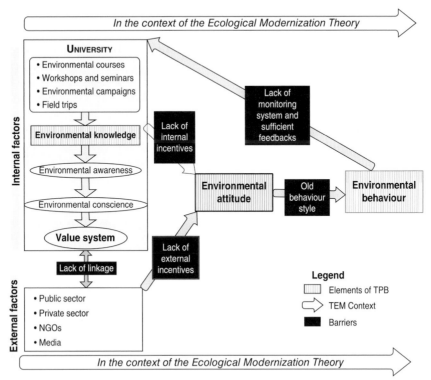

Fig. 10.1. Environmental education model (adapted based on TPB and TEM). TPB = theory of planned behaviour (Ajzen and Fishbein, 1980); TEM = theory of ecological modernization (Hajer, 1996)

Recently, TPB has been employed to support the linkage between attitude and environmental behaviour in various disciplines such as agriculture and ecology (Price and Leviston, 2014; Sulemana and James, 2014), business and marketing (Kalamas *et al.*, 2014), energy (Stigka *et al.*, 2014), hospitality (Chou, 2014), psychology (Sparks *et al.*, 2014) and education (Yasunaga *et al.*, 2014). In a recent study conducted by Gifford and Nilsson, knowledge and education were considered influential factors towards creating pro-environmental behaviour. In their words 'one is unlikely to knowingly be concerned about the environment or deliberately act in pro-environmental ways if one knows nothing about the problem or potential positive actions' (Gifford and Nilsson, 2014, p. 142).

As exhibited in Fig. 10.1, a model has been developed to provide a framework for this case study. As previously mentioned, the structure of the model is framed based on TEM and TPB. Two sets of variables/factors are identified as the machinery that is fundamental for setting the process in motion.

The first set consists of internal factors, which fall within the domain of the university, where different modules (environmental courses, workshops and seminars, environmental campaigns, field trips, etc.) will channel environmental knowledge, awareness and consciousness. This process will most likely result in an environmental value system among the students in regard to their attitude and behaviours (i.e. based on TPB) (Ajzen and Fishbein, 1980; Montano and Kasprzyk, 2008; Gifford and Nilsson, 2014). The *environmental knowledge construct* is highlighted as it encompasses all other modules.

The second set is composed of external factors, with an emphasis on the degree of linkages to internal factors. External factors are those that fall outside the university's sphere; however, they have an active and dynamic link to internal factors as public institutional spheres (e.g. the Ministry of Education). Consequently, the public institutions' policy change towards environmentalism is emphasized as structural (based on TEM) (Choy and Lau, 2013). Therefore, the strength of such a link, based on a partnership framework, is essential in the shift towards greening educational institutions (i.e. institutional policy transformation). In addition, external factors also encompass the private sector, non-governmental organizations (NGOs) and the media. Their role as partners in the process of transformation cannot be overemphasized.

The model also refers to the barriers to the process of transforming environmental behaviour. These barriers are a manifestation of the difficulties that are inevitably associated with change. Perhaps, in the context of EM, the nature of such change can be understood as follows: 'Consistent with democratic principles, students should be exposed to the plurality of environmental ideologies, and…through a process of inquiry, critique and reflection, they can be assisted to develop and defend their own set of environmental beliefs and values' (Stevenson, 2007, p. 143).

The Eastern Mediterranean University was established in 1979 as a technical college in the newly independent economy known as the Turkish Republic of North Cyprus (TRNC). The university has become an educational hub for international students, mainly from the Middle East, Central Asia, Africa and the Far East. EMU is the largest university on the island of Cyprus. At present, it has a student body of over 16,000, and this figure is increasing. The university has been awarded 41 international accreditations, recognitions and memberships by international organizations (http://ww1.emu.edu.tr/en/about-emu/memberships-and-accreditations/c/597).

10.3 Methodology

The assumption that frames the conceptual/discursive nature of this study lies in TEM, which is justified because it has become instrumental and is the focus of analysis for recognition of the legitimacy of change in the public sphere towards the ecological system. The proponents of TEM believe that this is possible through institutional transformation in all spheres of society (Eder, 1996; Hajer, 1996; Orr, 1996; Giddens, 1998; Jackson and Roberts, 1999; Huber, 2000; Mol, 2002; Steurer and Hametner, 2013). Therefore, we have focused on the case of an educational institution, a university, to explore the nature of environmental education as a learning culture. Furthermore, we assume that environmental education in the form of the provision of knowledge can lead to the development of an attitude that will result in behaviour that favours environmentalism (i.e. contextualized based on TPB) (Ajzen, 1991; Montano and Kasprzyk, 2008; Ajzen and Sheikh, 2013).

Six hundred questionnaires were distributed among undergraduate- and graduate-level students majoring in different fields. For this purpose, an instrument of 51 items was designed and tested. The instrument was adapted from Ivy *et al.* (1998) and was used to measure secondary students' environmental knowledge. The 51 questions contained 16 items to measure students' environmental knowledge, 13 that targeted their attitudes towards environmental concerns and 13 that gauged their environmental behaviour (four items on their green consumerism and nine on their general environmental behaviour). The remaining nine items assessed EMU's environmentally relevant modules within the curricula. In order to reduce common method bias, one of the procedural remedies proposed by Podsakoff *et al.* (2012) was applied to provide respondent anonymity. Therefore, students were assured about the confidentiality of the information that they provided in the questionnaire.

A non-random method of convenience sampling was applied. However, in this study, the instruments were readjusted to measure EMU's role in the provision of environmental education through different modules within the curricula. Samples selected from students of different age, educational level, gender and study were filed. In total, 277 questionnaires were returned, of which 241 items were valid and usable. Thus, the response rate was 40%. An independent *t*-test was used to check non-response bias. To ensure the clarity of the instruments, they were pilot tested on 20 respondents (12 undergraduates and 8 graduates) who were not included in the survey.

The pilot study result indicated that the questionnaire items were understandable and unambiguous. The reliability of the instruments was measured using Cronbach's alpha, and the reliability coefficients for three dimensions – environmental knowledge, attitude and behaviour – met the acceptable cut-off, indicating 0.61, 0.65 and 0.63, respectively (Cortina, 1993). Therefore, the results indicate the internal consistency of the measurement. For the purpose of descriptive and inferential statistical analysis, a *t*-test and a one-way analysis of variance (ANOVA) were applied. For the statistical analysis, SPSS (statistical package for social sciences) version 20 was utilized.

The majority of the students (78%) are between 18 and 27 years old, 19% of the students are 28–37 years old and the remainder (2.9%) are 38 years old and above. About 13% of the respondents study in a 2-year programme, 54% in a 4-year programme, 22% are in an MS programme and about 10% are PhD students. About 55% of the students are male and 44% are female. The major field of study of 60% of the students is in social sciences (tourism management). About 40% are majoring in engineering fields including: industrial engineering, mechanical engineering, civil engineering and electrical and electronic engineering.

10.4   Results

To meet the objective of the study, the mean scores for the students' environmental knowledge through the attributes of land, air, water, noise and global issues have been calculated and are presented as a percentage in Table 10.1.

The mean scores for the environmental attitude and behaviour of students by field of study, gender and nationality (continent) were compared using the *t*-test (see Table 10.2).

The ANOVA was employed to compare mean scores of the environmental attitude and behaviour of the respondents, in the context of four modules (i.e. courses, workshops, trips and campaigns) within the curricula, towards the dissemination of environmental education (see Fig. 10.2).

10.4.1   General environmental knowledge (Dimension 1)

The analysis of the respondents' knowledge regarding environmental facts and concepts, as well as global environmental issues (i.e. measured by 16 items), showed that 55% had an accurate knowledge of the specific issue of land-related environmental issues (measured by three items). The accuracy of their knowledge of air-related environmental issues was 51% (measured by six items). The respondents' knowledge of water-related environmental issues was 36% (measured by two items). However, the respondents' knowledge and information on the issue of noise was 10% (measured by one item). In relation to global environmental issues, respondents' knowledge was 28% (measured by four items) (refer to Table 10.1). Overall, the average scores of the respondents in relation to their awareness and knowledge of environmental issues was 36%. The results indicate that the general environmental knowledge and information of students at EMU is below average (36%). The consistency of our study is only similar to that conducted by Ivy *et al.* (1998) in terms of the knowledge of noise pollution as an environmental issue. In other cases, such as Blum (2008) and Richmond (1976), who measured the environmental knowledge and information of students in different countries, the result of our study is consistent with their findings. However, this is not the case when our results are compared with those of Ivy *et al.* (1998), who studied students from Singapore.

10.4.2   Environmental attitude (Dimension 2)

Students' learned attitude precedes their behaviour where the latter is associated with taking action on an issue of concern – in this case, environmental concern. The idea of attitude towards a behaviour is theorized and explained by Fishbein and Ajzen (1975) and Azjen (1991) through the TPB. Based on TPB and its sister theory, the theory of reasoned action (TRA), which have been explored by numerous scholars (Glanz *et al.*, 2008), knowledge through education results in an attitude towards a behaviour/action with a certain issue as the target. Thus, being knowledgeable of the environment can possibly result in an individual taking positive action towards

Table 10.1. Descriptive statistics of respondents' knowledge regarding environmental facts, concepts and global environmental issues.

Issues	Items	Answer options (%)					Total (%)
		1	2	3	4	Don't know	
Land	What is likely to be the most important worldwide source of energy for the future?	66.8*	4.6	7.9	12.9	7.9	55
	Which source of energy contributes the least to environmental problems?	48.1*	10.4	11.6	24.5	5.4	
	Which is a renewable resource?	8.7	10.8	9.5	49.8*	21.2	
Air	What is the effect of burning coal and oil?	4.1	11.6	11.6	56.4*	16.2	51
	What is the major air pollutant (by weight) discharged by motor vehicles?	39.4*	38.6	5.4	3.3	13.3	
	What are the major sources of air pollution in big cities?	7.9	7.9	73.0*	7.1	4.1	
	Why is carbon monoxide a serious air pollutant?	39.4*	32.8	11.6	6.2	10.0	
	What is the cause of the increase in carbon dioxide in the atmosphere?	46.9*	15.4	12.0	7.9	17.8	
	Which statement is true about air pollution?	29.9	10.8	9.5	39.0*	10.8	
Water	What is the major source of oil pollution in the oceans?	25.7	36.5*	15.8	9.1	12.9	36
	Why are fish killed when waste is thrown into bodies of water?	27.4	10.4	13.7	32.0*	16.6	
Noise	What does not contribute to an increase in noise levels?	24.5	29.5	10.0*	24.5	11.6	10
Global issues	What increases the acidity of rain?	15.4	18.3	13.3	25.7*	27.4	28
	What is the effect of deforestation?	5.8	24.9	10.0	41.1*	18.3	
	What caused the 'greenhouse effect'?	29.0*	17.0	12.0	16.2	25.7	
	Which statement about the ozone is not true?	16.2*	13.3	14.1	14.1	42.3	

Note: Correct answers indicated with an asterisk.[1]

the environment. One's attitude towards the environment is consequently a learned process, and it is the responsibility of educational institutions to generate such an attitude in students, who are the future scientists, policy makers, consumers and voters (Chaineux and Charlier, 1999). The composite scores of the 13 items that were allocated to measure students' environmental attitudes were computed, and the results

Table 10.2. Compared mean of environmental attitude and behaviour of respondents with different major, gender and continent of origin.

Mean comparisons	Field of study					Gender					Students' origin				
	Engineering		Tourism			Male		Female			African		Asian		
Variables	Mean	SD	Mean	SD	t-test	Mean	SD	Mean	SD	t-test	Mean	SD	Mean	SD	t-test
Environmental attitude	3.04	0.52	3.22	0.50	-2.65*	3.15	0.52	3.15	0.49	0.002[ns]	3.13	0.50	3.15	0.52	-0.26[s]
Environmental behaviour	2.86	0.46	2.86	0.44	-0.02[ns]	2.89	0.44	2.81	0.44	1.28[ns]	2.85	0.44	2.86	0.44	-0.26[ns]

Notes: *Significant at 0.01 level; ns = not significant.

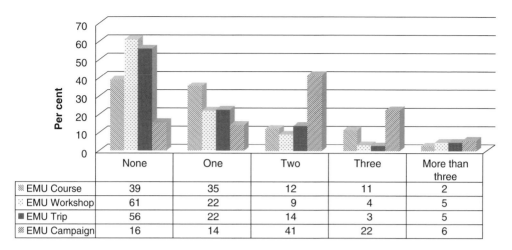

	None	One	Two	Three	More than three
▨ EMU Course	39	35	12	11	2
⸭ EMU Workshop	61	22	9	4	5
■ EMU Trip	56	22	14	3	5
▨ EMU Campaign	16	14	41	22	6

Fig. 10.2. Level of environmental activities of the EMU in line with TEM.

indicated that the average respondent's attitude was 3.15 (SD = 0.55) out of 5, which was the highest scale. The average score of students' environmental behaviour was relatively low (M = 2.86, SD = 0.44). The percentage rate of environmental knowledge that was obtained based on correct answers (through the Likert scale) showed a mean value of 1.8, which was very low (refer to Table 10.2). The results are in accord with the theoretical framework presented, which demonstrates that a low level of knowledge will possibly lead to poor environmental attitude and behaviour. This finding is in line with the study conducted by Monroe *et al.* (2013), where a positive correlation between environmental knowledge and attitudes/behaviour is demonstrated.

10.4.3   Environmental behaviour (Dimension 3)

This dimension was measured by 13 items in two categories, where the mean attitude and behaviour scores with standard deviation for engineering and tourism students were illustrated. In addition, the mean and standard deviation scores based on gender and nationality (continent) were shown (Table 10.2). The results of the *t*-test for the mean comparison of two groups of students revealed a significant difference between the environmental attitudes of engineering and tourism students (t = -2.65, $p < 0.01$). The environmental attitude of the tourism students (M = 3.22, SD = 0.50) is stronger than that of the engineering students (M = 3.04, SD = 0.52). However, the mean scores for the environmental behaviour of engineering and tourism students are not significantly different (t = -0.02, ns). The environmental attitude and behaviour of male and female students is not statistically different. A comparison of the environmental attitude and behaviour of African and Asian students revealed no significant differences between the two groups (t (241) = -0.26, ns) (refer to Table 10.2).

10.4.4   EMU's environmentally relevant modules/curricula (Dimension 4)

This dimension focuses on EMU's environmentally oriented modules and activities, as part of its curricula, with the aim of assessing the extent of the university's efforts towards the dissemination of environmental knowledge/awareness among the students. An ANOVA test was conducted to compare the means of the educational level of the students in regard to environmental attitude and behaviour. The analysis revealed no significant differences in the environmental attitude (F (3,241) = 0.54, ns) and behaviour (F (3,241) = 1.2, ns) of the students through four means of educational modules (i.e. courses, workshops, field trips and campaigns). Furthermore, no significant differences exist among the various levels of schooling, including 2-year programmes, 4-year programmes, master programmes and doctoral programmes.

As depicted in Fig. 10.2, 39% of the respondents claimed that they had taken no environmentally related/relevant modules, 59% stated that they had never participated in any workshop on environmental issues and 54% responded that they had never participated in any field trip for environmentally oriented educational purposes. Fifteen per cent of the students had never participated in any campaign related to an environmental issue. As depicted in the last column of Fig. 10.2, only 2% of the students had taken more than three environmentally oriented courses, 5% had attended more than three workshops, 5% had taken more than three field trips and 6% had taken part in campaigning for environmental purposes.

What is revealed through this dimension has profound implications for attitude and behaviour, as knowledge and attitude are considered antecedents of behaviour towards environmental actions (i.e. based on TPB) (Ajzen, 1985; Montano and Kasprzyk, 2008). Finally, yet importantly, the EM school of thought has been instrumental in environmental capacity building in various institutions around the world, and this has positive implications. It is time for transitional economies, such as north Cyprus, to embark on university and public sector partnerships geared towards what Weidner (2002) called the 'ecologicalization' of institutions and organizations in various social systems (and scientific disciplines), which is progressing slowly in the developing nations. It is hoped that this will pave the way to sustainable development.

Consonant with other empirical studies (Hartline *et al.*, 2000; Lindner *et al.*, 2001), an independent sample *t*-test was employed to check a non-response bias. Respondents were grouped as early and late respondents. The two groups were compared on their responses to the question items using a *t*-test. No apparent significant differences were found between the responses of early (i.e. 170 cases) and late (i.e. 70 cases) respondents; therefore, the results are generalizable to the target population. This is one of the highly used methods for controlling a non-response error in survey research (Lindner *et al.*, 2001). Based on the results of an independent test ($p < 0.01$), a non-response bias did not emerge in the data.

10.5   Conclusion

Notwithstanding the growth of environmentally oriented curricula in the past few decades, along with the establishment of environmentally relevant fields (Palmberg and Kuru, 2000; Shin, 2000), the following question remains: To what extent is environmental education deliberately designed to instil environmentalism behaviour in students?

The first major purpose of the present study was to test the degree of dissemination of environmental knowledge/education in the case of EMU. The second was to gauge the students' environmental awareness. For this purpose, the EM paradigm and TPB have been instrumental in advancing understanding of the role of the university's curricula towards environmentalism in the context of EM. The results revealed the extent of the university's efforts in this regard, as well as the students' environmental inclinations. It also contributed to the notion that, in the developed countries, through organizational/institutional differentiation/integration, capacity building has been elevated within the context of environmental modernization in science, culture, politics, economics and civil society by specializing in environmental matters where training and education play a decisive role (Weidner, 2002).

As an underpinning framework for this study, the convergence between TPB and EM is modelled (Fig. 10.1), and the dissemination of knowledge through educational institutions becomes fundamental to changing behavioural patterns towards environmental concerns. As the environmental crisis intensifies, it is becoming increasingly clear that addressing it requires a radical change in human behavioural patterns.

This study has presented a provisional approach to the effectiveness of the EM theory on educational institutions' dissemination of knowledge and the awareness of how best to safeguard the environment. The outcomes of such knowledge and awareness, as contextualized in TPB (Ajzen and Sheikh, 2013), will result in the generation of attitudes/behaviours among students geared towards upholding environmental values. As Stevenson (2007, p. 143) stated, 'Students should be exposed to the plurality of environmental ideologies, and…through a process of inquiry, critique and reflection, they can be assisted to develop and defend their own set of environmental beliefs and values'.

The study revealed that students at EMU scored poorly regarding their overall knowledge and awareness of environmental issues (47.3%). This is an indication of their lack of exposure to the subject in question. The students' responses to the issues of land, air, water, noise and globally related environmental issues scored 55, 51, 36, 10 and 28, respectively. This indicates that students, either prior to or during their attendance at EMU, have not developed adequate knowledge of the subject.

The findings indicate that the EM call for institutional policy change (i.e. curricular reform) in inspiring environmental valuation among students as future policy makers, planners, managers and consumers has fallen on deaf ears. Therefore, EMU has remained aloof to the EM theory as a school of thought that 'not only…contributes to environmental social sciences and policy, but also strengthen[s] the linkages between those trans-disciplinary pursuits and mainstream social science' (Mol and Sonnenfeld, 2000; Ismaili et al., 2014). The study has also revealed the inadequacy of EMU's environmentally oriented curricula regarding four dimensions: courses/modules, workshops/seminars, field trips and campaigns.

As depicted in Fig. 10.2, students' exposure and involvement in regard to these dimensions have remained minimal. This picture contradicts the principles of TPB – that is, that attitude and behaviour towards an issue are dependent on knowledge and information that is gained prior to commitment to the issue in question (Montano and Kasprzyk, 2008).

The results of the present study reveal that TEM and TPB are adequate frameworks for understanding and explaining the deficient environmental capacity building among students in an educational institution. Overall, these findings highlight the fact that the basic curriculum structure at EMU has ignored the validity of environmental education as the catalyst for future environmental behaviour.

Various scholars have discussed and analysed the role of educational institutions in instilling environmental awareness geared towards commitment to environmental sustainability among students enrolled in universities, colleges and primary/secondary education (Rickinson, 2001; Kollmuss and Agyeman, 2002). However, this study has contributed to the role of educational institutions by focusing on the modules/means that are essential for the construction of attitude/behaviour among students for the purpose of encouraging their environmental commitment in the future.

Environmental knowledge and awareness modules are considered as the policy imperatives that are associated with the public sector, as well as educational institutions' approach to generating positive environmental behaviour (Lozano *et al.*, 2013). Such environmental behaviour among students can be placed on a continuum. At one end, the worst case scenario of environmentalism, known as *anthropocentricity*, is the dominant behaviour. This is the behavioural state when students remain apathetic to their environs. At the opposite end, the ideal case scenario of environmentalism, known as *ecocentricity*, is dominant. This is the behavioural state when students graduate with compassion towards the environment (Baker, 2006).

This research is a cross-sectional study, which can be considered a limitation; however, we suggest further studies that adopt a longitudinal approach through a follow-up of students' environmental performance after graduation. Another idealistic suggestion for further research is to track the performance of the current students in their later working lives to identify the effect of the environmental knowledge injected into them by the university. However, as the current study has considered several factors out of the 18 social and personal factors that influence pro-environmental concern and behaviour noted by Gifford and Nilsson (2014), it is suggested that future research should measure all factors, in order to provide a more comprehensive view of the environment and education nexus. Another recommendation is to explore the performance of institutions (other than universities), as policy changes need to be made in the process of transformation towards EM.

Some of the implications of so-called 'greening' EMU's curriculum can be highly effective for tourism students based on the role they will take in their environmental agenda in the future. According to the classic meta-analysis of Hines *et al.*, knowledge and education are underlined as the two strongest predictors of responsible environmental behaviour (as cited in Gifford and Nilsson, 2014).

The findings of the study revealed that students in general lacked environmental knowledge and awareness, which encompassed students of tourism as well. Such discouraging levels of knowledge about issues of climate change, energy production and pollution will hamper making pro-environmental choices as an essential embryonic environmental greening towards sustainable tourism development. In fact, mass tourism, with all the critique of its negative environmental impact, is going to stay; however, environmental education in the context of a knowledge-based platform and concurrent with TEM is an initiative to accommodate a more complex and ambiguous array of sustainability options within the tourism industry (Weaver and Lawton, 1999).

This study should be considered a wake-up call for tourism educators at EMU that social equity, justice, ethics and environmentalism are values that demand their rightful place in the tourism curriculum. In the context of a knowledge-based platform and ecological modernization's call for institutional policy change, the present curriculum has remained short of an appreciation of the structural complexity and international nature of tourism as a socio-economic, political and environmental phenomenon.

Note

[1]Questions and answer options 1 to 4 for Table 10.1, measuring respondents' knowledge regarding environmental facts, concepts and global environmental issues. Correct answers indicated by ✓

What is likely to be the most important worldwide source of energy for the future?

1 Solar radiation. ✓
2 Tidal flow.
3 Geothermal sources.
4 Wind power.

Which source of energy contributes the least to environmental problems?

1 Solar. ✓
2 Coal.
3 Petroleum.
4 Nuclear.

Which of the following is a renewable resource?

1 Copper.
2 Coal.
3 Oil.
4 Water. ✓

As a result of burning coal and oil, the amount of carbon dioxide in the atmosphere is:

1 Decreasing, but will not affect the Earth's environment.
2 Decreasing, with possible serious effects on the Earth's environment.
3 Increasing, but will not affect the Earth's environment.
4 Increasing, with possible serious effects on the Earth's environment. ✓

What is the major air pollutant (by weight) discharged by motor vehicles?

1 Carbon monoxide. ✓
2 Carbon dioxide.
3 Sulphur dioxide.
4 Solid particles.

What are the major sources of air pollution in big cities?

1 Homes and industries.
2 Agriculture and industries.
3 Motor vehicles and industries.
4 Motor vehicles and homes. ✓

Why is carbon monoxide a serious air pollutant?

1 It is poisonous to humans. ✓
2 It causes atmospheric haze.
3 It is harmful to vegetation.
4 It is corrosive to metals.

What is the cause of the increase in carbon dioxide in the atmosphere?

1 Extensive deforestation and burning of fossil fuels. ✓
2 Use of aerosols and refrigerants found in air conditioners.
3 Breakdown of inorganic substances.
4 Use of chemical fertilizers.

Which of the following statements about air pollution is true?

1 Air pollution is caused by man-made processes only.
2 Only some pollutants are harmful to health.
3 Air pollution is confined to certain political boundaries.
4 Pollution may give rise to irreversible changes in the environment. ✓

What is the major source of oil pollution in the oceans?

1 Offshore drilling.
2 Oil tanker operation. ✓
3 Refineries.
4 Motor vehicle waste.

Waste thrown into bodies of water kills fish because the decaying waste:

1 Adds carbon dioxide to water.
2 Gives off a bad smell.
3 Removes the food eaten by fish.
4 Uses up oxygen needed by fish in respiration. ✓

What does not contribute to an increase in noise levels?

1 Rapid urbanization.
2 Rapid industrial development.
3 Rapidly ageing population. ✓
4 Rapid increase in vehicle population.

What increases the acidity of rain?

1 Chlorofluorocarbons (CFCs).
2 Carbon.
3 Methane.
4 Sulphur dioxide. ✓

What is the effect of deforestation?

1 Distortion of the rainfall.
2 Destruction of habitat and food species for wildlife.
3 Destruction of soil in the mountains due to erosion.
4 All of the above. ✓

What caused the 'greenhouse effect'?
1 An increased amount of carbon dioxide in the atmosphere, which traps the heat radiated from the ground. ✓
2 Increased vegetation on the surface of the Earth.
3 An increased rate of melting of polar ice caps due to increased temperature of the atmosphere.
4 Increased destruction of the ozone layer.

Which of the following statements about the ozone is not true?

1 Chlorine reacts with sunlight to produce pollutants like ozone. ✓
2 Ozone prevents the Earth's surface from absorbing too many ultraviolet rays from the sun.
3 CFCs and methane are ozone depleting gases.
4 Excess ultraviolet rays can cause skin cancer.

References

Ajzen, I. (1985) From intentions to actions: a theory of planned behavior. In: Kuhl, J. and Beckmann, J. (eds) *Action Control: From Cognition to Behavior.* Springer Verlag, New York, pp. 11–40.

Ajzen, I. (1991) The theory of planned behavior. *Organizational Behavior and Human Decision Processes* 50(2), 179–211.

Ajzen, I. and Fishbein, M. (1980) *Understanding Attitudes and Predicting Social Behavior*. Prentice-Hall, Englewood Cliffs, New Jeresy.

Ajzen, I. and Sheikh, S. (2013) Action versus inaction: anticipated affect in the theory of planned behavior. *Journal of Applied Social Psychology* 43(1), 155–162.

Baker, S. (2006). Sustainable development. Routledge, New York.

Ballantyne, R., Packer, J. and Falk, J. (2011) Visitors' learning for environmental sustainability: testing short- and long-term impacts of wildlife tourism experiences using structural equation modelling. *Tourism Management* 32(6), 1243–1252.

Beck, U. (1996) Risk society and the provident state. In: Lash, S., Szerszynski, B. and Wynne, B. (eds) *Risk, Environment and Modernity: Towards a New Ecology*. Sage, London, pp. 27–43.

Blum, N. (2008) Environmental education in Costa Rica: building a framework for sustainable development? *International Journal of Educational Development* 28(3), 348–358.

Castles, A. and Stratford, E. (2014) Planning reform in Australia's island-state. *Australian Planner* 51(2), 170–179.

Chaineux, M.C.P. and Charlier, R.H. (1999) Strategies in environmental education. *International Journal of Environmental Studies* 56(6), 889–905.

Chou, C.J. (2014) Hotels' environmental policies and employee personal environmental beliefs: interactions and outcomes. *Tourism Management* 40, 436–446.

Choy, E.A. and Catherine Lau, Y.P. (2013) Towards a sustainable campus: an ecological modernization perspective. *Asian Social Science* 9(15), 106–110.

Cortina, J.M. (1993) What is coefficient alpha? An examination of theory and applications. *Journal of Applied Psychology* 78(1), 98–104.

Eder, K. (1996) The institutionalization of environmentalism: ecological discourse and the second transformation of the public sphere. In: Lash, S., Szerszynski, B. and Wynne, B. (eds) *Risk, Environment and Modernity: Towards a New Ecology*. Sage, London, pp. 203–223.

Fidgeon, P.R. (2010) Tourism education and curriculum design: a time for consolidation and review? *Tourism Management* 31(6), 699–723.

Fishbein, M. and Ajzen I. (1975) *Belief, Attitude, Intention, and Behavior: An Introduction to Theory and Research*. Addison-Wesley, Reading, Massachusetts.

Giddens, A. (1998) *The Third Way: The Renewable of Social Democracy*. Polity Press, Cambridge, UK.

Gifford, R. and Nilsson, A. (2014) Personal and social factors that influence pro-environmental concern and behavior: a review. *International Journal of Psychology* 49(3), 141–157.

Glanz, K., Rimer, B.K. and Viswanath, K. (eds) (2008) *Health Behavior and Health Education: Theory, Research, and Practice*. Wiley, Hoboken, New Jersey.

Hajer, M.A. (1996) Ecological modernization as cultural politics. In: Lash, S., Szerszynski, B. and Wynne, B. (eds) *Risk, Environment and Modernity: Towards a New Ecology*. Sage, London, pp. 203–223.

Hartline, M.D., Maxham, J.G. III and McKee, D.O. (2000) Corridors of influence in the dissemination of customer-oriented strategy to customer contact service employees. *Journal of Marketing* 64(2), 35–50.

Huber, J. (2000) Towards industrial ecology: sustainable development as a concept of ecological modernization. *Journal of Environmental Policy and Planning* 2(4), 269–285.

Ismaili, M., Srbinovski, M. and Sapuric, Z. (2014) Students' conative component about the environment in the Republic of Macedonia. *Procedia-Social and Behavioral Sciences* 116, 95–100.

Ivy, T.G.C., Road, K.S., Lee, C.K.E. and Chuan, G.K. (1998) A survey of environmental knowledge, attitudes and behavior of students in Singapore. *International Research in Geographical and Environmental Education* 7(3) 181–202.

Jackson, T. and Roberts, P. (1999) Ecological modernization as a model for regional development: the changing nature and context of the Eastern Scotland Structural Fund Program. *Journal of Environmental Policy and Planning* 1, 61–75.

Kalamas, M., Cleveland, M. and Laroche, M. (2014) Pro-environmental behaviors for thee but not for me: Green giants, green Gods, and external environmental locus of control. *Journal of Business Research* 67(2), 12–22.

Kollmuss, A. and Agyeman, J. (2002) Mind the gap: why do people act environmentally and what are the barriers to pro-environmental behavior? *Environmental Education Research* 8(3), 239–260.

Kuo, S.Y. and Jackson, N.L. (2014) Influence of an environmental studies course on attitudes of under-graduates at an engineering university. *The Journal of Environmental Education* 45(2), 91–104.

Lindner, J.R., Murphy, T.H. and Briers, G.E. (2001) Handling nonresponse in social science research. *Journal of Agricultural Education* 42(4), 43–53.

Lozano, R., Lukman, R., Lozano, F.J., Huisingh, D. and Lambrechts, W. (2013) Declarations for sustainability in higher education: becoming better leaders, through addressing the university system. *Journal of Cleaner Production* 48, 10–19.

Mihalic, T. (2014) Sustainable-responsible tourism discourse – towards 'responsustable' tourism. *Journal of Cleaner Production*, doi:10.1016/j.jclepro.2014.12.062.

Mol, A.P.J. (2002) Ecological modernization and the global economy. *Global Environmental Politics* 2(2), 92–115.

Mol, A.P.J. and Sonnenfeld, D.A. (2000) Ecological modernization around the world: an introduction. *Environmental Politics* 9(1), 1–14.

Monroe, M.C., Agrawal, S., Jakes, P.J., Kruger, L.E., Nelson, K.C., *et al.* (2013) Identifying indicators of behavior change: insights from wildfire education programs. *The Journal of Environmental Education* 44(3), 180–194.

Montano, D.E. and Kasprzyk, D. (2008) Theory of reasoned action, theory of planned behavior, and the integrated behavioral model. *Health Behavior and Health Education: Theory, Research, and Practice* 4, 67–95.

Orr, D.W. (1996) Educating for the environment: higher education's challenge of the next century. *The Journal of Environmental Education* 27(3), 7–10.

Palmberg, I.E. and Kuru, J. (2000) Outdoor activities as a basis for environmental responsibility. *The Journal of Environmental Education* 31(4), 32–36.

Podsakoff, P.M., MacKenzie, S.B. and Podsakoff, N.P. (2012) Sources of method bias in social science research and recommendations on how to control it. *Annual Review of Psychology* 63, 539–569.

Potter, G. (2010) Environmental education for the 21st century: where do we go now? *The Journal of Environmental Education* 41(1), 22–33.

Price, J.C. and Leviston, Z. (2014) Predicting pro-environmental agricultural practices: the social, psychological and contextual influences on land management. *Journal of Rural Studies* 34, 65–78.

Richmond, J.M. (1976) A survey of environmental knowledge and attitudes of fifth year students in England. PhD dissertation, The Ohio State University. Available at: http://files.eric.ed.gov/fulltext/ED130864.pdf (accessed 7 November 2014).

Rickinson, M. (2001) Learners and learning in environmental education: a critical review of the evidence. *Environmental Education Research* 7(3), 207–320.

Saat, S.A. (2013) Solid waste management in Malaysia and ecological modernization theory perspective. *Journal of Sustainability Science and Management* 8(2), 268–275.

Shin, D.S. (2000) Environmental education course development for preservice secondary school science teachers in the Republic of Korea. *The Journal of Environmental Education* 31(4), 11–18.

Sparks, P., Hinds, J., Curnock, S. and Pavey, L. (2014) Connectedness and its consequences: a study of relationships with the natural environment. *Journal of Applied Social Psychology* 44(3), 166–174.

Steurer, R. and Hametner, M. (2013) Objectives and indicators in sustainable development strategies: similarities and variances across Europe. *Sustainable Development* 21(4), 224–241.

Stevenson, R.B. (2007). Schooling and environmental education: contradictions in purpose and practice. *Environmental Education Research* 13(2), 139–153.

Stigka, E.K., Paravantis, J.A. and Mihalakakou, G.K. (2014) Social acceptance of renewable energy sources: a review of contingent valuation applications. *Renewable and Sustainable Energy Reviews* 32, 100–106.

Sulemana, I. and James, H.S. Jr (2014) Farmer identity, ethical attitudes and environmental practices. *Ecological Economics* 98, 49–61.

Thapa, B. (2010) The mediation effect of outdoor recreation participation on environmental attitude-behavior correspondence. *The Journal of Environmental Education* 41(3), 133–150.

Weaver, D.B. and Lawton, L. (1999) *Sustainable Tourism: A Critical Analysis*. Pacific Asia Travel Association (PATA). CRC for Sustainable Tourism, Griffith University, Australia.

Weidner, H. (2002) Capacity building for ecological modernization lessons from cross-national research. *American Behavioral Scientist* 45(9), 1340–1368.

Yasunaga, A., Kawano, Y., Kamahori, Y. and Noguchi, K. (2014) Individual and environmental factors related to stage of change in exercise behavior: a cross-sectional study of female Japanese undergraduate students. *Journal of Physical Activity and Health* 11(1), 62–67.

Part III   Improving Tourism Destination Sustainability

11 Understanding the Seasonal Concentration of Tourist Arrivals: The Case of the South of Spain

José David Cisneros-Martínez * and Antonio Fernández-Morales

Universidad de Málaga, Málaga, Spain

11.1 Introduction

Seasonality is a phenomenon that affects many economic activities, including tourism. Regions or destinations where the tourism industry represents a significant part of their economies are indeed more affected by seasonal fluctuations. In Andalusia, the southern region of Spain, tourism is a very important economic industry, with 12.8% of the share in the regional gross domestic product (GDP) for 2013. Employment figures for 2013 indicate that there are 320,000 tourism-related jobs, which is 13% of the total regional employment. Moreover, it has been estimated that 22.4 million tourists visited Andalusia in 2013, of which 59% chose the Andalusian coastline; 'sun and beach' was the predominant product (Consejería de Turismo, Comercio y Deporte [CTCYD], 2013).

Thus, the entire Andalusian region must deal with the effects of seasonality. Both local and regional administration, as well as tourism business owners, are currently confronting this problem by implementing remedial measures to reduce seasonal concentration with the relentless pursuit of new formulas for product diversification. This can be corroborated by the recent observed coordination between public administration and the private sector to address this problem. Yet, for coordination to work efficiently, it needs to have both the knowledge as well as the adequate tools to measure seasonality.

The objectives of this chapter are: (i) to present a methodology for analysing seasonal concentration in tourism, designed as a control and monitoring measure which tourism planners and managers may use in destinations with a high seasonal concentration (by estimating the Gini index, applying an additive decomposition over tourism segments and estimating relative marginal effects over the annual indexes of the tourism segments); and (ii) to apply this methodology to the analysis

*E-mail: joscismar@uma.es

© CAB International 2016. *Destination Competitiveness, the Environment and Sustainability: Challenges and Cases* (eds A. Artal-Tur and M. Kozak)

of seasonal concentration in Andalusia over the period 1999–2013 to two tourism data sets, travellers visiting the coastal areas in Andalusia and passengers arriving in Andalusia.

11.2   Literature Review

There has been an almost general acceptance that seasonality is inevitably linked with tourism activity, which until recently somewhat inhibited the serious and extensive research agenda in this field (Allcock, 1994), especially regarding measurement techniques (Koenig-Lewis and Bischoff, 2005; De Cantis *et al.*, 2011). Moore (1989) defined seasonality as the displacements produced in a given period, during a specific time of the year and each occurring similarly. In addition, Butler and Mao (1997) identify two dimensions of seasonality: natural (including climate, weather, etc.) and institutional (mainly holiday and leisure calendar). The effects of tourism seasonality are related to these aspects, and for this reason, tourism managers have difficulty in establishing appropriate policies to reduce their impact.

The main problems caused by the effects of seasonality are the underuse of tourism facilities during the low season and, vice versa, their maximum occupancy to full capacity during the high season (Baum and Hagen, 1999; Pegg *et al.*, 2012). This fact is explained by the concentration of touristic flows during certain periods of the year, which represents a temporary mismatch between the supply and demand of tourism. This has negative consequences, resulting in an instability that causes various problems that business owners and tourism managers have to contend with: such as unstable employment, limits on the profitability of investments, reduction in business revenue, a mismatch in load capacity, fluctuation of prices, environmental degradation and various sociocultural effects among visitors and residents in a given destination (Butler, 2001).

Traditional measurement tools, such as seasonal variation and concentration indexes, including the Gini index (without a marginal decomposition), are focused on reproducing representative models of seasonality, reaching general conclusions about the level of seasonal concentration. However, these traditional tools do not allow one to know what type of tourist is truly favourable for the seasonal adjustment of a destination (Cisneros-Martínez and Fernández-Morales, 2015). Therefore, when tourism managers implement measures to reduce seasonality, they find it difficult to identify whether there is any type of tourist that can contribute significantly to the reduction of seasonality at a destination, and these (potential) tourists pass unnoticed due to the lack of a methodology that could identify them.

11.3   Methodology

The methodology used in this study is proposed as a control and monitoring measurement, which tourism managers may use in destinations with a high seasonal concentration. Specifically, it has been applied to tourist arrivals in Andalusia with the main purpose of checking quantitatively whether certain tourist segments can help reduce tourism seasonality. The additive decomposition of the Gini index provides information about the contribution of each tourist segment to the total seasonal concentration. Furthermore, by obtaining the measures of the relative marginal effects (RMEs), it is possible to identify to what extent a particular tourist segment can contribute to the reduction of seasonal concentration in the destination analysed. Likewise, by analysing the evolution of RMEs throughout the period of study, especially in the last year analysed, tourism managers could tailor tourism policies designed to alleviate seasonal concentration annually, anticipating each year how it will contribute to an increase of a type of tourist in the reduction of the overall Gini index that had previously been used to measure the degree of seasonal concentration.

The Gini index is a measure that has traditionally been used to measure the concentration of wealth in a particular country or area, but also in measuring the seasonal concentration of tourism (Sutcliffe and Sinclair, 1980; Lundtorp, 2001; Rosselló Nadal et al., 2004; Tsitouras, 2004; Fernández-Morales and Mayorga-Toledano, 2008; Cuccia and Rizzo, 2011; De Cantis et al., 2011; Halpern, 2011; Martín Martín et al., 2014). Furthermore, the additive decomposition of the Gini index was first used in tourism research to measure the concentration of hotel demand on the Costa del Sol (Fernández-Morales and Mayorga-Toledano, 2008). Later, it was also used to investigate the seasonal concentration demand of Spanish airport passengers (Halpern, 2011).

We use the additive decomposition proposed by Lerman and Yitzhaki (1985). This decomposition, as pointed out by Fernández-Morales and Mayorga-Toledano (2008), facilitates the estimation of the marginal effects produced by a given variation in some of the components analysed in the overall Gini index. For a monthly series with K additive components $Y = X_1 + X_2 + \cdots + X_K$, the RME quantifies, in relative terms, how much the overall Gini index increases or decreases when a small relative increase e^k (equally distributed throughout the year) occurs in component k. It can be calculated as follows:

$$RME_k \frac{\partial G}{\partial e^k} \frac{1}{G} = S_k \left(\frac{\Gamma_{k,Y} G_k}{G} - 1 \right)$$

where G_k is the annual Gini index of k, S_k is the annual participation of X_k in the annual value of Y, and $\Gamma_{k,Y}$ represents the Gini correlation between X_k and Y, $Cov\ X_k$, $F(Y)/Cov\ X_k$, $F(X_k)$ (Yitzhaki and Schechtman, 2013). This decomposition can be a very useful tool for tourism managers who establish measures to reduce seasonality (Cisneros-Martínez and Fernández-Morales, 2015). In addition, seasonal factors are also estimated to enhance the exploratory analysis, providing the seasonal patterns of the analysed series, prior to analysing the Gini indexes and their decompositions (De Cantis et al., 2011).

11.4 Results

The first application of our methodology in this study consists of analysing the impact of seasonality on the Andalusian coastline. The main tourism destinations in Andalusia are on the coast, which is traditionally visited by the majority of tourists.

Our study draws a distinction between the five different coasts, and the Andalusian coastal line is divided into: Costa de la Luz de Huelva, Costa de la Luz de Cádiz, Costa del Sol, Costa Tropical and Costa de Almería.

Travellers staying in hotels were chosen as the unit of measurement and, during the first stage, were distinguished between domestic and international. The data sources are the monthly series of the Hotel Occupancy Survey 'Encuesta de Ocupación Hotelera' published by the Spanish National Statistics Institute from January 1999 to December 2013 (Instituto Nacional de Estadística [INE], 2013b). This choice is motivated by the predominance of the hotel as the most relevant type of demand for tourist accommodation on the Andalusian coastline. In 2013, 84.7% of travellers that lodged in a regulated accommodation, as recorded by the INE (hotels, camping grounds and apartments for tourists) for this coastal destination, stayed in hotels (INE, 2013a,b).

The degree of seasonal concentration in all of Andalusia's coastal tourism showed a slightly increasing pattern for the observed period, reaching a Gini index in 2013 of $G_D = 0.24$ for domestic travellers, $G_I = 0.22$ for international travellers and $G_T = 0.21$ in total (Gini indexes in 1999 were $G_D = 0.20$, $G_I = 0.19$ and $G_T = 0.19$, respectively). These estimations are consistent with a previous work, Cisneros-Martínez and Fernández-Morales (2015), where it was also noted that international travellers showed a less concentrated seasonal pattern with data up to 2011. These findings indicate that the regional and local policies against seasonality have not been fully effective, at least in the coastal tourism sector.

The five coastal areas in Andalusia show a variable level of seasonal concentration. The lowest Gini indexes in 2013 correspond to the Costa del Sol ($G_D = 0.24$, $G_I = 0.22$, $G_T = 0.21$), which includes most of the mature and well-known destinations like Torremolinos, Marbella or Fuengirola, consolidated since the 1960s. Conversely, the highest ones are found in Costa de la Luz de Huelva ($G_D = 0.42$, $G_I = 0.41$, $G_T = 0.41$), which is a newer coastal destination. The other three areas, Costa de la Luz de Cádiz ($G_D = 0.31$, $G_I = 0.29$, $G_T = 0.30$), Costa Tropical ($G_D = 0.31$, $G_I = 0.25$, $G_T = 0.29$) and Costa de Almería ($G_D = 0.33$, $G_I = 0.32$, $G_T = 0.33$), remain in an intermediate position. It is worth noting that the estimated Gini indexes in the five coastal areas in 2013 are in all cases higher than the 1999 indexes.

An implication from the previous analysis could be that domestic travellers exhibit a more seasonally concentrated pattern than international travellers, and thus the international segment should be the focus of counter-seasonal policies. In fact, the estimation of the RME in 2013 for international travellers is $RME_I = -0.03$ ($RME_D = +0.03$ for domestic travellers). If one distinguishes by areas, in all the cases the RME is negative for international travellers, ranging from -0.08 in Costa Tropical to -0.01 in Costa de Almería. However, a recent study suggested that a more detailed segmentation could yield better results (Cisneros-Martínez and Fernández-Morales, 2015). Therefore, we also grouped travellers into segments according to their main travel motivation: sun and beach segment (weather and beach); cultural segment (popular festivals and folklore, and visiting monuments) and other segments (prices, nature and rural tourism, visiting family and friends, sports, etc.). Statistical data provided by the Turismo Andaluz Company (Sistema de Análisis y Estadísticas del Turismo en Andalucía, SAETA), which depends on regional government, were used for the segmentation.

To get accurate results, we used a double segmentation, both by travel motivation and origin. A first look into the seasonal factors of the six segments (Fig. 11.1) reveals remarkable differences between them. On the one hand, both domestic and international travellers are not homogeneous groups with respect to their seasonal patterns, especially in the domestic case. Among domestic travellers, those indicating sun and beach as their motivation exhibited a pronounced one-peak profile, highly concentrated in July and August, in Andalusia and in the five coastal areas (particularly intense in Costa Tropical). This profile contrasts with those corresponding to the cultural and other segments. There are also differences between the three international segments.

On the other hand, a single segmentation only of travel motivation does not seem to suffice because there are also notable differences within each of the three motivation segments, mainly between the international and the domestic sun and beach segments. Although the sun and beach segment traditionally concentrates in the summer months, international travellers in this segment present a longer season and are less concentrated in July and August than domestic ones. In addition, cultural and other segments also show different patterns depending on the traveller's origin, which is slightly flatter in the international case.

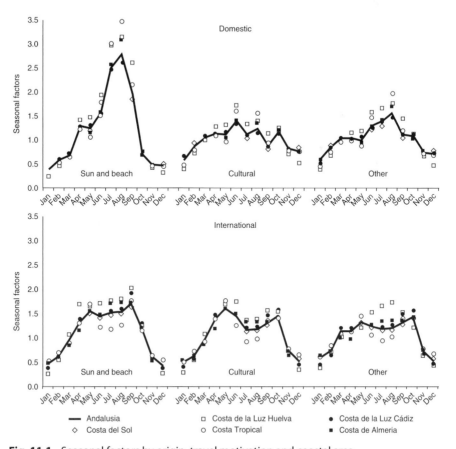

Fig. 11.1. Seasonal factors by origin, travel motivation and coastal area.

Gini indexes for the six segments have been estimated, and they show a general increasing trend for all the cases in the period 1999–2013, except in cultural segments, which experienced a slight decrease throughout the period in the international case and a relatively stable trend (with some oscillations) in the case of domestic travellers. Overall, in Andalusia and in the five coastal areas, the highest Gini indexes are found in the sun and beach segments, always greater in the domestic than in the international case. In Andalusia in 2013, the highest seasonal concentration corresponds to domestic sun and beach travellers, $G_{D-S \text{ and } B}$ = 0.32, followed by international sun and beach ones, $G_{I-S \text{ and } B}$ = 0.26. The same occurs in the rest of the areas, but at different levels; the lowest value being that of Costa del Sol ($G_{D-S \text{ and } B}$ = 0.32 and $G_{I-S \text{ and } B}$ = 0.26) and the highest ones that of Costa de la Luz de Huelva ($G_{D-S \text{ and } B}$ = 0.48 and $G_{I-S \text{ and } B}$ = 0.43).

Conversely, although domestic travellers (considered as a whole group) show a high level of seasonal concentration, as mentioned above, the segment of domestic travellers with a cultural motivation has the lowest Gini index when the double segmentation is applied in Andalusia (G_{D-C} = 0.15 in 2013), in the five coastal areas (from G_{D-C} = 0.15 in the Costa del Sol to G_{D-C} = 0.33 in the Costa de la Luz de Huelva), and practically throughout the complete observed period. This outcome confirms that segmentations that are too broad may obscure important features related to seasonal concentration as a result of aggregating different seasonal patterns into a group whose monthly distribution may be dominated by one predominant segment.

The additive decomposition of the Gini indexes performed (as explained in the previous section) to the double segmentation permits the estimation of the relative marginal effects over the Gini index of Andalusia or to the corresponding coastal area. Figure 11.2 shows the estimated RMEs in 2013, the last year of the observed period. In Andalusia, both the domestic and the international cultural segments are the ones that have the most significant effect against seasonal concentration, with negative marginal effects 'represented as solid circles' (RME_{D-C} = –0.04, RME_{I-C} = –0.05). The domestic cultural segment showed negative RMEs throughout the whole observed period, being even more important than the international cultural segment in some years, even though its share is smaller.

In contrast, the domestic sun and beach segment is the only one with a positive RME – represented with a dashed circle – for 2013 in Andalusia ($RME_{D-S \text{ and } B}$ = 0.10). Therefore, a potential increase in the share of this segment would have the significant effect of a greater seasonal concentration, as measured by the Gini index. This is due to the fact that this is the segment with the highest Gini index, as well as with the highest share. In addition, only the domestic sun and beach segment shows positive RMEs all over the observed period in Andalusia, reaching values of over 0.20 from 2004 to 2007.

Distinguishing by coastal areas, a common feature observed throughout the period studied is that the domestic sun and beach segment shows the highest RME. In 2013, it ranged from 0.06 in Costa de la Luz de Huelva to 0.12 in Costa Tropical. Thus, its potential impact to aggravate seasonal concentration is much higher in Costa Tropical. In contrast, the international sun and beach segment plays a different role in some coastal areas. While in 2013 it shows positive RMEs in Costa de Almería, Costa de la Luz de Cádiz and Costa del Sol, negative RMEs, although

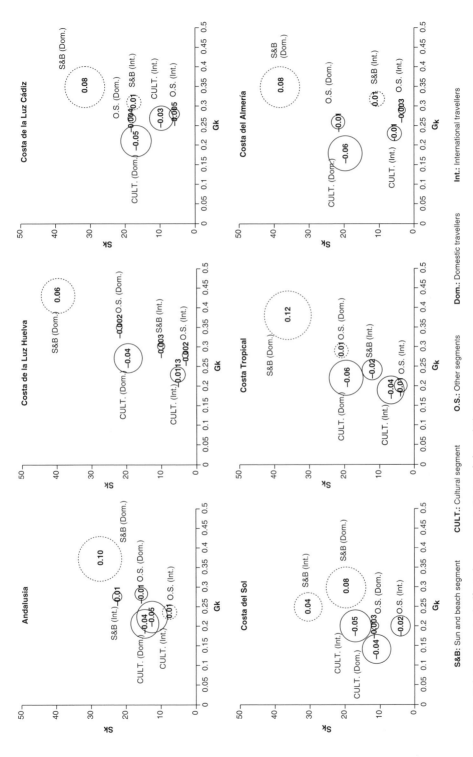

Fig. 11.2. Relative marginal effects by segment, Gini and share (%), 2013.

relatively small, are found in Costa Tropical and Costa de la Luz de Huelva (in this particular area, we see it throughout the whole period observed).

The domestic cultural segment shows negative RMEs in the five coastal areas for the entire period (with values from −0.04 to −0.06 in 2013), of which the highest negative figures for four of them were in 2013. Even though this segment is not the one with the smallest Gini index, in some areas (Costa Tropical and Costa de la Luz de Huelva), its high level of share counteracts its seasonal marginal effect. Therefore, this is the central segment to focus on when attempting to tackle seasonality in all the coastal areas of our study. Moreover, the share of the domestic cultural segment in the coastal areas hardly exceeds 20%, leaving enough room to encourage a greater development of this segment.

There are notable differences by area in the counter-seasonal role of the international cultural segment. Three areas (Costa del Sol, Costa Tropical and Costa de la Luz de Cádiz) show negative RMEs greater (in absolute value) than −0.03 in 2013, indicating that promoting this sector could be an effective policy to tackle seasonal concentration on these coasts. However, in Costa de la Luz de Huelva and Costa de Almería, the estimated RMEs are relatively small (RME_{I-C} = −0.01); thus indicating that in these areas the counter-seasonal effects are limited. The estimated marginal effects over seasonal concentration of the other segments are of little magnitude in all cases, but almost always negative (in 2013, only domestic other segments in Costa Tropical shows a positive RME).

Finally, it is important to note that, in addition to a sufficiently detailed segmentation, the peculiarities of each of the coastal areas demands a customized analysis to reveal some potential effects that are specific to those areas, such as the significant pro seasonal effect of the international sun and beach segment in the Costa del Sol, or the limited counter-seasonal effect of the international cultural segment in Costa de la Luz de Huelva and in Costa de Almería.

The second application of our methodology consists of analysing the seasonal concentration of passengers arriving at Andalusian airports by distinguishing domestic and international passengers. The statistical sources are the monthly series of the Spanish Airports and Air Navigation Company from January 1999 to December 2013 (Aeropuertos Españoles and Navegación Aérea, 2013). In this case, we focused our attention on the specific segment of airport passengers. This is especially relevant for the international component of visitors to Andalusia, since 81% of international tourists visiting the coastline of Andalusia use the airplane as their means of transport, whereas only 16% of domestic tourists chose this mode of transport (CTCYD, 2013). However, we have maintained the domestic segment in the analysis to keep the decomposition consistency, and to find out if this segment has specific seasonal characteristics.

Throughout the analysed period, the observed level of passenger seasonal concentration in Andalusia showed a relatively stable behaviour until 2007 (with Gini indexes between 0.12 and 0.14), which was followed by an increasing trend, reaching a Gini index of G_T = 0.17 in 2013. The same pattern is observed in the international segment, which is the major segment (71% in 2013), but with higher seasonal concentration indexes (between 0.17 and 0.19 until 2007, reaching G_I = 0.21 in 2013). These estimated Gini indexes are in the same range as those corresponding to the international segment of travellers visiting the Andalusian coastline, as analysed above and by Cisneros-Martínez and Fernández-Morales (2015). In contrast, the domestic segment shows a very low level of seasonal concentration, with Gini indexes varying from 0.04 to 0.09 (G_D = 0.06 in 2013). This is due to the fact that within the domestic visitors to Andalusia, those who come by airplane are a minority, with a well-differentiated seasonal distribution compared with the entire domestic segment.

By distinguishing by airports, first, we find that the evolution of the Gini index in Málaga Airport is very similar to that of Andalusia, as this is the main airport in the region, absorbing 69% of the regional arrivals in 2013. The second airport in relative terms is Sevilla (18% of the regional arrivals in 2013). In this airport, the levels of seasonal concentration are lower than in Málaga overall, but a greater concentration is also observed in the international segment. The remaining three small airports, Jerez, Almería and Granada (with shares of 5.5%, 4.9% and 2.4% in 2013), show higher levels of seasonal concentration and less stable patterns in the evolution of Gini indexes, due to their smaller dimension. A common feature observed in the five airports is that the national segment shows, in general, a low level of seasonal concentration.

To get a deeper insight, the seasonal factors have been estimated for both the domestic and the international segments in the five airports, and in the whole region (Fig. 11.3). The seasonal pattern of the domestic passengers segment, which explains its low Gini indexes, is clearly different from that unimodal one of the domestic sun and beach and domestic other segments of visitors to the coasts in Fig. 11.1. Therefore, this segment should be a good possible target for counter-seasonal policies. International passengers, however, exhibit distributions more concentrated in the summer, especially in smaller airports.

The results of the additive decomposition of the Gini indexes for the series of passengers according to origin, domestic and international revealed that in all the airports, the domestic segment yielded negative RMEs throughout the entire period analysed. In the larger airports, Málaga and Sevilla, the estimated relative marginal effects have been in the range of ($-0.07, -0.15$) in Sevilla and ($-0.07, -0.14$) in Málaga, with values in 2013 equal to RME_D = -0.08 and RME_D = -0.11, respectively. This result confirms the previous suggestion that domestic visitors choosing flying as their mode of transport should have a counter-seasonal effect in these two airports. Furthermore, in two of the smaller airports, Jerez and Almería, the RMEs are even higher, with estimations of RME_D = -0.43 in Almería Airport and RME_D = -0.38 in Jerez Airport for 2013.

Finally, we have performed the additive decomposition of the Gini index in the main airports (Málaga and Sevilla) and in all Andalusian airports as a whole in 2013, with a segmentation of international passengers by country (or group of countries in the case of the Baltic countries) of origin 'considering the main four origins in relative terms in each case' (Fig. 11.4). In Málaga Airport, we find that within the international passengers, the segment coming from the Baltic countries exhibit a negative RME (with a Gini index below 0.20), thus being a possible objective for counter-seasonal policies. In contrast, the highest RME among the international segment is found within passengers from the UK.

Regarding Sevilla Airport, there is also one international origin with a negative RME: Italy. However, these origins with negative RMEs should be considered locally, since from a regional point of view (considering the whole region of Andalusia),

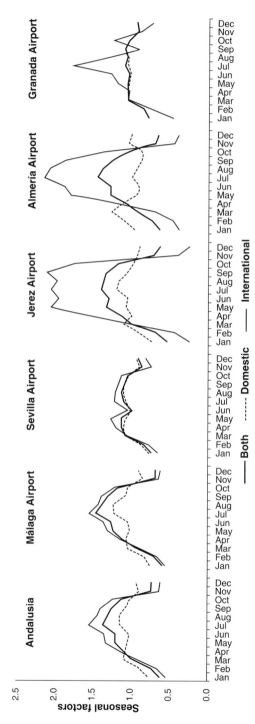

Fig. 11.3. Seasonal factors by airport and origin.

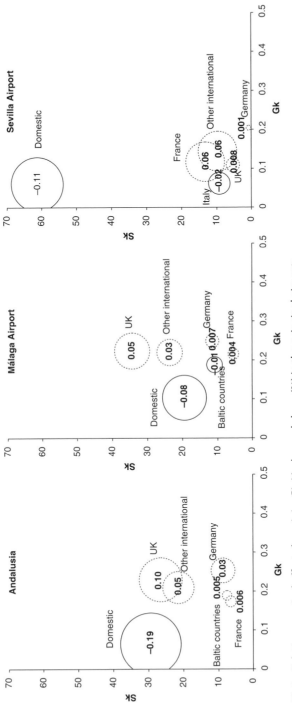

Fig. 11.4. Relative marginal effects by origin, Gini index and share (%) in the principal airports.

their RMEs are not negative. From a regional point of view, i.e. aggregating the figures of the five airports, the differences in the RMEs are more notable. The domestic RME, $RME_D = -0.19$, is clearly greater than what is estimated in larger airports, and conversely, the positive RME of the main origin, the UK (0.10), doubles the estimated figures for Málaga Airport (0.05).

11.5 Conclusion

The analysis of tourism seasonality, and particularly the levels of seasonal concentration in regions like Andalusia, where the tourism industry shares a significant portion of the employment and GDP, is of undoubted relevance. Yet adequate and efficient analytical tools are needed, as well as thorough data sets, to support coherent and successful policies against seasonality. The additive decomposition of the Gini index, and the estimation of the relative marginal effects over the indexes, have been found to be a very useful technique in this research by allowing one to identify segments of travellers or passengers with potential counter-seasonal effects.

Some of the outcomes of this study indicate that seasonal patterns and the consequent degree of seasonal concentration in the considered segments differ significantly when they are studied with a higher level of segmentation. Therefore, an adequate level of segmentation is essential to the approach taken with policies against seasonality. The use of a double segmentation by origin and travel motivation in the coastal areas has revealed very interesting results by allowing segments with interesting characteristics not visible in simpler segmentations to be identified. In particular, domestic travellers who visit the Andalusian coastal areas (considered as a whole segment) are pro seasonal, but within this group, the domestic cultural segment is counter-seasonal throughout the five coastal areas analysed, and even more so than the international cultural segment.

In addition, the analysis of the passengers' series also yielded some useful results, such as the potential counter-seasonal features of the domestic visitors who choose this mode of transport in all the airports studied and the identification of some countries of origin in Málaga and Sevilla Airports. However, a possible further line of research in this field with potentially useful results could be the use of a double segmentation by origin and type of airline company (traditional or low cost). Finally, the observed increasing trend of seasonal concentration indexes in many of the coastal areas and airports of Andalusia indicate that the counter-seasonal policies adopted in recent times have not been effective enough. Thus, more research is still needed in this area to inform policy makers and managers.

Acknowledgements

We would like to acknowledge the support given by the Ministerio de Educación of the Spanish government through its programme Formación del Profesorado Universitario (FPU) under grant AP2010-0532.

References

Aeropuertos Españoles and Navegación Aérea (2013) Estadísticas de tráfico aéreo. Available at: http://
    www.aena.es/csee/Satellite?pagename=Estadisticas/Home (accessed on 2 June 2014).
Allcock, J.B. (1994) Seasonality. In: Witt, S.F. and Moutinho, L. (eds) *Tourism Marketing and Management
    Handbook*. Prentice-Hall, Cambridge, UK, pp. 86–92.
Baum, T. and Hagen, L. (1999) Seasonality in tourism: understanding the challenges. *Tourism Economics*
    5(1), 5–8.
Butler, R.W. (2001). Seasonality in tourism: issues and implications. In: Baum, T. and Lundtorp, C. (eds)
    Seasonality in Tourism. Pergamon, New York, pp. 5–22.
Butler, R.W. and Mao, B. (1997) Seasonality in tourism: problems and measurement. In: Murphy, P.E.
    (ed.) *Quality Management in Urban Tourism*. Wiley, Chichester, UK, pp. 9–23.
Cisneros-Martínez, J.D. and Fernández-Morales, A. (2015) Cultural tourism as tourist segment for
    reducing seasonaliy in a coastal area: the case study of Andalusia. *Current Issues in Tourism* 18(8),
    765–784.
Consejería de Turismo, Comercio y Deporte (2013) Balance del año turístico en Andalucía 2013. Junta
    de Andalucía. Available at: http://www.turismoandaluz.com/estadisticas/ (accessed 8 April 2014).
Cuccia, T. and Rizzo, I. (2011) Tourism seasonality in cultural destinations: empirical evidence from
    Sicily. *Tourism Management* 32(3), 589–595.
De Cantis, S., Ferrante, M. and Vaccina, F. (2011) Seasonal pattern and amplitude – a logical frame-
    work to analyse seasonality in tourism: an application to bed occupancy in Sicilian hotels. *Tourism
    Economics* 17(3), 655–675.
Fernández-Morales, A. and Mayorga-Toledano, M.C. (2008) Seasonal concentration of the hotel de-
    mand in Costa del Sol: a decomposition by nationalities. *Tourism Management* 29, 940–949.
Halpern, N. (2011) Measuring seasonal demand for Spanish airports: implications for counter-seasonal
    strategies. *Research in Transportation Business & Management* 1(1), 47–54.
Instituto Nacional de Estadística (2013a) Encuesta de Ocupación en Campings; Encuesta de
    Ocupación en Apartamentos Turísticos. Available at: http://www.ine.es/inebmenu/mnu_hosteleria.
    htm (accessed 4 March 2014).
Instituto Nacional de Estadística (2013b) Encuesta de Ocupación Hotelera. Available at: http://www.ine.es/
    inebmenu/mnu_hosteleria.htm (accessed 4 March 2014).
Koenig-Lewis, N. and Bischoff, E.E. (2005) Seasonality research: the state of the art. *International
    Journal of Tourism Research* 7(4–5), 201–209.
Lerman, R.I. and Yitzhaki, S. (1985) Income inequality effects by income source: a new approach and
    applications to the United States. *The Review of Economic and Statistics* 67(1), 151–156.
Lundtorp, S. (2001) Measuring tourism seasonality. In: Baum, T. and Lundtorp, S. (eds) *Seasonality in
    Tourism*. Pergamon, Oxford, pp. 23–50.
Martín Martín, J.M., Jiménez Aguilera, J.D. and Molina Moreno, V. (2014) Impacts of seasonality on
    environmental sustainability in the tourism sector based on destination type: an application to
    Spain's Andalusia region. *Tourism Economics* 20(1), 123–142.
Moore, T.W. (1989) *Handbook of Business Forecasting*. Harper & Row, New York.
Pegg, S., Patterson, I. and Vila Gariddo, P. (2012) The impact of seasonality on tourism and hospitality
    operations in the alpine region of New South Wales, Australia. *International Journal of Hospitality
    Management* 31, 659–666.
Rosselló Nadal, J., Riera Font, A. and Sansó Rosselló, A. (2004) The economic determinants of seasonal
    patterns. *Annals of Tourism Research* 31(3), 697–711.
Sutcliffe, C.M.S. and Sinclair, M.T. (1980) The measurement of seasonality within the tourist industry:
    an application to tourist arrivals in Spain. *Applied Economics* 12, 429–441.
Tsitouras, A. (2004) Adjusted Gini coefficient and 'months equivalent' degree of tourism seasonality: a
    research note. *Tourism Economics* 10(1), 95–100.
Yitzhaki, S. and Schechtman, E. (2013) *The Gini Methodology*. Springer, New York.

12 Tourism Policy and the Challenge of Seasonality: The Case of the Balearic Islands

MARGARITA ALEMANY,* MARIA ANTONIA GARCÍA AND ÁNGELA AGUILO

University of the Balearic Islands, Palma de Mallorca, Spain

12.1 Introduction

The origin of tourism in the Balearic Islands dates from the end of the 19th century, but travelling to the Balearic Islands did not become a mass phenomenon until the late 1950s and 1960s. This was the so-called tourism boom, which led to a significant increase in hotel capacity and annual number of tourists. This new reality became the backbone of a unique economic model, which has almost always shown an upward trend, with only slight fluctuations such as the one caused by the energy crisis of the 1960s. This tourism model established itself as a successful production system, reaching a turning point in the 1980s when, as a consequence of the decentralization of state powers prompted by the Spanish constitution of 1978, the area of responsibility for tourism was transferred to the Autonomous Region. This led to the development of an independent tourism model for the notable creation of wealth, which, despite inevitable fluctuations from one year to another, has been the undisputed driver of the economy of the Balearic Islands from its creation to the present day.

In fact, the economic impact of the tourism industry on the Balearic economy is of great importance, as evidenced by the latest data from Impactur (2009), which estimated that 43.2% of the total GDP of the Balearic Islands (€11,032 million) could be attributed to tourism. On the labour market, 30.3% of total employment in the Balearic Islands (148,767 jobs) was attributed to tourism. Tourism activity accounted for 39.1% of the total tax revenue levied in the Balearic Islands in 2009, generating an income of €2,052 million for the government between direct and indirect taxes in the archipelago. Despite the previously mentioned figures, tourism activity in the Balearic Islands is of a highly seasonal nature; in fact, it has the strongest seasonal pattern within the Spanish territory (Aguiló and Rosselló, 2005), leading to a number of undesirable consequences.

*E-mail: marga.alemany@uib.es

12.2   Literature Review

One of the most widely accepted definitions of seasonality in tourism is that described by Butler (1994) as the temporary imbalance occurring in tourism, which can be expressed in terms of visitor numbers, tourist expenditure, traffic on motorways and the use of other forms of transport, employment and so on. For López and López (2007), seasonality is the variation in demand experienced throughout the seasons of the year, characterized by long periods of low demand and short periods of excessive demand.

Despite its unquestionable contribution to the economy, the characteristic seasonality of tourism generates several negative effects of great significance to the whole industry, such as: the increase in temporary contracts; environmental degradation during the months of mass tourism (air and noise pollution); saturation of public services during the period of maximum tourism activity; road congestion; uncertainty on the labour market; variations in hotel capacity (from minimums forcing hotels to close, to maximums where 100% of hotel vacancies are filled); and decreased profitability during the months of lower tourism activity, which makes it difficult to cover maintenance costs of properties, among others. Due to these distortions caused by seasonality, Nieto and Amate (2000) state that counteracting seasonality in tourism is one of the main objectives of the tourism policies of different administrations, and Lanquar (2001) affirms that seasonality is a constant concern for those responsible for marketing tourism destinations, striving to maintain seasonality within certain limits.

As the Balearic economy has a strong seasonal component, the authorities and tourism agents of the Balearic Islands have consistently been making proposals to combat seasonality, proposals which have been incorporated by the regional institutions into successive marketing plans approved by the Balearic government. These marketing plans will be reviewed in this study. Before analysing the seasonality of the tourism demand in the Balearic Islands, a review of the main contributions in the area of seasonal demand is necessary, a phenomenon rarely addressed in the field of economy and tourism research (Aguiló, 2010). The papers related to the seasonality of demand highlight four main aspects of this phenomenon: the determination of its causes; the problems or effects that arise; strategies to be adopted to mitigate these effects; and its measurement and modelling.

Various authors have enriched the contributions of Barón (1975) with regard to the causes or factors that determine the seasonality of demand (Butler, 1994; Baum and Hagen, 1999; De Querol et al., 2012). These studies suggest that the causes of seasonality include the following factors: climate; personal decisions of a socio-religious-cultural nature; social pressure or trends; sports seasons; inertia or tradition; business trips; adjustments to schedules; bank holidays in different countries; and so on. While the economic impact and positive externalities that tourism generates for some regional economies today is undeniable, it is also true that the seasonality suffered in some tourism destinations has effects of which attempts are being made to minimalize. In line with López and López (2007), this chapter highlights: economic effects (Getz and Nilsson, 2004; Rosselló et al., 2004; De Querol et al., 2012); labour effects (Krakover, 2000); ecological effects (Lusseau and Higham, 2004); and socio-cultural effects (Waitt, 2003; Kuvan and Akan, 2005). The strategies implemented to combat seasonality are mostly related to product policies (Baum and Hagen, 1999; Andriotis, 2005) and price and communication (Andriotis, 2005), and are promoted by the public institutions responsible for the tourism industry, with the support of the private sector.

12.3   Methodology

The purpose of this study is twofold: the first objective is to develop a qualitative review of the evolution of successive marketing plans in the Balearics between 1991 and 2015 in the framework of tourism policies. The second objective is to measure the seasonality of tourism demand in the Balearic Islands and suggest a possible relation between marketing stimuli set out in the various marketing plans and the behaviour of the seasonality of demand. The literature review suggests that, in order to mitigate the effects of seasonality, strategies based on product, price and communication policies be implemented. The approach to the study of the aforementioned marketing plans will focus on these aspects, in order to show their evolution over this period. For the second objective, seasonality will be measured from the point of view of demand. The variable used is the number of tourists in the Balearic Islands, considered with a monthly regularity. The indicator used to carry out this measurement is the Gini coefficient, possibly the most common indicator used for this type of work (Lundtorp, 2001; Fernández, 2003). The Gini coefficient is defined as:

$$Gini = 1 + \left(\frac{1}{n}\right) - \left(\frac{2}{n^2 \overline{y}}\right)(y_1 + 2y_2 + 3y_3 + \cdots + ny_n)$$

where $y_1 \geq y_2 \geq y_n$ corresponds to each monthly observation.

The Gini coefficient was chosen to measure the inequality of distribution because, as noted in Aguiló and Sastre (1984), it satisfies the condition of the Pigou–Dalton principle of transfers. This condition, in terms of tourism, indicates that the transfer of tourists from a month with a higher occupation to a month with a lower occupation would cause a decrease in the coefficient, and therefore a decrease in the indication of seasonality.

12.4   Results

A marketing plan is usually presented as a tool with proposals to enable the optimization and greater efficiency of the resources of public administrations in collaboration with agents of the private sector. This has been the case in the recent history of the Balearic Islands – different marketing plans have been developed successively but not continuously: 1991–1993, 2001–2005, 2009–2012 and the Comprehensive Tourism Plan of 2012–2015, currently in force. In some way, they have all influenced the future of tourism in the Autonomous Region. The most significant aspects of the plans, such as their objectives, policies, geographical markets and guidelines, will now be described, with particular reference to those strategies implemented to combat seasonality, which are linked in the literature to product, price and communication policies.

The evolution of the objectives of the various plans is placed in context for each of the periods under study. Thus, the first marketing plan (1991–1993) was created with the clear mission of serving the institutions, the private sector and the whole of the Balearic society, and set operational goals referring to: the social area (to enhance physical safety and freedom, and improve the interrelation between tourists and residents); the economic sector (to ensure sufficient air and sea transport capacity, modernize and restructure accommodation, and improve infrastructures and public services); and the environmental area (to promote protected areas and reduce environmental degradation). The second marketing plan of the Balearic Islands (2001–2005) presented a thorough analysis of the competitive environment in which the tourism destination of the Balearic Islands was immersed during this period, as well as an assessment of the challenges facing one of the most developed tourism destinations worldwide. This plan reflects a strong economic component and the impulse given to commercial and communication strategies. The third marketing plan for the Balearic Islands (2009–2012) emphasized increasing sales during the mid- and low seasons in order to improve the profitability of the industry, given that a large part of its production capacity remained inactive for too many months, generating various types of negative effects, widely commented on in the literature.

The Comprehensive Tourism Plan (2012–2015) proposes the introduction of a model of responsible tourism based on the principles of sustainability, on the balance of social standards, on the conservation of the destination's resources, and in which economic aspects acquire prominence. This plan aims to be more than just a marketing plan, as, in addition to assisting in the planning of tourism policies for the destination, it incorporates elements for the measurement of the results of these strategies and also includes aspects related to land management within the legal framework of the industry, quality and training. The set of marketing strategies designed in recent years has more similarities than differences. The satisfaction of the needs and desires of tourists and of the local community is a point of reference in each and every one of the planning tools. Strengthening the relationship with the tourist, strengthening ties with intermediaries, diversifying tourism products in order to reduce dependence on the monoculture of sun and sand in order to correct the imbalances generated by the highly seasonal nature of this product, the application of segmentation and branding techniques, as well as progression towards new methods of promotion based on telecommunication technologies: these features are all shared, to a greater or lesser degree, by all the marketing plans mentioned.

Andriotis (2005) and Baum and Hagen (1999) suggest that strategies to combat seasonality are focused mainly on the policy of product diversification. In order to show how the marketing plans of the Balearics address product policy, a summary of the portfolio of products and the priority or classification established for each is illustrated below (Table 12.1). The lack of consistency in the choice of classification criteria obliges the use of various typologies. For the first two marketing plans, priority A (high-priority products to maintain leadership), priority B (high-priority products to be promoted) and priority C (products to be developed) were used. For the plans of 2009–2012 and 2012–2015, the classification was made according to the phase of

Table 12.1. Comparison of the product portfolio.

Products	1991–1993	2001–2005	2009–2012	2012–2015
Accessible tourism				E
Active tourism				S
Cinematographic				E
City break or short break	A	B		
Congresses and conventions	B	B	S	S
Cruises		C		
Cultural or heritage		B	E	S
Cycle tourism		C		M
Educational				E
Elite or luxury tourism				E
Equestrian				E
Family		A		
Gastronomic		B		E
Golf	A	C	S	S
Health, beauty and wellness	C	B		S
Healthcare (medical)				E
Hiking				S
Language learning				E
Major events		C		E
Nature tourism			E	
Nautical	A	A	S	M
Nightlife				E
Nordic walking				E
Ornithological				E
Religious and spiritual				E
Residential				
Rural		B		M
Senior tourism		A		
Shopping				S
Sports tourism	A			
Sports training		C		
Sun and beach	A	A	M	M
Touring	B			
Urban				S
Wine tasting				E

Notes: A = priority A; B = priority B; C = priority C; S = strong; M = mature; E = emerging.

the product life cycle: mature (established products), strong? (products in the growth phase), and emerging (products in the introduction phase).

In the marketing plan of 1991–1993, there were eight products in the portfolio, five of which (short break, golf, nautical, sports tourism, and sun and beach) were given high priority, although further development of the product policy focused mainly on the four dimensions of the sun and beach area (relaxing, sea, fun, landscape/culture), with the aim of becoming the undisputed leader in terms of the relationship between quality and price, seeking differentiation with respect to other competing destinations. In the marketing plan of 2001–2005, the product policy included some new features with respect to the previous plan. The predominance lay once again in the sun and beach product, but aimed for a greater diversification of products as a complementary strategy, assigning nautical, family and senior tourism to the high-priority group to maintain leadership. The products of wellness, culture, nature, gastronomy, conventions, rural tourism and short breaks were classified as high priority to achieve leadership in the mid- and long term.

The contribution of this second marketing plan was precisely to highlight the need to target marketing towards the priority segments, stimulating interactivity between customers and the destination, offering new products adapted to new holiday motivations detected at the time. In the marketing plan of 2009–2012, the excellent flight connections at the time encouraged managers to develop off-season products to boost business, nautical and golf tourism, while also making efforts to create tourism products related to culture and nature. This product strategy related to the five previously mentioned activities sought to generate a positive crossover effect on to sun and beach tourism, influencing the seasonality of the destination, by offering products during mid- and low season, as well as improving the image of the islands. In addition, during this period, a major reorganization of the institutions responsible for tourism promotion was undertaken, with the appearance of Product Clubs and Product Managers.

In the Comprehensive Tourism Plan of 2012–2015, the product policy once again emphasizes diversification and differentiation, as well as its connection with the brand, establishing a management model based on the Boston Consulting Group Matrix, and territorial identification. Tactics such as the relaunching, updating or extension of the maturity phase are the commitments of this plan to reinvent products. Proof of this is the wide range of products on offer, including traditional products, updated products and newly conceived products related to active tourism (Table 12.1).

The three marketing plans and the Comprehensive Tourism Plan, all of which are instruments for tourism planning, assess the competitive position of the Balearic Islands and ascertain the market attractiveness of each source market, taking into account aspects such as tourism expenditure by nationality, market volume and its potential for growth, seasonality and sensitivity to the price variable. The target markets are then selected and a specific strategic priority allocated. The marketing plan of 1991–1993 focuses its efforts on the following markets, classified under separate categories with different budgets, as previously mentioned: priority A (Germany, UK, Spain); priority B (Sweden, Norway, Finland, Denmark, Benelux, Italy); and priority C (Switzerland, Austria, France, Ireland). The 2001–2005 plan mainly focuses its activities on three countries in two categories: priority A (Germany and UK) and priority B (Spain), substantially reducing the size of its scope.

The 2009–2012 plan once again diversifies and expands its line of intervention towards potentially attractive markets in different categories: priority A (Germany,

UK, Spain); priority B (Nordic countries, Benelux, France, Italy); and priority C (Russia, rest of Europe). The Comprehensive Plan of 2012–2015 has not only broadened its target markets considerably but also has introduced changes when categorizing and organizing its portfolio of policies to achieve the most suitable positioning for each market. The markets in this plan have been categorized in a different way, according to their level of development: consolidated (National, UK, Germany, France, Italy); developing (Switzerland, Denmark, Belgium, Austria, Ireland, the Netherlands, Portugal, Norway, Sweden, Finland); emerging (Russia, Poland, Israel, Bulgaria, the Czech Republic, Ukraine); and overseas (Canada and the USA). Germany, the UK and the domestic market historically have been, and still are, the priority source markets, generating a greater volume of tourists for the Balearic Islands, offering better flight connections and having a long tradition of trade with the destination.

The main strategies and commercialization promoted in the various marketing plans will now be summarized. The marketing plan of 1991–1993, in the area of commercialization and communication, focused its efforts on the standardization of the corporate identity and addressed specific programmes to intermediaries such as tour operators and travel agencies. The various programmes included: direct commercialization programmes; customer, user and agent pull programmes; and push programmes directed towards tour operators. In addition to the creation of a corporate identity for Mallorca, the plan tried to standardize all the elements that formed the identity of a tourism destination. The production of merchandizing and audio-visual materials, product catalogues, monographic catalogues, television, radio, press and magazines comprised the communication mix designed at this stage.

The marketing plan of 2001–2005 was oriented towards: increasing sales by using commercialization channels other than tour operators; the satisfaction and creation of customer loyalty; the creation of public relations in source markets, representative offices; the improvement of tourist services at the destination; the development of the portal VISITABALEARS.COM; or the launch of loyalty programmes. These were the most important aspects of the area of communication included in this plan. Another important aspect was the effort made to incorporate a strong technological component, with information systems to improve the management of the destination.

In the marketing plan of 2009–2012, the clear impulse towards the most innovative technologies of information and communication became evident in the area of distribution and communication. With the purpose of carrying out an effective push action on intermediaries, the Trade-Plus programme was launched, aimed at developing new partnerships and strengthening relationships with intermediaries in the source markets. Furthermore, it set out to boost a sales system that became a pioneer platform allowing user interaction. These systems were intended to increase the effectiveness of communication, to capture new segments of demand, as well as to build the image and positioning of the destination for 365 days of the year, by using a combination of traditional media in conjunction with online media.

The Comprehensive Tourism Plan of 2012–2015 includes a wide range of strategies. In addition to marketing issues (related to product, market research and promotion), other aspects are involved, such as: land management; the introduction of a new legal framework for regulating the actions of the tourism industry; quality; and training. The territory and its efficient use have become essential factors in the new era of tourism in the Balearic Islands, the implementation of zoning indicators has been proposed, and diagnostics and contexts that allow the identification of and intervention in mature areas has been introduced. In the specific case of promotion, it is of note that this stage is oriented towards adapting to new consumer behaviours, as well as towards various digital positioning platforms to attract tourists towards a differentiated, motivational and experiential destination. Management of the destination brand and forward planning of promotional activities are important features of this latest plan.

12.4.1 Measuring the seasonality of demand

In addition to the analysis of the marketing plans, the second objective of this study is to measure the seasonality of tourism demand in the Balearic Islands between the years 1992 and 2012. To do so, the Gini coefficient of the monthly number of tourists in the Balearic Islands has been calculated. The decisive years are 1999, 2003 and 2007 (Table 12.2). During these years, changes in the seasonality cycles (Fig. 12.1)

Table 12.2. The Gini coefficient of tourism demand in the Balearic Islands.

Year	Gini tourism in the Balearic Islands	Index numbers (%)	Gini tourism national	Index numbers (%)	Gini tourism international	Index numbers (%)
1992	0.414	100.00	0.271	100.00	0.438	100.00
1993	0.415	100.33	0.256	94.60	0.442	100.70
1994	0.405	97.77	0.214	79.06	0.428	97.60
1995	0.389	94.07	0.195	72.09	0.412	94.04
1996	0.383	92.60	0.213	78.89	0.403	91.91
1997	0.385	92.91	0.213	78.70	0.404	92.24
1998	0.375	90.46	0.190	70.34	0.394	89.88
1999	0.359	86.59	0.230	84.98	0.374	85.24
2000	0.384	92.79	0.171	63.04	0.417	95.07
2001	0.383	92.61	0.156	57.51	0.424	96.68
2002	0.394	95.27	0.234	86.59	0.425	96.87
2003	0.398	96.06	0.291	107.48	0.423	96.47
2004	0.379	91.62	0.300	110.80	0.398	90.69
2005	0.374	90.42	0.297	109.67	0.396	90.20
2006	0.365	88.09	0.237	87.51	0.405	92.41
2007	0.358	86.52	0.235	86.78	0.406	92.55
2008	0.366	88.40	0.255	94.11	0.405	92.31
2009	0.383	92.48	0.302	111.59	0.411	93.79
2010	0.424	102.43	0.347	128.43	0.447	101.87
2011	0.432	104.28	0.344	127.24	0.458	104.36
2012	0.444	107.32	0.373	137.97	0.464	105.84

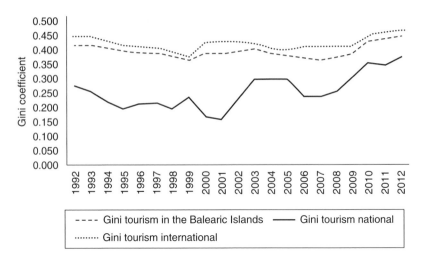

Fig. 12.1. Evolution of the Gini coefficient of tourist demand.

occurred. The analysis starts in 1992 at a value of 0.414, which descends during the 1990s, until the beginning of this century when it increases, to then decrease again from 2003 to 2007. From 2008 to 2012, at the end of the series, an upward trend is noted (seasonality increases).

The same development was experienced by the Gini coefficient of national and international tourism demand, from which it can be concluded that:

- Both national and international tourism demand have similar cyclical behaviour (high and low periods generally match).
- The values of the Gini coefficient of domestic tourism demand have a more volatile behaviour (standard deviation of 0.059) than international tourism demand (standard deviation of 0.022).
- International tourism demand, according to the Gini coefficient, is more seasonal (average value 0.418) than national tourism demand (average value 0.253).

When attempting to explain the cyclical behaviour of seasonality, the coincidences with Aguiló and Sastre (1984) cannot be overlooked. They claim that there is a clear association between tourism growth and reduced seasonality, and that at the beginning of an economic crisis, an increase in seasonality takes place. The authors state that it seems clear that tourism has now reached such a degree of maturity that, in relative terms, tourism during the low season is more affected by seasonality than tourism in the high season, possibly because tourism in the peak season has become a basic commodity and is therefore less subject to changes of income (Aguiló and Sastre, 1984). In the same vein, Rosselló *et al.* (2004) conclude that the visits of German and British tourists (representing approximately two-thirds of the international tourism in the Balearic Islands) have a lower seasonal pattern as their income increases.

12.5 Conclusion

The development of mass tourism led to a significant change in the economic model of the Balearic Islands. Tourism became the backbone of the economy, but its seasonal nature still creates several problems for the main economic agents. In order to mitigate the adverse effects of seasonality, one of the main approaches taken by the Autonomous Region of the Balearic Islands has been the ongoing development of a wide range of tourism products, whether complementary or alternative to traditional sun and beach tourism. In recent years, interest has grown in tourism products for which the principal demand is in the off season. For decades, considerable amounts of human and financial efforts have been made to design and develop marketing plans. These planning tools, which have increased progressively in areas of responsibility and budgetary allocation, require an analysis of the extent to which their implementation has been effective and of benefit to Balearic society as a whole.

The initial approach of this chapter led to a review of the marketing plans developed in the last two decades in the Balearic Islands, and to determining the evolution of the seasonality of tourism demand by applying the coefficient of variation and the Gini coefficient to tourist arrivals. The following points summarize the results briefly.

The lack of continuity and even absence of marketing plans for a large part of the period under study has hampered the objective set. From the analysis of seasonality and successive marketing plans, it is difficult to establish a direct relationship between the two. One of the main limitations of this study is the absence of information concerning the degree of implementation of the measures included and achievement of the goals outlined in the various marketing plans.

In spite of being unable to establish a link between the main features of the marketing plans and the behaviour of demand, a coincidence has been found between expansive economic cycles and periods of reduction in seasonality. Two periods of decreased seasonality can be identified (the 1990s and 2003–2007), coinciding with periods of economic boom. It should be noted that from 2008, beset by the current severe economic situation, seasonality indicators have soared. An essential aspect of policies and instruments that are directly linked to combating seasonality is the product portfolio. In this sense, it is necessary to structure, communicate and market specific products for the non-summer season.

The increase in tourism seasonality in times of economic recession makes it clear that the sun and beach product, of a seasonal nature, has become a basic commodity for a large percentage of consumers; difficult to forego even in an economic downturn. However, those products positioned in the months of lower demand are more sensitive to changes in disposable income (higher elasticity).

It is necessary to promote a strategic agreement between destination management, hoteliers, complimentary services, tour operators and airlines. This agreement should allow for the design of a rigorous plan to combat seasonality. This plan, in operational terms, must be translated into product configuration and into quantitatively establishing a possible time-related and geographical distribution of tourists, catering to their motivations and preferences. In the Balearic Islands, the price variable has not been addressed from the perspective of a corrective measure for seasonality, but rather from an environmental and sustainability oriented perspective, as in the case of the controversial eco-tax of 2001, since abolished. The high level of dependency on tour operators as intermediaries, their strong bargaining power due to the high volume of tourists that travel, in addition to requirements in terms of a certain quota of all-inclusive holidays, may have been one of the constraints of using this variable in strategies for reducing seasonality.

Social tourism initiatives, both nationally (Imserso) and in Europe (Calyso), have provided an excellent opportunity to generate economic activity and improve seasonality patterns. In the 1990s, the impulse given to these programmes made a significant contribution towards the reduction in the seasonality of domestic tourism demand, which is why the Balearic Islands and other Spanish coastal destinations have traditionally called for their continuity and asked for similar initiatives in Europe.

The evidence gathered through this research leads to the conclusion that the tourism planning of the Balearic Islands requires the inextricable combination of aspects related to consumer behaviour with aspects related to the tourism products on offer. The design of new, alternative options to the sun and beach product for the low season would be key factors in order to lengthen the tourist season and counteract the negative effects of seasonality on the economic model of the Balearic Islands.

References

Aguiló, E. (2010) Una panorámica de la Economía del Turismo en España. *Cuadernos de Economía* 33(91), 5–42.

Aguiló, E. and Rosselló, J. (2005) Host community perceptions: a cluster analysis. *Annals of Tourism Research* 27(3), 925–941.

Aguiló, E. and Sastre, A. (1984) La medición de la estacionalidad del turismo: el caso de Baleares. *Estudios Turísticos* 81, 79–88.

Andriotis, K. (2005) Seasonality in Crete: problem or a way of life? *Tourism Economics* 11(2), 207–224.

Barón, R.V. (1975) *Seasonality in Tourism: A Guide to the Analysis of Seasonality and Trends for Policy Making.* The Economist Intelligence Unit, London.

Baum, T. and Hagen, L. (1999) Responses to seasonality: the experiences of peripheral destinations. *International Journal of Tourism Research* 1(5), 299–312.

Butler, R. (1994) Seasonality in tourism: issues and problems. In: Seaton, A. (ed.) *Tourism. The State of the Art.* Wiley, Chichester, UK, pp. 332–340.

De Querol, N., Barquero, M. and Maqueda, F.J. (2012) Importancia de la estacionalidad y del conocimiento de la demanda turística para las empresas familiares españolas. *Revista de Empresa Familiar* 2(1), 33–44.

Fernández, A. (2003) Decomposing seasonal concentration. *Annals of Tourism Research* 30(4), 942–956.

Getz, D. and Nilsson, P.A. (2004) Responses of family businesses to extreme seasonality in demand: case of Bornholm, Denmark. *Tourism Management* 25, 17–30.

Impactur (2009) Estudio del impacto económico del turismo sobre la economía y el empleo de las Illes Balears. Government of the Balearic Islands, Spain.

Krakover, S. (2000) Partitioning seasonal employment in the hospitality industry. *Tourism Management* 2(3), 461–471.

Kuvan, Y. and Akan, P. (2005) Resident's attitudes toward general and forest-related impacts of tourism: the case of Belek, Antalya. *Tourism Management* 26(5), 691–706.

Lanquar, R. (2001) *Marketing turístico: de lo global a local.* Ariel, Barcelona, Spain.

López, J.M. and López, L.M. (2007) Variabilidad estacional del mercado turístico en Andalucia. *Estudios y perspectivas en turismo* 16, 150–172.

Lundtorp, S. (2001) Measuring tourism seasonality. In: Baum, A. and Lundtorp, S. (eds) *Seasonality in Tourism.* Pergamon, Oxford, UK, pp. 23–50.

Lusseau, D. and Higham, J.E.S. (2004) Managing the impacts of dolphin-based tourism through the definition of critical habitats: the case of bottlenose dolphins in Doubtful Sound, New Zealand. *Tourism Management* 25(6), 657–667.

Nieto, J.L. and Amate, I. (2000) Análisis de la estacionalidad de la demanda turística en la Comunidad Andaluza. *Papers de Turisme* 28, 42–64.

Rosselló, J., Riera, A. and Sansó, A. (2004) The economic determinants of seasonal patterns. *Annals of Tourism Research* 31(3), 697–711.

Waitt, G. (2003) Social impacts of Sydney Olympics. *Annals of Tourism Research* 30(1), 194–215.

13 Expenditure and Stay Behaviour of Nature-based Visitors: The Case of Costa Rica

ANDRES ARTAL-TUR* AND ANTONIO JUAN BRIONES-PEÑALVER

Technical University of Cartagena, Cartagena, Spain

13.1 Introduction

The tourism industry has shown an important development in Central America in recent years, with arrivals growing 7% annually between 1995 and 2013, from 2.6 to 7.9 million people. According to UNWTO forecasts, 14 million people are expected to arrive in the region in 2020, and 22 million in 2030 (United Nations World Tourism Organization (UNWTO), 2014). Nature-based tourism is highly extended in this area. Green forest and wildlife richness attract international visitors to this place, one of the most important world reserves of the biosphere. In this chapter, we gain a deeper understanding of the particularities of tourists coming to a nature-based destination. Building on a survey of more than 14,000 questionnaires for the years 2009–2011, we investigate the behaviour of tourists coming to a salient destination of this region, Costa Rica.

With this objective, we estimate two equations explaining the expenditure and stay patterns of international tourists arriving in the country. In particular, we test for the role played by time and budget restrictions, the socio-economic features of visitors, destination characteristics and previous knowledge of the country. In doing so, we are able to compute the cross-elasticity between expenditure and stay duration. All these findings help us to improve the knowledge on the behaviour of visitors arriving at a nature-based tourist location, obtaining interesting conclusions for improving destination management on a sustainable basis.

13.2 Literature Review

In this section, we review the related literature briefly and describe the data set employed throughout the study. Our objective is to estimate the main factors explaining

---

*E-mail: andres.artal@upct.es

the expenditure and stay duration patterns of international visitors coming to Costa Rica. According to Bahar *et al.* (2008), there is still no consensus among researchers on how to confront the study of the variable, 'tourist spending'. Some authors employ the average annual expenditure per tourist as the unit of analysis, using time-series data on total expenditures and number of arrivals (Song and Witt, 2000). This type of study traditionally focuses on forecasting analysis, i.e. for the number of tourist arrivals or the total expenditure, providing in this way relevant information for the managers of the destination. Other authors employ a micro-focus when analysing the expenditure pattern of tourists by using survey data. This type of study explains the daily expenditure pattern of tourists by taking into account the personal characteristics of the visitors, allowing them to understand the factors underlying the consumption behaviour of tourists (Juaneda and Aguiló, 2000; Pol *et al.*, 2006).

Moreover, some researchers seek to characterize the type of tourist according to his or her total expenditure throughout the trip, accounting for the so-called 'size of the party', purpose of the visit, or stay duration at the destination (Kozak, 2001; Jang *et al.*, 2004). In the present study, we will focus on understanding the daily tourist expenditure, building on survey data. Our data set contains information on individual tourist profiles, the type of holiday selected (organization, accommodation used, number of stages, places visited, company, etc.) and the activities developed while travelling. We will employ an ordinary least squares (OLS) modelling strategy, correcting for some estimation bias arising in the model, such as collinearity or heteroskedasticity.

Moving to the literature explaining tourists' length of stay, the original contributions of Fleischer and Pizam (2002) and Alegre and Pou (2006) employed discrete choice models, logit and tobit, respectively, to quantify the probability of a tourist to stay a certain number of days at one particular destination. The authors approached the study of stay duration by intervals of time, i.e. a weekend, an entire week, a month. This methodology, although interesting as a seminal contribution, is somehow limited for tourism destination management purposes, where companies may be more interested in understanding the factors underlying the stay duration of a tourist by single days, then constructing their own intervals of time.

Other authors begin to apply a complementary approach in the analysis of tourist stay, introducing models of duration or survival analysis, which identify the factors that influence the duration of an event, such as a tourist's stay at a destination (Gokovali *et al.*, 2007). Duration models have become commonplace in studies of stay, being employed in the analysis of new products such as island tourism, golf tourism or low-cost travel (Martínez-Garcia and Raya, 2008; Menezes *et al.*, 2008; Barros *et al.*, 2009). In this study, we build on count-data models for the analysis of stay duration, which will allow us to predict the stay of tourists by single days (Cameron and Trivedi, 1998).

13.2.1 The profile of tourists visiting Costa Rica

The Costa Rican Tourism Institute (ICT) provides the database employed in this study. It consists of annual surveys of tourists that leave the country through the

Juan Santamaria International Airport.[1] The descriptive analysis of tourists visiting Costa Rica in 2009–2011 in Table 13.1 shows that the most common visitor is a male (61% of the sample), between 25 and 44 years (40%), married (49%) or single (45%), coming for leisure purposes (70%), followed by business tourists and those visiting friends and relatives (VFR) at 20% and 10%, respectively. The visitor is a resident of the USA (34.5%), Europe (29%), Canada (7%), Central and rest of Latin America (28%) or the Caribbean (1%). The level of study is university (Bachelor or Diploma in 63% of cases) and tertiary education (22%).

The analysis of the trip characteristics shows that around 40% of the sample has visited Costa Rica for the very first time. The average stay is for 9 nights, whereas those staying from 1 to 10 nights are 67% of the sample and 86% from 1 to 15 nights. Arrivals are concentrated mostly in the last two quarters of the year. In terms of organization of the travel, the bulk of tourists decided to organize the journey themselves, either in their home country (40%) or once in Costa Rica (27%). Tourist packages also appear to be relevant as a way of organizing travel (30%). Visitors travel alone (43%), with friends (24%) or with their family (14%). Regarding the type of accommodation used, and given that the tourist's trip can include several stages, we find that most tourists use hotel/cabin/camping accommodation (83%), stay at the houses of friends and relatives (20.5%), at rented houses (3.5%) or at their own houses (2.2%).

In terms of the activities undertaken, and considering that the same tourist can engage in several activities throughout the trip, Table 13.1 shows that the most pursued activity is that of sun and sand (64%) and visiting national parks (63%), followed by wildlife sightseeing (49%), going shopping (38%), canopy tours (30%), thermalism (23%) and cultural tourism (12%). Moreover, the most visited tourist spots in the country seem to be the Arenal Volcano (30%), Manuel Antonio Park (20%), Corcovado Park (12%) and Tortuguero Village (10%). Reviewing the most visited areas, and considering that tourists visit several of them while on holiday, the most visited areas are those of the Central Valley (79%), the northern region (30%), the Pacific area (30%), Guanacaste (20%), the Caribbean Sea (14%) and Puntarenas golf (11%).

13.3   Analysis of Factors Explaining the Expenditure and Stay Behaviour of Tourists

In this section, we estimate the factors explaining the expenditure and stay behaviour of international tourists visiting Costa Rica.

13.3.1   Modelling the daily expenditure of international tourists visiting Costa Rica

In order to analyse the expenditure pattern of tourists, we employ a pooled OLS method. In addition, we control for heteroskedasticity by using the correction proposed by White (1980). The empirical model takes the following form:

$$\ln Y_i = \beta_0 + \beta_k X_{ki} + \varepsilon_1$$

Table 13.1. Descriptive analysis of international tourists visiting Costa Rica.

Tourist profile

Gender		Age		Marital status	
Female	38.8%	Under 25 years	10.6%	Single	44.7%
Male	61.2%	25–34 years	35.7%	Married	49.1%
		35–44 years	22.7%	Others	6.2%
		45–54 years	17.3%		
		Over 55 years	13.7%		
Level of education		**Country (residence)**		**Purpose of visit**	
Primary/Secondary	14.9%	USA	34.5%	Leisure	70%
Bachelor/Diploma	63.3%	Canada	7.3%	Business	20%
Master/Doctor	21.8%	Central America	11.0%	VFR	10%
		Rest of Latin America	16.9%		
		Caribbean	1.1%		
		Europe	29.2%		

Trip characteristics

First visit	39.4%	**Arrivals per quarter**		**Travel arrangements**	
		Q1	21.8%	Package at origin	15.1%
		Q2	22%	Package in Costa Rica (CR)	1.4%
Length of stay		Q3	27.5%	On my own at origin	40.5%
9 nights (mean)		Q4	28.7%	On my own at CR	27%
1–10 nights	67%			Company travel	10%
1–15 nights	86%			Another institution	6%
Company during the trip		**Year of arrival**		**Accommodation**	
Alone	43.4%	2009	36.3%	Hotel/cabin/camping	83.4%
Family	14.5%	2010	44%	Rent house	3.4%
Friends	14.6%	2011	19.7%	Family house	20.5%
Couple	24.1%			Own house	2.2%
Workmates	3.4%				
Main tourist points		**Most visited areas**		**Activities**	
Arenal Volcano	30%	Central Valley	79%	Sun and sand	64%
Manuel Antonio Park	20%	Northern area	28%	National parks	63%
Corcovado Park	12%	Pacific area	30%	Wildlife	49.3%
Tortuguero Village	10%	Guanacaste	20%	Shopping	38.2%
Cahuita	5%	Caribbean Sea	14%	Canopy	29.8%
		Puntarenas golf	11%	Thermalism	23.9%
				Cultural activities	12.1%

Note: VFR = visiting friends and relatives.

where ln Y_i is the natural log of real daily expenditure per tourist, X_{ki} is the vector of explanatory variables and ε_I is the error term. Given the logarithmic nature of the model, we obtain elasticities from the estimation results.

As shown in Table 13.1, the explanatory variables in our empirical model include the sociodemographic profile of tourists, their budget and time constraints, the characteristics of the trip, the attributes of the region of the country and tourist points visited, and the activities undertaken on the trip. For both empirical models, we will test for the following working hypotheses:

- Hypothesis 1: Tourist spending and duration of stay are influenced by the time and budget constraints of visitors (Nicolau and Más, 2005).
- Hypothesis 2: Tourist spending and duration of stay are influenced by the activities undertaken at the destination (Woodside and MacDonald, 1993; García-Sánchez and Fernández-Rubio, 2013).
- Hypothesis 3: Tourist spending and individuals' duration of stay are influenced by sociodemographic characteristics or visitors' profiles (Barros et al., 2008).
- Hypothesis 4: Tourist spending and individuals' duration of stay are influenced by trip characteristics (Rodrigues et al., 2011).
- Hypothesis 5: Tourist spending and individuals' duration of stay are influenced by the place visited (García Sánchez and Fernández-Rubio, 2013).
- Hypothesis 6: Tourist spending and individuals' duration of stay highly influence each other (Alegre and Pou, 2006).

In general terms, the empirical models attempt to test the validity of the six working hypotheses. Further, the groups of explanatory variables for the expenditure function are detailed in Table 13.2.

The analysis needs a reference category in order to avoid perfect collinearity problems. This is defined as 'a leisure tourist, coming to the country for the first time, in the first quarter of the year, with job colleagues, with the trip being organized by other institutions (university, etc.), staying at a hotel/cabin/camping, being male, aged over 55 years, with a civil state other than married or single and a tertiary level of studies (Master degree or doctorate), while coming from an European country'.

The results of the estimation are included in Table 13.3. The specification of the whole model appears to be good, with the joint model showing a significant I-test, and the R^2 fit is of 0.55. In general, the most important factors explaining the daily expenditure of tourists in regard to the profile of the tourist are his or her geographical origin, the age of the visitor and the purpose of the trip. From trip characteristics, estimates show the leading role of the type of organization of the visit, the type of accommodation and company while travelling, together with the length of stay. From activities, going shopping and canopy touring increase daily spending, and in terms of regions visited, Corcovado Park, the Pacific area and Guanacaste receive the most visitor spending. Length of stay is perhaps the most important variable leading daily spending, together with the type of organization of the trip, according to the marginal effects obtained in the model, as shown in Table 13.3.

After analysing the determinants of the daily expenditure of tourists visiting Costa Rica, we compute the 'expenditure–stay elasticity' in Fig. 13.1 and Table 13.4, measuring the percentage change that the daily expenditure experiences in response to a percentage change in a given tourist stay.

Table 13.2. Variables in the model of international tourists visiting Costa Rica.

(i) Variables regarding the profile of the tourist:
• *Income:* in US$/year.
• *Purpose of visit:* leisure, business, visiting friends and relatives (VFR).
• *Gender:* female, male.
• *Age:* under 25 years, 25–34 years, 35–44 years, 45–54 years, over 55 years.
• *Civil state:* single, married, other (divorced, widowed, etc.).
• *Education:* primary + secondary, university degree, Master–doctorate studies.
• *Origin of the tourist (country of residence):* USA, Canada, Central America, rest of Latin America, Caribbean, Europe, rest of the world.
• *Annual earnings:* in thousands of US$.
(ii) Trip characteristics:
• First visit or not.
• Quarter of the visit: 1st, 2nd, 3rd, 4th quarters.
• Year of visit: 2009, 2010 and 2011.
• Stay duration: number of nights spent on the whole trip.
• Organization of the trip: tour package (taken in home country or in Costa Rica), on their own (independent travel arrangements in home country or in CR), organized by your company or by other institutions (university, church, etc.).
• Type of accommodation used: hotel/cabin/camping, rented house, VFR house, own house.
• Company while travelling: alone, family, friends, couple, work colleagues.
(iii) Activities pursued by tourists:
Sun and sand, shopping, canopy tour, wildlife, thermalism, MICE (meetings, incentives, conferences and exhibitions), cultural tours, visiting national parks.
(iv) Places of visit:
• *The most visited tourist points in the country:* Arenal Volcano, Cahuita, Manuel Antonio Park, Tortuguero Village, Corcovado Park.
• *Areas of the country:* includes all regions of the country, namely Central Valley, Guanacaste, Puntarenas golf, Pacific area, Caribbean Sea and Monteverde.

In general, we see that the (negative) elasticity of daily expenditure increases when the stay exceeds 3–4 nights. In Table 13.4, we can see that for the first and second days of stay, the elasticity is in the range of –0.5, moving to –0.6 for stays of 3–5 days, to –0.7 for 8–13 days and to a value of around –0.75 for more than 13 days. According to this, when the stay increases from 1 to 22 nights, the range of elasticities varies from –50% to –75%, with the consequent reduction of daily expenses. In any case, tourists with stays higher than 15 days reduce their daily spending greatly in comparison with those staying less than 2 weeks, and more significantly compared with those staying for just 1–3 days. Table 13.4 reflects in this way the existence of a clear differing expenditure behaviour by intervals of stay, i.e. 1–3 days, 1–2 weeks and more than 2 weeks. As a result, it would be necessary to define particular marketing policies for each segment of tourists in the sample, in coping with their stay and expenditure behaviour.

Table 13.3. Function of the daily spending of international tourists visiting Costa Rica.

Category of reference	Dependent variable: daily expenditure	Coefficient	Significance	Standard deviation	t-statistic	p > t
Tourist profile						
Purpose: leisure	Business tourist	0.0813	*	0.0337	2.41	0.016
	VFR tourist	−0.1682	***	0.0297	−5.66	0.000
Male	Female	−0.0937	***	0.0130	−7.20	0.000
More than 55 years old	Age under 25	−0.2901	***	0.0303	−9.56	0.000
	Age 25–34	−0.1055	***	0.0225	−4.69	0.000
	Age 35–44	−0.0188		0.0229	−0.82	0.410
	Age 45–54	0.0191		0.0231	0.83	0.409
Other than married or single	Single	−0.0388		0.0301	−1.29	0.197
	Married	0.0193		0.0294	0.66	0.511
Tertiary education	Bachelor (university)	−0.0060		0.0153	−0.39	0.696
	Primary + secondary	−0.0438	*	0.0221	−1.98	0.048
Origin: European	USA	−0.0217		0.0186	−1.17	0.243
	Canada	0.0337		0.0258	1.30	0.192
	Central America	0.0378		0.0279	1.35	0.176
	Rest of Latin America	0.2279	***	0.0239	9.54	0.000
	The Caribbean	−0.0332		0.0745	−0.45	0.656
Annual earning	Income	0.0198	**	0.0057	3.46	0.001
Trip characteristics						
	First visit	−0.0007		0.0256	−0.03	0.979
Q1	Q2	−0.0792	***	0.0196	−4.05	0.000
	Q3	−0.1155	***	0.0184	−6.27	0.000
	Q4	−0.0994	***	0.0186	−5.35	0.000
Year: 2009	Year_2011	0.0298		0.0207	1.44	0.150
	Year_2010	0.0322		0.0167	1.93	0.054
	Log stay	−0.5122	***	0.0521	−9.84	0.000
	Log stay squared	−0.0399	**	0.0123	−3.24	0.001
Trip organized by other type of company	Package ORIGIN	−0.3268	***	0.0644	−5.07	0.000
	Package Costa Rica	−0.2482	**	0.0741	−3.35	0.001
	OWN ORIGIN	−0.5255	***	0.0628	−8.36	0.000
	OWN Costa Rica	−0.5900	***	0.0633	−9.33	0.000
	Company	−0.0889		0.0637	−1.40	0.163

Continued

Table 13.3. Continued.

Category of reference	Dependent variable: daily expenditure	Coefficient	Significance	Standard deviation	t-statistic	p > t
Staying at hotel/ cabin/camping	House_rented	0.1826	***	0.0360	5.07	0.000
	Own_house	−0.1439	**	0.0527	−2.73	0.006
	House_VFR	−0.3298	***	0.0238	−13.89	0.000
Travelling with work colleagues	Alone	−0.0467		0.0377	−1.24	0.215
	Family	−0.2777	***	0.0431	−6.45	0.000
	Friends	−0.1167	**	0.0422	−2.76	0.006
	Couple	−0.2093	***	0.0416	−5.03	0.000
Activities	Sun and sand	−0.0023		0.0186	−0.12	0.902
	Shopping	0.0727	***	0.0132	5.49	0.000
	Canopy	0.0966	***	0.0145	6.65	0.000
	Wildlife	0.0138		0.0180	0.77	0.441
	Thermalism	0.0234		0.0174	1.35	0.178
	Cultural	−0.0322		0.0202	−1.60	0.111
	National parks	0.0262		0.0228	1.15	0.249
Tourist points	Arenal Volcano	0.0022		0.0216	0.10	0.919
	Cahuita	−0.0934	**	0.0269	−3.48	0.001
	Manuel Antonio Park	0.0004		0.0214	0.02	0.985
	Tortuguero Village	−0.0104		0.0317	−0.33	0.743
	Corcovado Park	0.1285	**	0.0423	3.04	0.002
Country zones	Central Valley	−0.0671	***	0.0176	−3.81	0.000
	Guanacaste	0.0523	**	0.0180	2.90	0.004
	Puntarenas golf	−0.0235		0.0197	−1.19	0.233
	Pacific Area	0.0729	***	0.0179	4.07	0.000
	Caribbean Sea	0.0426		0.0303	1.41	0.160
	Monteverde	−0.0562	**	0.0199	−2.83	0.005
	_cons	62.866	***	0.1225	51.34	0.000

Notes: number of obs = 10,498; R-squared = 0.557; $F(71,10426) = 158.32$; prob > F = 0.0000; *$p < 0.05$; **$p < 0.01$; ***$p < 0.001$; VFR = visiting friends and relatives.

The analysis of spending behaviour has allowed us to accept the six working hypotheses previously defined. In this regard, tourist profile (origin, age) and trip characteristics (organization of travel, purpose of visit, type of accommodation) appear to be the leading variables driving the expenditure of tourists (Hypotheses 3 and 4). The length of stay is the most important determinant of spending (Hypothesis 6). The other three hypotheses do not show that relevance in explaining the expenditure

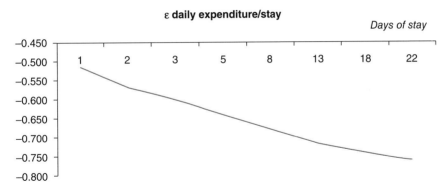

Fig. 13.1. Daily spending–stay elasticity of tourists visiting Costa Rica.

Table 13.4. Daily spending–stay elasticity of tourists visiting Costa Rica.

δ daily expenditure–stay	Stay of tourist (nights)	Daily expenditure (in US$)
−0.512	1	793
−0.567	2	521
−0.600	3	373
−0.641	5	212
−0.678	8	146
−0.717	13	107
−0.743	18	77
−0.759	22	60

of tourists, although we cannot reject them. In this way, budget and time constraints matter for tourist spending (H1), as well as the place of visit (H5) and activities undertaken while travelling (H2), but estimated coefficients are much lower than those of the preceding covariates.

13.3.2 Modelling the length of stay of international tourists in Costa Rica

The international tourism industry is currently facing major changes, one of the most notable being the reduction in the length of stay of tourists in traditional destinations. For example, in the Spanish case, and according to the Hotel Occupancy Survey of the INE (Spanish National Institute of Statistics), there has been an accumulated decrease in the average stay of tourists of 18% since 1999. The situation is not unique to Spain, being shared by many European and international destinations (UNWTO, 2013). In this subsection, we seek to understand better the factors influencing the length of stay of tourists arriving in Costa Rica.

With this objective in mind, we employ count-data models, as the variable of analysis (stay) takes non-zero positive integer values (Cameron and Trivedi, 1998).

We employ the truncated-at-zero version of the model, since the stay variable does not include null values, given that, by definition, a tourist must spend at least one night of stay at the destination. The hypotheses to be tested are, in this case, similar to those of the expenditure model (H1–H6), as well as the set of explanatory variables employed in the analysis (*Xi*). The dependent variable is now the number of nights at the destination. Starting with a Poisson model specification, we ran the appropriate tests, leading to a rejection of the null hypothesis of overdispersion in data, so we decided to estimate a negative binomial model truncated at zero, with the results shown in Table 13.5.

As shown in Table 13.5, the significance of the model is high for the joint and individual specification of the covariates, with results presented in terms of *incidence rates response* (IRR). The interpretation of the IRR for dummy variables of the model with various categories (age, gender, etc.) shows the percentage change in the variable defined regarding the category of reference, as usual in this type of model. We have to subtract one point value to the coefficient in order to get the marginal effect of the covariate on stay duration. Coefficients above one show an increasing expectancy of stay duration of tourists in Costa Rica, while those below one show a decreasing stay effect. For continuous variables (expenditure, tourist points, geographical zones, holiday activities), we have to retain the sign of the coefficient in general terms.

Testing for overdispersion in the Poisson specification
H0: variance = mean (overdispersion tests)
Deviance in goodness-of-fit: 18,566.87
Prob > chi^2 (10,433): 0.0000
Pearson goodness-of-fit: 20,331.62
Prob > chi^2 (10,433): 0.0000

Factors that seem to increase expectancy of stay in regards to tourist profile seem to be those of the (more distant) origin of the tourist, (higher) age and (lower) level of studies. Daily expenditure also influences stay duration, in an endogenous relationship with stay, as we have seen in the previous section. From trip characteristics, the most important variables are those of purpose of the visit, type of accommodation and organization of the trip. Finally, the place of visit is also important, given the distance from the starting point of the trip, usually being the capital of the country, San Jose, and the activities undertaken (sun and sand, and visiting national parks).

In general, the results are consistent with those obtained by other studies on the determinants of the length of stay (Alegre and Pou, 2006; Gokovali *et al.*, 2007; Barros *et al.*, 2009). Stay–expenditure elasticity remains negative (inverse relationship), and the duration of stay of tourists appears to be related robustly to the characteristics of the vacational time planned. For example, those tourists staying around the capital used to stay for short periods of 2–3 days, spending higher daily amounts, as we have seen previously. Visitors arriving in more distant places in the south of the country (the Pacific area, Guanacaste or Corcovado Park) spend more time and extend the duration of their stay. Budget restrictions also influence the duration of stay, with longer stays associated with tourists organizing their travel themselves, coming alone and arriving from nearby countries with cheaper travel costs (American countries).

Some types of activities (sun and sand, wildlife, national parks), as well as those tourist profiles linked to less time restrictions (older age) and particular trip purposes

Table 13.5. Function of stay duration of international tourists visiting Costa Rica. Truncated negative binomial regression model. Truncation point: 0; dispersion = mean.

Category of reference	Dep. variable: duration of stay	IRR	Sign.	s.e.	z-statistic	p > z
	Log daily expenditure	11.185	***	0.0353	3.55	0.000
	Log daily expenditure squared	0.9482	***	0.0034	−14.79	0.000
Tourist profile						
Purpose: leisure	Business tourists	1.2245		0.0249	0.91	0.363
	VFR tourists	0.9919		0.0165	−0.49	0.626
Male	Female	1.0277		0.0094	0.29	0.771
More than 55 years old	Age under 25	0.9052	***	0.0181	−4.99	0.000
	Age 25–34	0.8919	***	0.0139	−7.35	0.000
	Age 35–44	0.9140	***	0.0145	−5.65	0.000
	Age 45–54	0.9347	***	0.0155	−4.08	0.000
Other than married or single	Married	0.9366	**	0.0179	−3.43	0.001
	Single	0.9427	**	0.0185	−3.00	0.003
Tertiary education	Bachelor	1.0562	***	0.0125	4.61	0.000
	Primary + secondary	1.1068	***	0.0172	6.54	0.000
Origin: European	USA	0.8029	***	0.0100	−17.57	0.000
	Canada	0.9262	***	0.0170	−4.19	0.000
	Central America	0.7620	***	0.0156	−13.27	0.000
	Rest of Latin America	0.9606	*	0.0151	−2.56	0.011
	Caribbean	0.8609	**	0.0391	−3.30	0.001
Trip characteristics						
	First visit	0.9385	***	0.0105	−5.65	0.000
Q1	Q2	0.9949		0.0139	−0.37	0.713
	Q3	0.9621	**	0.0129	−2.88	0.004
	Q4	0.9797		0.0131	−1.53	0.126
Year 2009	Year_2011	0.9502	***	0.0128	−3.80	0.000
	Year_2010	0.9435	***	0.0099	−5.53	0.000
Trip organized by other companies	Package from ORIGIN	0.8680	**	0.0442	−2.78	0.005
	Package in Costa Rica	0.9473		0.0582	−0.88	0.378
	On my OWN from ORIGIN	0.8413	**	0.0419	−3.47	0.001
	On my OWN once in Costa Rica	0.8223	***	0.0412	−3.91	0.000
	Company trip	0.9643		0.0486	−0.72	0.471

Continued

Table 13.5. Continued.

Category of reference	Dep. variable: duration of stay	IRR	Sign.	s.e.	z-statistic	p > z
Staying at hotel/cabin/camping	House_rented	1.0118	***	0.0319	15.28	0.000
	Own_house	1.2261	***	0.0359	6.97	0.000
	House_VFR	1.1626	***	0.0145	4.46	0.000
Travelling with work colleagues	Alone	1.0723	*	0.0354	2.11	0.035
	Family	0.9646		0.0347	−1.00	0.317
	Friends	0.9826		0.0350	−0.49	0.622
	Couple	0.9677		0.0342	−0.93	0.352
Activities	Sun and sand	12.081	***	0.0150	15.18	0.000
	National_Parks	10.824	***	0.0164	5.24	0.000
	Wildlife	10.546	***	0.0136	4.13	0.000
	Shopping	10.328	**	0.0101	3.30	0.001
	Canopy	10.320	**	0.0117	2.78	0.005
	Thermalism	10.352	**	0.0133	2.70	0.007
	Cultural activities	10.371	**	0.0144	2.64	0.008
Tourist points	Arenal Volcano	0.9866		0.0139	−0.96	0.340
	Cahuita	10.860	***	0.0199	4.49	0.000
	Manuel Antonio Park	0.9973		0.0143	−0.19	0.852
	Tortuguero Village	0.9779		0.0218	−1.00	0.315
	Corcovado Park	10.997	**	0.0340	3.07	0.002
Country region	Central_Valley	0.9479	***	0.0115	−4.42	0.000
	Guanacaste	11.131	***	0.0138	8.65	0.000
	Puntarenas_golf	11.274	***	0.0156	8.67	0.000
	Pacific area	10.769	***	0.0138	5.77	0.000
	Caribbean Sea	10.885	***	0.0231	3.99	0.000
	North region	10.558	***	0.0156	3.66	0.000
	Monteverde	10.563	***	0.0149	3.89	0.000
	_cons	19.114	***	18.089	31.18	0.000

Notes: number of obs = 10,498; AIC = 5,657.3; log-likelihood = −28,220; LR chi^2(64) = 8,192.6; pseudo R^2 = 0.1268; prob > chi^2 = 0.0000; *$p < 0.05$; **$p < 0.01$; ***$p < 0.001$; VFR = visiting friends and relatives.

(leisure versus business trips), clearly influence the duration of stay, as shown in Table 13.5. In general, all these results lead to accepting (not rejecting) working hypotheses H1–H6, with H3 (origin of tourist), H4 (organization of travel, type of accommodation) and H5 (places of visit) appearing to be the most important in determining the duration of stay of tourists visiting Costa Rica.

13.4   Conclusion

Managing a tourism destination is always a complex task. The availability of information regarding the visitors and their behaviour is of paramount relevance in order to help managers to make necessary decisions. In the case of a nature-based destination, this is even more relevant, given the special characteristics and fragility of the environment. In this chapter, we have focused on providing that relevant information for the case of Costa Rica, an increasingly visited green destination in Central America. The analysis has been divided into two parts, one for the analysis of the daily expenditure of international tourists arriving in this destination and the other for the study of the factors influencing the duration of their stay.

The expenditure function has revealed differences in the level of daily spending of tourists according to their stay behaviour (1–3 days versus more than 2 weeks of stay). In particular, estimation results have shown that variables associated with the socio-economic profile of the tourist (age, origin), and mainly those linked to the characteristics of the trip (length of stay, travel organization, accommodation, company and purpose of the visit), are the main factors leading to tourist spending. To a lesser extent, the activities on the trip (shopping, canopy tour) and the place visited also determine tourists' daily expenditure. Obviously, longer stays result in a reduction of daily expenditure, with results showing a negative elasticity between expenditure and stay of between 0.5 and 0.75.

Regarding the results on the duration of stay, the empirical model has shown that the primary factors influencing that variable are those of the visitor's profile (origin, age) and trip characteristics (purpose and organization of the trip). In this case, the place of visit and the activities undertaken on the trip acquire a higher relevance in explaining the length of stay, given its geographical location. Arriving in more distant places and certain types of vacational activities (sun and sand, visiting national parks) are linked closely with longer stays of tourists.

The main conclusion arising from the results of this chapter is the existence of different segments of tourists inside the full flow of visitors arriving in the country. In particular, short-stayers show the highest spending per day, and perhaps the lower environmental impact given the limited distance range of their movements. Longer-stayers move around the country, and correspondingly adjust their daily spending to the longer duration of the trip. In this way, they can be considered more nature-related visitors in comparison with short-stayers, more focused on visits around the capital of the country or to the seaside destinations of the north and mid-Pacific area for a couple of days' stay. As has been shown, these two segments of tourists differ significantly in their expenditure and stay behaviour. Correspondingly, the managers of Costa Rica as a tourism destination would have to seek for the combination of length of stay–daily tourist spending that can result in optimal global tourism revenue for the country, both in economic terms and for sustainability issues (human footprint). This question becomes of pivotal relevance for a country where tourism is based largely on the management of renewable natural resources and where the presence of tourists exerts a considerable impact on wildlife conditions.

Note

[1]Extensive details on the survey can be found at: http://www.visitcostarica.com/ict/paginas/modEst/estudios_demanda_turistica.asp?ididioma=1.

References

Alegre, J. and Pou, L. (2006) The length of stay in the demand for tourism. *Tourism Management* 27, 1343–1355.

Bahar, O., Kozak, M. and Gokovali, U. (2008) Estimating the determinants of tourist spending: a comparison of four models. *Tourism Analysis* 13(2), 143–155.

Barros, C.P., Correia, A. and Crouch, G. (2008) Determinants of the length of stay in Latin American tourism destinations. *Tourism Analysis* 13(4), 329–340.

Barros, C.P., Butler, R. and Correia, A. (2009) The length of stay of golf tourism: a survival analysis. *Tourism Management* 31(1), 13–21.

Cameron, A.C. and Trivedi, P.K. (1998) *Regression Analysis of Count Data*. Cambridge University Press, Cambridge, UK.

Fleischer, A. and Pizam, A. (2002) Tourism constraints among Israeli seniors. *Annals of Tourism Research* 29, 106–123.

García-Sánchez, A. and Fernández-Rubio, E. (2013) Daily expenses of foreign tourists, length of stay and activities: evidence from Spain. *Tourism Economics* 19(3), 613–630.

Gokovali, U., Bahar, O. and Kozak, M. (2007) Determinants of the length of stay: a practical use of survival analysis. *Tourism Management* 28, 736–746.

Jang, S., Bai, B., Hong, G.S. and O'Leary, J.T. (2004) Understanding travel expenditure patterns: a study of Japanese & pleasure travelers to the United States by income level. *Tourism Management* 25(3), 331–341.

Juaneda, C. and Aguiló, E. (2000) Tourist expenditure for mass tourism markets. *Annals of Tourism Research* 27(3), 624–636.

Kozak, M. (2001) An analysis of tourist spending and its determinants. *Anatolia: An International Journal of Hospitality and Tourism Research* 12(2), 196–202.

Martínez-Garcia, E. and Raya, J.M. (2008) Length of stay for low-cost tourism. *Tourism Management* 29, 1064–1075.

Menezes, A., Moniz, A. and Vieira, J. (2008) The determinants of length of stay of tourists in the Azores. *Tourism Economics* 14, 1–18.

Nicolau, J. and Más, F. (2005) Stochastic modelling: a three-stage tourist choice process. *Annals of Tourism Research* 32, 49–69.

Pol, A.P., Pascual, M.B. and Vázquez, P.C. (2006) Robust estimators and bootstrap confidence intervals applied to tourism spending. *Tourism Management* 27(1), 42–50.

Rodrigues, A.I., Correia, A. and Kozak, M. (2011) A multidisciplinary approach on destination image construct. *Tourismos: An International Multidisciplinary Journal of Tourism* 6(3), 93–110.

Song, H. and Witt, S.F. (2000) *Tourism Demand Modeling and Forecasting: Modern Econometric Approaches*. Pergamon, Oxford, UK.

United Nations World Tourism Organization (2013) *Tourism Market Trends*. United Nations World Tourism Organization, Madrid.

United Nations World Tourism Organization (2014) *Tourism Highlights 2013*. United Nations World Tourism Organization, Madrid.

White, H. (1980) A heteroskedasticity-consistent covariance matrix estimator and a direct test for heteroskedasticity. *Econometrica* 48(4), 817–838.

Woodside, A.G. and MacDonald, R. (1993) General system framework of customer choice processes of tourism services. In: Gasser, R. and Weiermair, K. (eds) *Spoilt for Choice*. Kultur Verlag, Austria.

14 Socio-economic Profile of Sustainable Tourists and Expenditure at Destinations: A Local-based Analysis in Andalusia, Spain

PABLO JUAN CÁRDENAS-GARCÍA* AND JUAN IGNACIO PULIDO-FERNÁNDEZ

University of Jaén, Spain

14.1 Introduction

The core around which all economic impacts revolve is tourism expenditure (Cárdenas-García, 2012; Brida and Scuderi, 2013), which is therefore considered a key variable in the analysis of the tourism market, even though its assessment is becoming increasingly complex (Aguiló and Juaneda, 2000).

In fact, tourists have specific characteristics – such as age, origin, income, occupational status, etc. – that usually determine the tourism expenditure linked to a particular tourism activity. Thus, the study of the underlying causes that explain such expenditure becomes crucial to guide both the private sector and those responsible for setting tourism policy, inasmuch as it would be possible to know in advance the tourism expenditure that will be performed by a consumer according to his or her specific characteristics (Woodside and Dubelaar, 2002).

The trend of research in recent years has been to analyse tourism expenditure on the basis of the different attributes of tourism demand – socio-demographic characteristics, motivations, trip characteristics, etc. – by means of various econometric tools (Brida and Scuderi, 2013).

However, so far, except for some papers dealing with expenditure in the destination (Vaughan *et al.*, 2000; Mehmetoglu, 2007; Medina-Muñoz and Medina-Muñoz, 2012), most of the research works studying tourism expenditure have used total tourism expenditure as the variable for analysis, which includes products and services in origin – transport, intermediaries, etc. – as well as products and services in the destination – accommodation, restaurants, leisure activities, shopping, etc.

*E-mail: pcgarcia@ujaen.es

Under this premise, the results obtained, in most cases, are too limited to allow the development of effective proposals that improve the management of the destination, given that a component of the total tourism expenditure is not spent in the destination.

Therefore, the aim of this study is to identify, by means of a regression model with dummy variables, the determinants of tourism expenditure in the destination, on the basis of the sociodemographic characteristics of sustainable tourists visiting a particular destination – medium-sized cities of Andalusia (Spain) – using the results obtained from 1180 surveys of tourists who visited this tourism destination during 2013. Thus, the major academic contribution of this study is the creation of an explanatory model of tourism expenditure in the destination in order to establish tourism policy proposals aimed at improving the tourism management of emerging urban cultural destinations, given that, so far, this issue has not been addressed in the literature.

14.2 Literature Review

Many contributions of the scientific literature have analysed whether the different sets of attributes – psychological factors: motivation, need or perception; demographic factors: age, origin or income; or the characteristics of the trip themselves: length, distance to destination, means of transport used – affect tourism expenditure (Wu *et al.*, 2013).

The explanation of tourism expenditure according to these explanatory variables has been studied from different points of view: (i) research works dealing with total expenditure per tourist in each tourism destination; (ii) studies analysing total expenditure in the destination, including all group members travelling with the respondent; and (iii) studies that attempt to explain the daily expenditure per tourist in the destination (García-Sánchez *et al.*, 2013).

Among all the categories of factors with the capacity to influence tourism expenditure, most of these research contributions have dealt with the analysis of how the different sociodemographic characteristics of the consumer affect tourism expenditure. The most studied characteristics include: geographical origin, gender, age, educational level, occupation (or professional status) and income level (Hellstrom, 2006; Medina-Muñoz and Medina-Muñoz, 2012), which are also, except for geographical origin, the variables selected in this research.

The analysis of these socio-economic factors as explanatory variables of tourism expenditure has been included in numerous research works carried out to date (Table 14.1).

Tourists' gender has been a factor that has received little attention in the scientific literature as a potential determinant of tourism expenditure. Moreover, those research works that have dealt with this variable have been unable to establish clearly whether gender influences tourism expenditure. In fact, there is a group of studies that conclude that this variable does not have any impact on tourism expenditure (Fredman, 2008; Barquet *et al.*, 2011; Boman *et al.*, 2013), while another group of studies determine precisely the opposite (So and Morrison, 2004; Bilgic *et al.*, 2008; Anderson, 2011; Zheng and Zhang, 2013).

Tourists' age is among those factors most frequently mentioned when trying to explain tourism expenditure, yet there is no unanimity among researchers regarding its possible impact. On the one hand, some of the literature argues that middle-aged

Table 14.1. Determinants of socio-economic profile (literature review).

Literature	Gender	Age	Education level	Occupation	Income level
Boman et al. (2013)	N	Y	Y	–	Y
García-Sánchez et al. (2013)	–	Y	Y	–	Y
Vietze (2011)	–	–	Y	–	Y
Zheng and Zhang (2013)	Y	N	Y	Y	Y
So and Morrison (2004)	Y	Y	–	–	Y
Anderson (2011)	Y	Y	–	–	Y
Fredman (2008)	N	Y	–	–	Y
Park and Yoon (2009)	–	–	Y	–	Y
McHone and Rungeling (1999)	–	N	Y	–	Y
Tchetchik et al. (2009)	N	N	Y	–	–
Villena (2011)	–	–	Y	Y	Y
Wang and Lee (2011)	N	N	Y	N	Y
Barquet et al. (2011)	N	Y	–	–	–
Downward et al. (2009)	–	–	–	–	Y
Bilgic et al. (2008)	Y	N	–	Y	Y
Lee (2001)	–	N	–	–	Y
Eugenio and Campos (2014)	–	Y	Y	Y	–
Alegre et al. (2013)	–	Y	–	Y	–

Notes: Y = determinant of tourism expenditure; N = not related to tourism expenditure; – = not analysed.

tourists allocate more of their budget to tourism activities (So and Morrison, 2004; Fredman, 2008; Anderson, 2011; Barquet et al., 2011; Alegre et al., 2013; Boman et al., 2013; García-Sánchez et al., 2013; Eugenio and Campos, 2014). On the other hand, there are also studies concluding that tourists' age does not influence tourism expenditure (Lee, 2001; Bilgic et al., 2008; Zheng and Zhang, 2013).

Concerning the educational level of tourists, according to the results obtained from the studies that have examined it, it can be concluded that it is a determinant of tourism expenditure, since there is a positive relationship between tourists' educational level and the amount they spend in the destination (Park and Yoon, 2009; Vietze, 2011; Villena, 2011; Boman et al., 2013; García-Sánchez et al., 2013; Zheng and Zhang, 2013; Eugenio and Campos, 2014).

Tourists' occupation and professional status are two of the variables that are less commonly used in research works. Nevertheless, those studies in which these factors have been analysed determine that there are certain occupations and/or professional groups that have a clear impact on tourism expenditure, although there is no general agreement among these studies when concluding on specific items (Bilgic *et al.*, 2008; Villena, 2011; Zheng and Zhang, 2013). However, those studies that have analysed the decrease in tourism expenditure in situations of economic crisis have determined, as it seems clear, that being unemployed contributes to a reduction in tourism expenditure (Eugenio and Campos, 2014).

Finally, along with age, tourists' level of income is one of the factors that have been studied most extensively when trying to explain tourism expenditure. In addition, there is a broad consensus on its effect on tourism expenditure, as might be expected. Most studies show that there is a positive relationship between level of income and tourism expenditure, resulting in significant differences between the expenditure by tourists with a higher income level and the expenditure by tourists with a lower income level – that difference in expenditure, though still significant, decreases between middle-income and low-income tourists (Lee, 2001; Bilgic *et al.*, 2008; Fredman, 2008; Downward *et al.*, 2009; Park and Yoon, 2009; Tchetchik *et al.*, 2009; Vietze, 2011; Boman *et al.*, 2013; García-Sánchez *et al.*, 2013; Zheng and Zhang, 2013).

Therefore, the scientific literature has shown that there are specific factors that explain tourism expenditure, having developed, in recent years, different models that have allowed the analysis of this issue. Yet, the tourism policy implications of these findings have been few (Jang and Ham, 2009).

14.3 Methodology

There are an increasing number of studies on tourist behaviour (TUI, 2004; Travelhorizons, 2009; Kuoni, 2011; Wehrli *et al.*, 2011), indicating that there is a growing awareness of the environmental, social and cultural impacts that tourism activity can generate. Previous research has shown an existing relationship between individuals' values, attitudes and behaviour (Steg *et al.*, 2005; Wurzinger and Johansson, 2006; Hansla *et al.*, 2008; Bergin-Seers and Mair, 2009; Mehmetoglu *et al.*, 2010), as well as the growing consciousness among society in general, and tourists in particular, of the environmental, social and cultural impacts that tourism can generate in a destination.

Consumers' perception and behaviour when choosing a destination show trends towards the consumption of green brands and interest in green products in general, along with sustainability, as important factors when booking holidays (Adlwarth, 2010; Dodds *et al.*, 2010; Hedlund, 2011; Wehrli *et al.*, 2011).

In fact, there are many studies that demonstrate that there are tourists who are willing to pay more due to issues related to sustainability from different perspectives (hotels, transport, products, etc.) (Rivera, 2002; Dodds *et al.*, 2010; Chung *et al.*, 2011; among others).

Therefore, as recognized by Edgel (2006), destinations are trying to address these new requirements and show a greater concern for developing a more sustainable tourism model. Miller (2003) is committed to the idea that consumers make purchasing decisions based on the environmental, social and economic quality of the products and are keen to transfer these habits to the purchase of tourism products.

The most comprehensive study undertaken in recent years is that by Wehrli *et al.* (2011), which is based on 6000 surveys conducted in eight countries and aims to identify the most relevant aspects of sustainable tourism from the perspective of tourists. The main objective of this study was to ascertain tourists' level of understanding of sustainability.

Based on this study, a battery of questions were included in our survey, with the aim of facilitating the segmentation of the sample and the identification of a group of 'sustainable tourists' that enables the analysis of the extent to which their socio-economic characteristics affect tourism expenditure at the destination. These questions were divided into three groups: (i) understanding of the implications of sustainable tourism; (ii) assessment of the ecological attributes of the destination and its tourism offer; and (iii) consideration of ecological, social and economic attributes in their purchasing behaviour. Respondents were requested to rate, on a Likert scale of 1–7, the issues about which they were asked. Those who had given a minimum rating of 6 to at least 80% of these aspects were considered 'sustainable tourists'.

14.3.1   Data collection

This research study differs from others – with respect to most of the studies existing within the scientific literature – in that it only analyses expenditure by tourists in the destination; the variable 'geographical origin' has not been used as an explanatory variable of tourism expenditure. In this regard, as argued by some authors (Leones *et al.*, 1998; Lee, 2001), the geographic origin of visitors is a determinant, but just of total tourism expenditure, since the greater the distance between the place of residence and the destination, the higher the transport costs. However, this variable has no connection at all to the tourism expenditure in the destination itself.

In view of the impossibility of identifying the object of this study (all sustainable tourists who visit these cities), a simple random sampling has been suggested in which the only selection criterion is having spent at least one night in the destinations in which the survey was conducted. The study focuses on a subset of 3835 respondents who travelled to one of the medium-sized cities of Andalusia analysed; however, since the aim of this study is to determine the factors influencing tourism expenditure by sustainable tourists – including, thus, only those who show the characteristics listed in the previous paragraph – we have worked with a sample of 1180 tourists. Sustainable tourists represent, therefore, 30.77% of the total tourists visiting the destinations analysed.

The survey was conducted between January and December of 2013. The sample selection was, by stratified sampling, proportional to the value of an index published by La Caixa – La Caixa is a Spanish bank that, since 1996, publishes a statistical yearbook, which includes, among others, an index that synthesizes tourism development in the municipalities of Spain, synthesizing the tourism development data that are available for all the municipalities of Spain (Table 14.2). Therefore, a cross-sectional series has been used, as the values correspond to different subjects at the same moment in time.

This survey also provides basic information on the characteristics of tourists with different expenditure levels. Therefore, the extent to which different factors such as nationality, age, profession, gender, income, educational level, etc. affect tourism expenditure can be studied. As a result, the differences in the level of expenditure between the different groups can be set.

Table 14.2. Survey data.

Population	Sustainable tourists staying overnight
Scope	Medium-sized cities in the centre of Andalusia
Type of survey	Structured survey conducted by face-to-face interview
Sample size	1180 respondents
Maximum sampling error	±2.853%
Confidence level	95% ($p = q = 0.50$)
Period analysed	January to December 2013

As mentioned in a previous section, there are three approaches to the definition of tourism expenditure in the destination: total tourism expenditure per person, total tourism expenditure per group and daily tourism expenditure per person. This research can be included in the third research group, so that the variable to be explained is the daily tourism expenditure per person.

In order to try to explain tourism expenditure according to the socio-economic characteristics of tourists, and in line with the majority of studies published to date – that use the ordinary least squares (OLS) method to estimate expenditure (Brida and Scuderi, 2013) – a multiple linear regression model has been used, which makes it possible to explain the variable of tourism expenditure on the basis of the variables of socio-economic profile considered.

In this sense, since the relationship between expenditure and tourists' socio-economic variables is usually heteroskedastic in nature, it is appropriate to use logarithms, as the assumption of homoskedasticity is satisfied in those models that apply logarithms to the endogenous variable; that is, while the conditional distribution of Y is often heteroskedastic, ln (Y) is homoskedastic (Uriel, 2013). Thus, the predicted value of the response variable is always a real value. Accordingly, the general equation model is the following – using a significance level of 0.05:

$$E[Y_i|\beta, X_i] = \beta_0 + \beta_{1xi1} + \beta_{2xi2} + \ldots + \beta_{kxik}, i = 1, \ldots, n$$

being: Y_i = the logarithm of daily expenditure per person travelling corresponding to the individual $i = 1, \ldots, n$; β_j = the parameter associated with the variable $j, j = 1, \ldots, k$.

Furthermore, as the model includes explanatory variables of categorical content (sex, occupation or educational level), it is necessary to include dummy variables (Hamilton, 1994; Wooldridge, 2009). In this sense, all adjustment variables xj have been treated as dummy variables. That is, xij (value of the variable j on the individual (i)) takes the values 0 and 1, being the reference category for each one of them the first position shown in each descriptive table (Table 14.3).

14.4 Results

The results obtained have allowed us to understand the behaviour of the respondents regarding expenditure in the destination, as well as the socio-economic factors determining such expenditure, identifying those that boost it or, to the contrary, contain it.

Table 14.3. Average daily expenditure per person.

Variable		N	Per cent	Expenditure (€)	CL 95%	
Sex	Man	679	57.5	73.6	69.9	77.2
	Woman	502	42.5	81.6	77.1	86.1
Age	18–30	266	22.5	70.3	64.6	76
	31–40	357	30.2	87.9	82.0	93.9
	41–50	288	24.4	75.4	70.2	80.6
	51–80	269	22.8	70.8	65.3	76.2
Education level	Can read and write and have been to school	19	1.6	90.0	70.3	109.7
	Completed elementary post-secondary education	85	7.2	70.1	60.1	80.2
	Advanced post-secondary education	135	11.4	76.0	68.3	83.8
	VTI, intermediate VT or industrial technician	53	4.5	128.6	102.9	154.2
	VTII, advanced VT, industrial mastery or equivalent	134	11.4	84.4	75.3	93.5
	Diploma degree, architecture or technical engineering	215	18.3	80.5	74.2	86.9
	University degree	493	41.8	67.8	64.1	71.4
	PhD, Master's degree	46	3.9	87.2	72.1	102.3
Occupation	Employed	983	83.3	80.4	77.2	83.6
	Unemployed	18	1.5	57.8	45.8	69.9
	Retired	80	6.8	73.2	60.9	85.5
	Housework	25	2.1	76.5	61.3	91.6
	Student	70	5.9	40.9	36.0	45.7
	Others	5	0.4	42.0	29.8	54.2
Professional status	Professional (lawyer, doctor, architect, etc.)	247	20.9	76.1	69.8	82.3
	Entrepreneur	115	9.7	82.9	73.1	92.7
	Manager	66	5.6	79.1	62.7	95.4
	Civil servant with a university degree	250	21.2	71.6	66.3	77.0
	Middle management (manager, etc.)	117	9.9	107.2	95.4	119.1
	Skilled worker (plumber, maître d', bank employee, etc.)	187	15.8	76.3	70.0	82.6
	Unskilled worker (labourer, kitchen helper, etc.)	48	4.1	88.2	73.0	103.5
	Civil servant without an academic qualification	14	1.2	68.2	47.4	89.1
	Others	136	11.5	54.0	49.2	58.8

Continued

Table 14.3. Continued.

Variable		N	Per cent	Expenditure (€)	CL 95%	
Income level	<€600	19	1.6	65.1	47.5	82.7
	€600–€900	23	1.9	63.8	48.4	79.2
	€900– €1200	121	10.2	77.8	70.1	85.6
	€1200–€1500	176	14.9	81.2	75.0	87.4
	€1500–€1800	185	15.7	75.6	69.2	81.9
	€1800–€2100	211	17.9	74.9	68.0	81.8
	€2100–€3000	224	19.0	72.7	66.3	79.1
	>€3000	221	18.7	82.9	74.6	91.2
Total		1180	100	77.0	74.1	79.8

Notes: N = frequency; CL = confidence level; VT = vocational training; maître d' = head waiter.

In a first approach, this analysis reveals that the expenditure by tourists visiting these cities is low. The average daily expenditure per person amounts to €77.

As can be seen in Table 14.3, gender is an important variable that needs to be taken into account when studying tourism expenditure in these cities. The average daily expenditure of women is €81.6, which is 10.87% higher than that of men. This is significant, as Pulido-Fernández and López-Sánchez (2011, p. 278) state that 'women have a growing influence on all key consumption decisions, including tourism. And it is also observed a process of feminization of holiday travel'.

As can be observed, nearly 55% of respondents are aged between 31 and 50. We are dealing, therefore, with a middle-aged tourist (member of the so-called Generation X) travelling as a couple with his or her partner in most cases. The age segment with a higher average daily expenditure, as shown in Table 14.3, is the 31–40 year age group, who spend €87.9/day (14.16% more than the average, and 16.58% more than the next segment that spends the most, the 41–50 year age group).

Table 14.3 also lists the results obtained from the analysis of this variable and reveals interesting aspects of tourists' educational level. A striking aspect is that the highest average daily expenditure is associated with tourists with vocational training (€128.6) and with those with a basic level of education, limited to knowing how to read and write (€90).

Relative to tourists' type of occupation, it was found that, first, 83.3% of respondents were employed: this is a logical result since travelling costs money, which requires having some source of income. Second, a reading of Table 14.3 suggests that, as might be expected, the highest daily expenditure corresponds with the employed (€80.4; 4.42% above the average), while the average daily expenditure of retired people is €73.2, and students, the third largest group analysed, spend only €40.9/day.

Professional status is another variable that could be considered as explanatory of tourism expenditure. Table 14.3 reveals that middle managers (with €107.2), unskilled workers (with €88.2) and entrepreneurs (with €82.9) show a higher average daily expenditure above the average in all three cases.

Finally, the other variable that is usually considered in studies on tourism expenditure is the income level of the respondents. That is, tourists with a level of income between €600 and €900 show an average daily expenditure of €63.8 (below the average), which amounts to €77.8 (similar to the average) for the bracket between €900 and €1200. It increases again to €81.2 when dealing with the income bracket between €1200 and €1500. However, from there, contrary to what might be thought, tourism expenditure in these cities decreases until the last income bracket considered, earning more than €3000, when it increases again (€82.9; the highest amount).

14.4.1   Regression model

Table 14.4 shows the results of the regression model estimated by OLS, robust to heteroskedasticity. This analysis confirms, as already noted in the review of the tables previously presented, that women spend more money than men, as well as the 31–40 year age group. In both cases, these are dependent variables of tourism expenditure with a very high significance, so both influence tourists' expenditure decisions.

Regarding educational level, it is worth highlighting two different groups with similar behaviour with respect to expenditure, which is precisely an average daily expenditure significantly lower than the reference category. The result obtained for university graduates (who, besides, represent 41.8% of the total sample) is especially interesting. This segment shows, by far, the lower expenditure, a fact which must be taken into consideration given that it can be very significant in explaining the subsequent behaviour. The other group is made up of tourists with primary education. As in the previous case, this is a segment that spends a much lower amount of money.

The results obtained for all the other segments considered for this variable (educational level) (with p-values well above 0.05, even 0.1) show the lack of dependence on tourism expenditure, which calls into question the fact that this variable could be significant. Thus, finally, it is not possible to conclude that educational level is a factor that does not have the capacity to influence the expenditure behaviour of tourists visiting these cities.

The variable occupations, however, seem to have an obvious relationship with tourism expenditure in the destination. As expected, the unemployed and the students spend less than the reference category (employed). The professional category also determines tourism expenditure in the medium-sized Andalusian cities. In this case, skilled workers spend less, while middle managers spend more.

Finally, as already anticipated in the initial analysis, the level of income is not associated with the average daily expenditure by tourists who visit these cities. Put another way, contrary to what has been shown by all studies used as references for this research work, the level of income is not a determinant of tourism expenditure in the cities analysed.

To justify this, we should analyse the income elasticity of demand. It seems clear that the quantity of offered goods and services demanded in these cities is insensitive to changes in the income level of those demanding them. Moreover, based on the information provided in Table 14.4, it is found that the tourism offer in these cities can be considered as an inferior good, at least for certain demand segments, given that, for those with an income over €1500, an increase in tourists' level of income results in a decrease in the quantity demanded.

Table 14.4. Regression model estimated by OLS robust to heteroskedasticity.

Socio-economic variables		Beta	CL 95%		p-value
Gender	Woman	0.086	0.022	0.150	0.008
Age	31–40	0.105	0.017	0.193	0.019
	41–50	0.032	−0.063	0.126	0.511
	51–80	−0.038	−0.144	0.069	0.489
Educational level	Completed elementary post-secondary education	−0.299	−0.551	−0.048	0.020
	Advanced post-secondary education	−0.186	−0.435	0.063	0.143
	VTI, intermediate VT or industrial technician	0.049	−0.236	0.334	0.734
	VTII, advanced VT or industrial mastery	−0.248	−0.500	0.003	0.053
	Diploma degree or technical engineering	−0.156	−0.400	0.087	0.209
	University degree	−0.369	−0.613	−0.126	0.003
	PhD, Master's degree	−0.057	−0.333	0.218	0.683
Occupation	Unemployed	−0.246	−0.470	−0.021	0.032
	Retired	−0.110	−0.260	0.040	0.152
	Housework	0.105	−0.121	0.331	0.363
	Student	−0.525	−0.681	−0.368	0.000
	Others	−0.573	−0.995	−0.152	0.008
Professional category	Entrepreneur	0.059	−0.050	0.168	0.287
	Manager	−0.074	−0.217	0.069	0.309
	Civil servant with a university degree	−0.081	−0.171	0.009	0.078
	Middle management (manager, etc.)	0.131	−0.005	0.268	0.060
	Skilled worker (plumber, bank employee, etc.)	−0.124	−0.240	−0.008	0.037
	Unskilled worker (labourer, kitchen helper, etc.)	−0.100	−0.320	0.120	0.372
	Civil servant without an academic qualification	−0.288	−0.600	0.024	0.071
	Others	−0.181	−0.316	−0.045	0.009
Income level	€600–€900	−0.311	−0.662	0.041	0.083
	€900–€1200	−0.106	−0.384	0.173	0.457
	€1200–€1500	−0.064	−0.338	0.209	0.646
	€1500–€1800	−0.089	−0.360	0.181	0.517
	€1800–€2100	−0.122	−0.394	0.149	0.378
	€2100–€3000	−0.110	−0.381	0.162	0.428
	> €3000	−0.057	−0.332	0.218	0.685
Constant		4.375	4.005	4.746	0.000

In this regard, we must remember that most of the cities analysed are considered emerging urban cultural destinations. That is, they still have a very basic tourism offer, which, in many cases, is limited to the provision of accommodation, catering and some tourism attraction. In most cases, there is no tourism production process, so there is not a finished and consolidated tourism product, which can generate tourism expenditure. Consequently, it is easy to find substitute tourism products of better quality.

In summary, Table 14.4 shows the factors that determine the expenditure of the tourists visiting medium-sized Andalusian cities: gender, age and occupation (including professional status). We are unable to confirm, however, that educational level influences expenditure; and, besides, it is clear that the level of income does not determine the tourism expenditure in the cities analysed.

These last two variables are two of the most significant variables included in most studies carried out to date on tourism expenditure. These two factors usually determine the expenditure of tourists visiting any destination, but in this case, they do not, or at least, it has not been possible to verify it by means of the analysis performed.

It should be borne in mind, in this regard, that we have analysed tourism expenditure in the destination; and, moreover, that the cases that have been studied correspond, in most cases, to emerging destinations, with a very basic tourism offer, still developing and in an initial state of tourism production. These two factors determine, undoubtedly, the results obtained. The fact that, from a certain income level (€1500), expenditure in the destination begins to decrease justifies the need to focus the explanation for these results on the tourism offer. There is not a sufficiently attractive offer in these destinations that encourages an increase in expenditure that goes beyond accommodation, catering and some basic tourism activities (tickets to tourism resources, museums and little else).

Finally, in order to guarantee the reliability of the results, we studied the overall model fit. As an absolute measure of goodness of fit, we calculated the typical residual error, whose value was 0.342. In addition, as a relative measure of the goodness of fit, we calculated the adjusted coefficient of determination (R^2aj), giving 0.0776, which indicated that 7.76% of the variance of the dependent variable was explained by the model. Lastly, the F ratio makes it possible to test empirically the hypothesis that the proportion explained by the model is not significant. In this case, the value of the F-test $[F(31,2935) = 8.31; p < 0.001]$ leads to the rejection of the null hypothesis and allows us to affirm that the model explains a significant part of the variance of the dependent variable.

14.5 Conclusion

The results obtained can be highly useful for policy makers and the managers of these tourism destinations. On the one hand, they allow us to identify the segments of tourists with a higher average daily expenditure, so that decision processes on the type of products to be created to respond to these profiles are facilitated. The aim would be to develop a portfolio of products that would enable each city to maximize its productivity in terms of expenditure.

On the other hand, the results facilitate the development of more effective promotion and marketing strategies in the cities analysed that, as already noted, are not at the same level of tourism development. This would make it possible to target specific products to specific segments, without squandering the good amount of money that is devoted to generic promotion actions, which are often ineffective.

In fact, as mentioned by Jang *et al.* (2004), travel expenditure patterns are vital to travel tour operators and destination promoters. For instance, a tourism policy that is compatible with sustainable tourism must include the daily expenditure per tourist as a marketing goal, rather than trying to achieve the maximum possible number of tourists. Consequently, the results obtained in this chapter will facilitate the implementation of tourism strategies, either public or private, aimed at seeking an increase in the expenditure per capita, rather than in the absolute number of tourists.

The results of this research work reflect the inability of the cities analysed to generate expenditure by those segments with middle or upper-middle income level, as well as by tourists with a high educational level, who are expected, therefore, to be more demanding regarding their tourism experience. These segments are precisely those, as has already been seen, showing a lower level of expenditure in the cities analysed.

The most interesting tourism expenditure profile at these destinations is that of a woman, aged between 31 and 40, with a university degree and holding an intermediate management position.

Consistent with this information, the stakeholders of the destinations analysed should make an effort to develop an attractive tourism product with the capacity to boost the expenditure of visitors who fit, especially, this profile. It must be a product for couples (66.4% of respondents travel with their partner), highly motivating, and which facilitates different tourism consumption options, thereby ensuring maximum multiplier effect on the local economy.

The scientific literature on tourism consumer behaviour often distinguishes three steps in the trip decision-making process. In the first step, the crucial decision is to travel. After that, the decisions made before travelling affect the choice of the destination, accommodation, means of transport, transport company, time of year to travel and trip duration (Fessenmaier, 1995). Finally, once at the destination, tourists make decisions regarding tourism attractions or special places to visit, routes, costs, places to eat or rest (Dellaert *et al.*, 1998). As Barlés and Matutes (2012) point out, the destination includes the decisions made having arrived at the chosen site, such as hiring a guide or attending activities; or decisions about the time spent at each specific location, the selection of restaurants or the cost of purchases, etc.

Therefore, these are the kind of decisions to which the cities analysed should pay special attention, by generating a wide and attractive offer that is able to encourage tourism expenditure beyond a simple visit to their most emblematic resources, as currently occurs.

This offer must, of course, take into consideration that these tourists have a special interest in the consumption and undertaking of 'sustainable' services and activities. Therefore, the managers of these destinations should make an effort to respond to these new requirements and develop a tourism offer that meets the highest standards of sustainability. Otherwise, it will not be possible to ensure that these tourists are satisfied with the experience generated by their visit to these cities, and thus be willing to pay more for it.

References

Adlwarth, W. (2010) Corporate social responsibility: customer expectations and behaviour in the tourism sector. In: Conrady, R. and Buck, M. (eds) *Trends and Issues in Global Tourism*. Springer, New York, pp. 101–103.

Aguiló, E. and Juaneda, C. (2000) Tourist expenditure for mass tourism markets. *Annals of Tourism Research* 27(3), 624–637.

Alegre, J., Mateo, S. and Pou, L. (2013) Tourism participation and expenditure by Spanish households: the effects of the economic crisis and unemployment. *Tourism Management* 39, 37–49.

Anderson, W. (2011) Enclave tourism and its socio-economic impact in emerging destinations. *Anatolia: An International Journal of Tourism and Hospitality Research* 22(3), 361–377.

Barlés, M.J. and Matutes, J. (2012) El papel de la mujer en la compra: una tipología del consumidor basada en las decisiones vacacionales. *PASOS, Revista de turismo y Patrimonio Cultural* 10(5), 543–551.

Barquet, A., Brida, J.G., Osti, L. and Schubert, S. (2011) An analysis of tourists' expenditure on winter sports events through the Tobit censorate. *Tourism Economics* 17(6), 1197–1217.

Bergin-Seers, S. and Mair, J. (2009) Emerging green tourists in Australia: their behaviours and attitudes. *Tourism and Hospitality Research* 9, 109–119.

Bilgic, A., Florkowski, W.J., Yoder, J. and Schreiner, D.F. (2008) Estimating fishing and hunting leisure spending. *Tourism Management* 29, 771–782.

Boman, M., Fredman, P., Lundmark, L. and Ericsson, G. (2013) Outdoor recreation – a necessity or a luxury? Estimation of Engel curves for Sweden. *Journal of Outdoor Recreation and Tourism* 3, 49–56.

Brida, J.G. and Scuderi, R. (2013) Determinants of tourist expenditure: a review of microeconometric models. *Tourism Management Perspectives* 6, 28–40.

Cárdenas-García, P.J. (2012) El turismo como instrumento de desarrollo económico (Doctoral dissertation). Available at: http://ruja.ujaen.es/bitstream/10953/363/1/9788484396635.pdf (accessed 5 December 2014).

Chung, J.Y., Kyle, G.T., Petrick, J.F. and Absher, J.D. (2011) Fairness of prices, user fee policy and willingness to pay among visitors to a national forest. *Tourism Management* 32(5), 1038–1046.

Dellaert, B.C., Ettema, D.F. and Lindh, C. (1998) Multi-faceted tourist travel decisions: a constraint-based conceptual framework to describe tourists' sequential choices of travel components. *Tourism Management* 19(4), 313–320.

Dodds, R., Graci, S.R. and Holmes, M. (2010) Does the tourist care? A comparison of tourists in Koh Phi Phi, Thailand and Gili Trawangan, Indonesia. *Journal of Sustainable Tourism* 18(2), 207–222.

Downward, P., Lumsdon, L. and Weston, R. (2009) Visitor expenditure: the case of cycle recreation and tourism. *Journal of Sport and Tourism* 14(1), 25–42.

Edgel, S.D. (2006) *Managing Sustainable Tourism: A Legacy for the Future*. Haworth Hospitality Press, New York.

Eugenio, J.L. and Campos, J.A. (2014) Economic crisis and tourism expenditure cutback decision. *Annals of Tourism Research* 44(1), 53–73.

Fessenmaier, D. (1995) *A Preliminary Examination of the Complex Tourism Decision Making Process*. University of Urbana-Champaign, Illinois.

Fredman, P. (2008) Determinants of visitor expenditures in mountain tourism. *Tourism Economics* 14(2), 297–311.

García-Sánchez, A., Fernández-Rubio, E. and Collado, M.D. (2013) Daily expenses of foreign tourists, length of stay and activities: evidence from Spain. *Tourism Economics* 19(3), 613–630.

Hamilton, J.D. (1994) *Time Series Analysis*. Princeton University Press, New Jersey.

Hansla, A., Gamble, A., Juliusson, A. and Gärling, T. (2008) The relationships between awareness of consequences, environmental concern, and value orientations. *Journal of Environmental Psychology* 28, 1–9.

Hedlund, T. (2011) The impact of values, environmental concern, and willingness to accept economic sacrifices to protect the environment on tourists' intentions to buy ecologically sustainable tourism alternatives. *Tourism and Hospitality Research* 11(4), 278–288.

Hellstrom, J. (2006) A bivariate count data model for household tourism demand. *Journal of Applied Econometrics* 21, 213–226.

Jang, S. and Ham, S. (2009) A double-hurdle analysis of travel expenditure: baby boomer seniors versus older seniors. *Tourism Management* 30(3), 372–380.

Jang, S., Bai, B., Hong, G.S. and O'Leary, J.T. (2004) Understanding travel expenditure patterns: a study of Japanese pleasure travelers to the United States by income level. *Tourism Management* 25(3), 331–341.

Kuoni (2011) Holiday Report: Daring to be Different: Holiday-Makers Cut Loose Madrid. Available at: http://www.kuoni.com/docs/kuoni_global_holiday_report_2011_1.pdf (accessed 10 December 2014).

Lee, H.C. (2001) Determinants of recreational boater expenditures on trips. *Tourism Management* 22, 659–667.

Leones, J., Colby, B. and Crandall, K. (1998) Tracking expenditures of the elusive nature tourists of Southeastern Arizona. *Journal of Travel Research* 36, 56–64.

McHone, W.W. and Rungeling, B. (1999) Special cultural events: do they attract leisure tourists? *International Journal of Hospitality Management* 18(2), 215–219.

Medina-Muñoz, D.R. and Medina-Muñoz, R.D. (2012) Determinants of expenditures on wellness services: the case of Gran Canaria. *Regional Studies* 46(3), 309–319.

Mehmetoglu, M. (2007) Nature-based tourists: the relationship between their trip expenditures and activities. *Journal of Sustainable Tourism* 15(2), 200–215.

Mehmetoglu, M., Hines, K., Graumann, C. and Greibrokk, J. (2010) The relationship between personal values and tourism behavior: a segmentation approach. *Journal of Vacation Marketing* 16(1), 17–27.

Miller, G. (2003) Consumerism in sustainable tourism: a survey of UK consumers. *Journal of Sustainable Tourism* 11(1), 17–39.

Park, D.B. and Yoon, Y.S. (2009) Segmentation by motivation in rural tourism: a Korean case study. *Tourism Management* 30(1), 99–108.

Pulido-Fernández, J.I. and López-Sánchez, Y. (2011) Tourism: analysis of a global phenomenon from a perspective of sustainability. In: Pachura, P. (ed.) *The Systemic Dimension of Globalization*. InTech Open Access Publisher, Rijeka, pp. 267–288.

Rivera, J. (2002) Assessing a voluntary environmental initiative in the developing world: the Costa Rican certification for sustainable tourism. *Policy Sciences* 35, 333–360.

So, S.I. and Morrison, A.M. (2004). The repeat travel market for Taiwan: a multi-stage segmentation approach. *Asia Pacific Journal of Tourism Research* 9(1), 71–87.

Steg, L., Dreijerink, L. and Abrahamse, W. (2005) Factors influencing the acceptability of energy policies: a test of VBN theory. *Journal of Environmental Psychology* 25, 415–425.

Tchetchik, A., Fleischer, A. and Shoval, N. (2009) Segmentation of visitors to a heritage site using high-resolution time-space. *Journal of Travel Research* 48(2), 216–229.

Travelhorizons (2009) American Travelers More Familiar with 'Green Travel' but Unwilling to Pay More to Support It. Available at: http://www.ustravel.org/news/press-releases/american-travelers-more-familiar-%E2%80%98green-travel%E2%80%99 (accessed 12 December 2014).

TUI (2004) A Future-Gazing Study of How Holidays Are Set to Change Over the Next 20 Years. Available at: http://www.ahp-monitor.pt/?data=download_file.objfid=111 (accessed 10 December 2014).

Uriel, E. (2013) *Regresión lineal múltiple: estimación y propiedades*. Universidad de Valencia, Valencia, Spain.

Vaughan, D.R., Farr, H. and Slee, R.W. (2000) Estimating and interpreting the local economic benefits of visitor spending: an explanation. *Leisure Studies* 19, 95–118.

Vietze, C. (2011) What's pushing international tourism expenditures? *Tourism Economics* 17(2), 237–260.

Villena, M. (2011) Análisis del gasto diario de los turistas de negocios: duración de la estancia y categoría profesional. MSc thesis. University of Cartagena, Murcia, Spain.

Wang, S.T. and Lee, Y.S. (2011) Expenditure differences among conference and regular tourists in Taiwan: the role of situational factors. *Journal of Convention and Event Tourism* 12(4), 290–312.

Wehrli, R., Egli, H., Lutzenberger, D., Pfister, J., Scwarz, J., *et al.* (2011) *Is There Demand for Sustainable Tourism?* Study for the World Tourism Forum Lucerne 2011, ITW. Working Papers Series Tourism 2001/2011. Lucerne University of Applied Sciences and Arts, Lucerne, Switzerland.

Woodside, A.G. and Dubelaar, C. (2002) A general theory of tourism consumption systems: a conceptual framework and an empirical exploration. *Journal of Travel Research* 41(2), 120–132.

Wooldridge, J.M. (2009) *Introductory Econometrics: A Modern Approach*, 4th edn. South-Western Cengage Learning, Mason, Ohio.

Wu, L., Zhang, J. and Fujiwara, A. (2013) Tourism participation and expenditure behaviour: analysis using a scobit-based discrete–continuous choice model. *Annals of Tourism Research* 40, 1–17.

Wurzinger, S. and Johansson, M. (2006) Environmental concern and knowledge of ecotourism among three groups of Swedish tourists. *Journal of Travel Research* 45, 217–226.

Zheng, B. and Zhang, Y. (2013) Household expenditures for leisure tourism in the USA, 1996 and 2006. *International Journal of Tourism Research* 15(2), 197–208.

15 Networking for Sustainable Cultural Tourism Activities and Dynamics: The Case of Oporto

Ivana Stević* and Zélia Breda

University of Aveiro, Aveiro, Portugal

15.1   Introduction

'We live in a networked world' (Scott *et al.*, 2008, p. 1), with constantly getting in touch with the term 'network' in our everyday lives, yet not thinking about what it actually represents and using it without a second thought. We have our networks of friends, family members and colleagues with whom we interact, interrelate and cooperate. We all are parts of a complex global system that functions on the basis of connections and interrelations, both people and industries, with tourism being no exception. Tourism is a phenomenon, an industry, an activity, an international business, an income generator, a development mechanism, a poverty alleviator. It can be studied and defined from the demand side (e.g. Frechtling, 2001; Eurostat, Organisation for Economic Co-operation and Development, United Nations and World Tourism Organization, 2001), from the supply side (e.g. Smith, 1988, 1991, 1993, 1995), as a system composed of supply and demand (e.g. Mill and Morrison, 1985; Leiper, 1990; Wall and Mathieson, 2006), from a community perspective (e.g. Murphy, 1985; Murphy and Murphy, 2004), or from a market perspective (e.g. Hall, 2003).

As an utterly global phenomenon, tourism generates impacts of unprecedented proportions, including lucrative sources of revenue for a destination but also having major negative impacts on it (United Nations Educational, Scientific and Cultural Organization (UNESCO) office in Venice, n.d.). It transforms both the demand and the supply side, that is, it influences those practising tourism, as well as those offering tourism products and working in the tourism industry, not to mention its impact on the resources that are the basis of the entire industry. Growth of one party can, but does not necessarily, generate the growth of another, but, to the contrary, the more one grows, the more other(s) can be endangered. Likewise, the growth of tourism reflects on the sustainability and protection of both cultural and natural heritage.

*E-mail: ivana.stevic87@ua.pt

Tourism can impose different sets of changes on the host country and the local communities, such as environmental, social, cultural, economic, as well as joint sociocultural and socio-economic, political and moral (Mill, 1990; Archer and Cooper, 1998; Archer *et al.*, 2005; Cooper *et al.*, 2005, 2008), and these changes raise issues and consequences for both visitors and hosts. According to the UNESCO office in Venice (n.d.), each of these impacts can be reduced, if not fully eradicated, by undertaking different management and organizational measures that can be effective only if the impacts have previously been identified, measured and evaluated. In order for this to be done successfully, stakeholders cannot act separately, without collaboration and knowledge sharing between them. This is where networking comes into effect.

This study aims to understand the role of networks and partnerships in cultural tourism activities and dynamics, and to examine if they exist and in what form, in the particular case of the Historic Centre of Oporto, classified as a World Heritage Site by UNESCO. More specific objectives are: (i) to understand and discuss the importance of networking at the cultural tourism level; (ii) to identify if there is an official network of stakeholders involved in management, planning, organization, strategic decisions and protection of the site in focus, or merely collaboration between them; and (iii) to identify the main difficulties and challenges when it comes to management, preservation and protection of cultural heritage and sustainable tourism development at the site.

15.2   Literature Review

There is a growing body of tourism literature on the concept of networks and the importance of collaboration between the participants of the tourism system on different levels. Developing networks and partnerships within the tourism industry is a significant tool of meeting the challenges resulting from the constant changes on the global tourism market. The following sections discuss the importance of collaboration, cooperation and network relationships in tourism, for more successful tourism management, particularly when it comes to cultural tourism, protection of cultural heritage and sustainable tourism development.

15.2.1   Conceptualizing networks

The academic literature that uses networks as a theoretical framework for research focused on the social and political sciences, information studies, public administration, management, etc., has exploded in recent years (Berry *et al.*, 2004). Networks embracing public and private sectors have become of extreme importance for a successful functioning of individual businesses, but also of entire industries, with the tourism industry being no exception. Long-standing researches on science and society interactions emphasize the role of networks, partnerships and deliberative experiments in bringing governments, industries, educational institutions and civil society actors together (Torfing *et al.*, 2012).

The concept of networks is generally based on relationships between different entities – whether organizations or people – and the properties of networks relate to the structure of these relationships (Scott *et al.*, 2008). Among the most important elements that characterize the shape and behaviour of the physical and social world as we understand it, there are relationships and connections, with most parts of the natural and social sciences being essentially founded on the study of relationships (Baggio *et al.*, 2008). Networks were originally a metaphor for the complex interactions between people of a certain community, later on becoming formalized and related to mathematical theory and afterwards transferred into sociology (Scott *et al.*, 2008). Klijn and Koppenjan define them as '[…] more (or less) stable patterns of social relations between interdependent actors, which take shape around policy problems and/or policy programme' (as cited in Jordan and Schout, 2006, p.34).

The network theory emerged from the policy subsystems' theory, that is, the theory about different areas of public policy, with policy subsystems being powerful organizing perspectives, created in efforts to understand communicative conceptions of policy making (Dredge, 2003). This theory challenges the 'stagist' approach to policy making (Dredge, 2003), based on the assumption that there is a clear sequence of stages through which public policies proceed and which, therefore, constitute the policy process (Dorey, 2005). This approach, however, does not make a distinction between separate areas of public policy, or convey the extent to which different policies involve different actors and modes of interaction or influence, providing an inaccurate account of how policies are made, because it depicts policy making as a linear process with clearly defined stages (Dorey, 2005). Both policy making and planning are dynamic and recursive processes involving a multitude of business, government and community actors and agencies, this being the notion that the network theory is based on (Dredge, 2003).

Network theory recognizes that policy making occurs in open, flexible and fluid systems that span across public and private sectors, different branches and levels of government in federal systems, where 'networks of actors, committed to a particular set of ideas, constantly identify, discuss and negotiate policy issues and ideas with a view to influencing formal policy making structures and procedures' (Dredge, 2003, p. 359). In this context, networks can be observed as 'sets of relatively stable ongoing and non-hierarchical relations built up around certain policy issues or problems, where policy actors mobilize diverse resources for some shared common good' (Dredge, 2003, p. 359).

Networks can also be defined in the context of governance, as important forms of co-governance (Kooiman, 2003) or multi-organizational governance (Provan and Kenis, 2007), or simply one of the new forms of governance that unlocks the potential for economic growth and increased competitiveness of markets (Beaumont and Dredge, 2010). The advantages of network coordination in both the public and private sectors are manifold and extensive, including enhanced learning, more efficient use of resources, increased planning capacities and greater aptitude for addressing complex problems, better provision of services and, generally, greater competitiveness (Provan and Kenis, 2007).

According to Dredge (2003, p. 360), networks can be characterized by: (i) a variety of network participants that transcend organizational boundaries and structures; (ii) commitment to common objectives; (iii) non-hierarchical interaction, with no established or formal hierarchy of power or responsibility; (iv) pooling and mobilization of diverse resources to achieve the common objectives; (v) stability, where 'quasi-institutional' structures may develop over time; and (vi) the capacity to influence decision making through transfer of knowledge and ideas and through the use of power and influence, emphasizing that networks are not, however, decision-making bodies.

In the core of a successful networking practice lays concepts of collaboration and cooperation. Managing a good set of collaborative relationships is critical for the achievement of economic development objectives (Baggio, 2011a). Nordin (as cited in Baggio, 2011a) stresses the need for the development of collaboration and cooperation strategies, so as to gain a long-term competitive advantage. The strength of collaborative relationships is derived from the capacity of individuals and agencies to work not only conjointly but also individually towards achieving common goals, while still maintaining their individual intents and autonomy (Dredge, 2006); that is to say, only strong individuals can make a strong group. If the stakeholders are not successful in their individual conducts, they are not likely to be successful outside their autonomy, although acting with a group can enhance and improve their performance. Even at the individual level, the ability to establish and develop successful relationships with other companies is an important factor of success (Baggio, 2011a).

When it comes to tourism in particular, Dredge, Ford and Whitford (2010) suggest that collaboration provides important opportunities for maximizing the strength and synergy of the existing tourism planning, marketing and management activities, whereby the success and well-being of the whole overshadow individual interests. Additionally, collaboration represents an essential forerunner to the issue-based network approach to local tourism planning and management, which, if conducted effectively between local governments, can lead the decision-making process towards reflecting the interests of local communities and strengthening the local organizational capacity (Dredge *et al.*, 2010) – all of the former fully applying to the concept of cooperation, as well. All things considered, there is no 'one size fits all' model for local (government) collaboration, nor is there a prescribed solution for the development of issue-based networks; different models of collaboration reflect different particular issues, opportunities, resources and objectives that councils bring to the process (Dredge *et al.*, 2010, p. 124).

15.2.2   Tourism networks and partnerships

Tourism has always been a networked industry, characterized by fragmentation and geographical dispersion, with a pervasive set of business and personal relationships between actors, such as tourism intermediaries, accommodation facilities, transportation companies, food and beverage establishments, attractions, etc. (Scott *et al.*, 2008). There is a growing body of tourism literature on the concept of networks (Dredge, 2006; Scott *et al.*, 2008; Beaumont and Dredge, 2010) and the importance of collaboration between the participants of the tourism system at different levels (Hall, 1999; Bramwell and Lane, 2000; Morrison *et al.*, 2004; Lazzeretti and Petrillo, 2006; Baggio *et al.*, 2008; Cooper *et al.*, 2009; Dredge *et al.*, 2010; Presenza and Cipollina,

2010; Baggio, 2011a,b), putting the main focus on the tourism destination as an essential element to analyse in order to understand the tourism system as a whole (Baggio *et al.*, 2008).

In the tourism literature, the concepts of networks can be divided into two main streams of application that necessarily overlap (Presenza and Cipollina, 2010). First, networks are seen as 'a useful framework for analysing the evolution of business, product development, packaging and opportunities for further development', as argued by Tinsley and Lynch (as cited in Presenza and Cipollina, 2010, p. 17). Second, networks are understood as 'an important conduit for managing public–private relationships and understanding structures of tourism governance', as argued by Palmer, Pforr, and Tyler and Dinan (as cited in Presenza and Cipollina, 2010, p. 17). The first concept has the accent on the analysis, while the second one stresses the importance of management and understanding. Adding the presumption of information and knowledge possession by each stakeholder, as well as the dimensions of planning and innovation, networking can embody a powerful tool for long-term success, driven by the sustainable development of a tourism destination.

Today's global challenges are too immense for one organization to struggle individually (UNESCO office in Venice, n.d.), especially when it comes to small and medium-sized tourism enterprises (SMTE) that cannot survive harsh competition without strategically planning in advance and creating partnerships with different stakeholders Buhalis and Cooper, 1998). Breda *et al.* (2006) and Bieger (as cited in Presenza and Cipollina, 2011) argue that the interdependence between different actors of the tourism system enables these enterprises to diminish their size disadvantage. Subsequently, there is a pressing need for partnerships, bringing together international organizations, from both the public and private sectors, and joining them into networks, with special attention being paid to enhancing the effectiveness of international cultural cooperation on both global and country (local/regional) levels (UNESCO, n.d.).

Coordination, collaboration and cooperation within an industry are improved by shared knowledge and understanding (Organisation for Economic Co-operation and Development (OECD), 2012). Developing networks and partnerships within the tourism industry is a significant tool for meeting the challenges resulting from the constant changes on the global tourism market (Breda *et al.*, 2006). Cooperation and the formation of alliances among different actors, with the objective of improving competitiveness beyond the incidental effects that promote gathering, are considered the most important aspect of cluster functioning, according to Andersson *et al.* (2004) and Mishan (as cited in Baggio *et al.*, 2008). A tourism destination may be considered an example of one such cluster (Baggio *et al.*, 2008).

When it comes to sites classified as World Heritage Sites by UNESCO, strategic collaboration and partnership between the key actors is of crucial importance in addressing principal tourism policy and management issues, such as coordination between heritage management and tourism organizations, extending benefits to local communities, reducing tourism congestion and environmental impacts, increasing site financing and enhancing the interpretation and communication of heritage values through tourism (United Nations World Tourism Organization, n.d.).

Tourism is an increasingly important factor in the planning and management processes of UNESCO World Heritage Sites (Pedersen, 2002). Therefore, the development of tourism that is sustainable in economic, environmental, social and cultural terms, requiring involvement and collaboration between many actors, has been recommended repeatedly by researchers, argues Paskeleva-Shapira (as cited in Timur and Getz, 2008). According to the World Tourism Organization (as cited in Timur and Getz, 2008), there is a large body of literature on sustainable tourism development, but most of it has focused on natural protected areas, despite the fact that the majority of travel takes place in cities and urban areas, due to most of the world's population living in these areas.

There is a mutual dependence between tourism and cultural heritage. Heritage creates a basis for tourism growth, while tourism has the power to generate funds that make the conservation of cultural heritage possible. Consequently, developing strong public sector management capabilities and a multi-actor system of governance, including public–private partnerships and a greater horizontal and vertical coordination of relevant government bodies, has been marked as a priority in many of the world's economies (OECD, 2012).

15.3 Methodology

Choosing the approach to the research and the methods for conducting the research depends on the nature of the topic in the focus of the study. It is the result of predetermined objectives and research questions, formed hypothesis, the pertinence and pragmatism between the former and the problem stated, as well as the appropriateness of the researcher. In the case of a detailed study of opinions and attitudes and the perceptions of individuals regarding a certain topic, the most appropriate approach is the qualitative one, due to the possibility for the researcher to achieve a greater insight into and understanding of the problem (Cooper *et al.*, 2005, 2008).

Qualitative methods are more adaptable to dealing with multiple (and less aggregate) realities, because such methods expose more directly the nature of the transaction between the researcher and the respondent. Therefore, they make the assessment of the extent to which the phenomenon is described easier, in terms of the researcher's personal perspective, and, likewise, because they are more adaptable to the many mutually shaping influences and value patterns that may be encountered during the research (Lincoln and Guba, 1985). The research approach and methods chosen to base the study on were purely qualitative, guided by the constructivist paradigm. Qualitative methodology was considered the most fitting for achieving the pre-stated objectives and reaching certain conclusions on the topic.

After a thorough literature review on the topic, the necessary information was first collected from secondary data, consisting of legal documentation, official manuals, reports, strategic and management plans for the Historic Centre of Oporto (Portugal), and then sorted and analysed by means of content analysis. Primary data collection was completed through personal communication, that is, semi-structured and semi-formal interviews with the representatives of the entities in charge of strategic decisions and management of the site: (i) Porto VIVO SRU – *Sociedade de Reabilitação Urbana* (Society for Urban Rehabilitation); (ii) the Cultural Department of Oporto City Council; and (iii) the Tourism Department of Oporto City Council.

Findings and conclusions of the overall research were expressed in a descriptive way, with the writing style of the reporting being narrative.

15.4   Results

The study unveiled the existence of strong collaboration and cooperation between the parties of interest, although it was not possible to define an official network structure, but merely a network-like structure, due to there not being an officially assigned protocol between the entities. However, it was learned that even a network-like structure improved organization, management and functioning, not only of the tourism industry but also of the general prosperity of an area. It caused a superior level of productivity of each actor individually, due to constant information and knowledge sharing. From examination of the literature on network structures, they are regarded as the most optimal form of governance when it comes to governing composite and multifaceted areas such as those classified as World Heritage Sites, as is the case of the Historic Centre of Oporto. The existing governance and management structure of the site is just as successful in meeting the challenges as if it was defined as an official network structure.

As emphasized by Pedersen (2002), the process of developing a management plan can encourage the participation of stakeholders, but only with the purpose and approach of identifying what is needed from the public, and what a site can offer them in return, and not merely releasing a draft management plan for public comment. These were the principles that led the Porto VIVO SRU to develop the Management Plan for the Historic Centre of Oporto World Heritage, declaring that it aimed to satisfy various groups of actors, including: (i) residents; (ii) visitors; (iii) employees; (iv) investors; (v) the Oporto City Council, responsible for the major part of the Historic Centre; (vi) the Portuguese State, which is the signatory of the convention; and (vii) UNESCO, the final recipient of the Management Plan.

The tourism industry is one of the principal drivers of economic development of the city of Oporto, making its successful management imperative for ensuring the balance between the impacts generated by the tourism industry, the undisturbed life of the local community and spatial harmony. The complexity of issues and interests, however, which form the basis of tourism policy making, complicates the matter. Therefore, the process of planning needs to be in accordance with the interests of all parties involved, not forgetting the environmental aspects, and keeping in mind that successful planning leads to the successful application of public policy.

When it comes to the question of the sustainable development of tourism, and cultural tourism in particular, it is included in the key strategic areas within the action plan for the Historic Centre of Oporto. It includes the efforts of preserving, conserving and restoring the heritage of the site; maintaining, enhancing and improving the public spaces; raising awareness and educating the local community on the importance of the Historic Centre; involving both public and private actors in the activities related to the site; improving tourism activities and incentivizing the creation of new places of interest; encouraging creative industries, entrepreneurship, knowledge sharing and technological development; and improving the activities related to the Douro River.

As regards the assurance of the long-term sustainable development of the area, the biggest challenge is how to control tourism without affecting the community in economic terms. It has become problematic to attract the rapidly decreasing population and to increase the occupancy of the buildings, improve access for vehicles and increase energy efficiency, which, in most cases, is inconsistent with the policies of heritage protection, which include many constraints in this aspect.

15.5   Conclusion

Networking enhances collaboration, cooperation and joint action between various stakeholders, and joint action leads to knowledge sharing, greater efforts and greater engagement in the fulfilment of objectives, due to them being collective and not particular. Collaboration and cooperation between the network actors increase the information flow and, again, the knowledge sharing between the stakeholders, enhancing awareness on the importance of sustainability between the actors, who further communicate the importance to individuals outside the network.

Even network-like structures improve the organization, management and functioning of both the tourism industry and the area where tourism is practised. They can be just as successful in meeting the organizational, management and planning challenges as if they were defined as official network structures, with duly assigned protocols between the actors. Joint action increases productivity, due to a greater deal of responsibility and commitment held by each stakeholder, leading to a more ethical and conscientious governance, organization and management of World Heritage Sites.

Based on the particular case of Oporto, which was discussed in this study, it can be said that the impacts affecting the enduring success and development of World Heritage Sites are inevitable in today's globalized world. They would be encountered independently by the management and organization structures, due to the complexity of these sites, as well as the socio-economic and political factors that generally dominate in this type of area. Meeting the challenges brought by modern times is almost inevitably inconsistent with the policies of heritage protection. Therefore, the biggest challenge of all is to try to reconcile the old with the new by accepting the fact that changes are inevitable, but embracing these changes through a professional, ethical and conscientious management, ensuring long-term sustainability.

References

Archer, B. and Cooper, C. (1998) The positive and negative impacts of tourism. In: Theobald, W.F. (ed.) *Global Tourism*, 2nd edn. Butterworth-Heinemann, Oxford, UK, pp. 63–81.

Archer, B., Cooper, C. and Ruhanen, L. (2005) The positive and negative impacts of tourism. In: Theobald, W.F. (ed.) *Global Tourism*, 3rd edn. Elsevier Inc, Burlington, Massachusetts, pp. 79–102.

Baggio, R. (2011a) Networks and tourism: the effect of structures and the issues of collaboration. In: Bachinger, M., Pechlaner, H. and Widuckel, W. (eds) *Regionen und netzwerke: Kooperationsmodelle zur förderung von branchenübergreifender kompetenzentwicklung.* Gabler-Springer, Wiesbaden, Germany, pp. 47–62.

Baggio, R. (2011b) Collaboration and cooperation in a tourism destination: a network science approach. *Current Issues in Tourism* 14(2), 183–189.

Baggio, R., Scott, N. and Cooper, C. (2008) Network science and socio-economic systems: a review focused on a tourism destination. Dondena Working Paper No 7. Carlo F. Dondena Centre for Research on Social Dynamics, Bocconi University, Milan, Italy.

Beaumont, N. and Dredge, D. (2010) Local tourism governance: a comparison of three network approaches. *Journal of Sustainable Tourism* 18(1), 7–28.

Berry, F.S., Brower, R.S., Choi, S.O., Goa, W.X., Jang, H., *et al.* (2004) Three traditions of network research: what the public management research agenda can learn from other research communities. *Public Administration Review* 64(5), 539–552.

Bramwell, B. and Lane, B. (2000) *Tourism Collaboration and Partnerships: Politics Practice and Sustainability.* Channel View Publications, Clevedon, UK.

Breda, Z., Costa, R. and Costa, C. (2006) Do clusters and networks make small places beautiful? The case of Caramulo (Portugal). In: Lazzeretti, L. and Petrillo, C. (eds) *Tourism Local Systems and Networking.* Elsevier, Oxford, UK, pp. 67–82.

Buhalis, D. and Cooper, C. (1998) Competition or co-operation: SMTE at the destination. In: Laws, E., Faulkner, B. and Moscardo, G. (eds) *Embracing and Managing Change in Tourism.* Routledge, London, pp. 324–346.

Cooper, C., Fletcher, J., Fyall, A., Gilbert, D. and Wanhill, S. (2005). *Tourism: Principles and Practice,* 3rd edn. Pearson Education Limited, Harlow, UK.

Cooper, C., Fletcher, J., Fyall, A., Gilbert, D. and Wanhill, S. (2008) *Tourism: Principles and Practice* 4th edn. Pearson Education Limited, Harlow, UK.

Cooper, C., Scott, N. and Baggio, R. (2009) Network position and perceptions of destination stakeholder importance. *Anatolia: An International Journal of Tourism and Hospitality Research* 20(1), 33–45.

Dorey, P. (2005) *Policy Making in Britain: An Introduction.* Sage, London.

Dredge, D. (2003) Networks, local governance and tourism policy: local tourism associations under the microscope. In: Braithwaite, R.L. and Braithwaite, R.W. (eds) *CAUTHE 2003: Riding the Wave of Tourism and Hospitality Research.* Southern Cross University, Lismore, New South Wales, Australia, pp. 359–374.

Dredge, D. (2006) Networks, conflict and collaborative communities. *Journal of Sustainable Tourism* 14(6), 562–582.

Dredge, D., Ford, E.J. and Whitford, M. (2010) The managing local tourism master class: communicating and building sustainable tourism management practices across local government divides. Paper presented at BEST EN Think Tank X: Networking for Sustainable Tourism, MODUL University, Vienna, 27–30 June 2010. Available at: http://3ws1wk1wkqsk36zmd6ocne81.wpengine.netdna-cdn.com/files/2012/09/3111_Dredge-Ford-Whitford.pdf (accessed 26 November 2014).

Eurostat, Organisation for Economic Co-operation and Development, United Nations, and World Tourism Organization (2001) Tourism Satellite Account: Recommended Methodological Framework. Available at: http://unstats.un.org/unsd/publication/SeriesF/SeriesF_80e.pdf (accessed 29 November 2014).

Frechtling, D.C. (2001) *Forecasting Tourism Demand: Methods and Strategies.* Butterworth-Heinemann, Oxford, UK.

Hall, C. (1999) Rethinking collaboration and partnership: a public policy perspective. *Journal of Sustainable Tourism* 7, 274–289.

Hall, C.M. (2003) *Introduction to Tourism: Dimensions and Issues,* 4th edn. Hospitality Press, Frenchs Forest, NSW, Australia.

Jordan, A. and Schout, A. (2006) *The Coordination of the European Union: Exploring the Capacities of Networked Governance.* Oxford University Press, New York.

Kooiman, J. (2003) *Governing as Governance.* Sage, London.

Lazzeretti, L. and Petrillo, C.S. (eds) (2006) *Tourism Local Systems and Networks.* Advances in Tourism Research Series. Elsevier, Oxford, UK.

Leiper, N. (1990) Tourist attraction systems. *Annals of Tourism Research* 17(3), 367–384.

Lincoln, Y.S. and Guba, E.G. (1985) *Naturalistic Inquiry*. Sage, Newbury Park, California.

Mill, R.C. (1990) *Tourism: The International Business*. Prentice-Hall, Englewood Cliffs, New Jersey.

Mill, R.C. and Morrison, A.M. (1985) *The Tourism System: An Introductory Text*. Prentice-Hall, New Jersey.

Morrison, A., Lynch, P.E. and Johns, N. (2004) International tourism networks. *International Journal of Contemporary Hospitality Management* 16, 197–202.

Murphy, P.E. (1985) *Tourism: A Community Approach*. Routledge, Oxon, UK.

Murphy, P.E. and Murphy, A.E. (2004) *Strategic Management for Tourism Communities: Bridging the Gaps*. Channel View Publications, Clevedon, UK.

Organisation for Economic Co-operation and Development (OECD) (2012) OECD Tourism Trends and Policies 2012. OECD Publishing, Paris. Available at: http://tiaontario.ca/uploads/2012%20-%20Tourism%20Trends%20and%20Policies.pdf (accessed 15 November 2014).

Pedersen, A. (2002) *Managing Tourism at World Heritage Sites: A Practical Manual for World Heritage Site Managers*. UNESCO World Heritage Centre, Paris.

Presenza, A. and Cipollina, M. (2010) Analysing tourism stakeholders networks. *Tourism Review* 65(4), 17–30.

Provan, K.G. and Kenis, P. (2007) Modes of network governance: structure, management, and effectiveness. *Journal of Public Administration Research and Theory* 18(2), 229–252.

Scott, N., Baggio, R. and Cooper, C. (2008) *Network Analysis and Tourism: From Theory to Practice*. Channel View Publications, Clevedon, UK.

Smith, S.L.J. (1988) Defining tourism: a supply-side view. *Annals of Tourism Research* 15(2), 179–190.

Smith, S.L.J. (1991) The supply side definition of tourism: reply to Leiper. *Annals of Tourism Research* 18, 312–318.

Smith, S.L.J. (1993) Return to the supply-side. *Annals of Tourism Research* 20(2), 226–229.

Smith, S.L.J. (1995) *Tourism Analysis: A Handbook*. Longman, New York.

Timur, S. and Getz, D. (2008) A network perspective on managing stakeholders for sustainable urban tourism. *International Journal of Contemporary Hospitality Management* 20(4), 445–461.

Torfing, J., Peters, B.G., Pierre, J. and Sørensen, E. (2012) *Interactive Governance: Advancing the Paradigm*. Oxford University Press Inc, New York.

United Nations Educational, Scientific and Cultural Organization (UNESCO) (nd.) Partners. Available at: http://www.unesco.org/new/en/culture/communities/partners/ (accessed 13 November 2014).

UNESCO Office in Venice (n.d.) *Sustainable Tourism Development in UNESCO Designated Sites in South-Eastern Europe*. Available at: http://portal.unesco.org/en/files/45338/12417872579Introduction_Sustainable_Tourism.pdf/Introduction_Sustainable_Tourism.pdf (accessed 17 November 2014).

United Nations World Tourism Organization (n.d.) Cultural heritage. Available at: http://sdt.unwto.org/en/content/cultural-heritage-1 (accessed 15 November 2014).

Wall, G. and Mathieson, A. (2006) *Tourism: Change, Impacts, and Opportunities*. Pearson Education Limited, Harlow, UK.

16 Facing the Challenges of Sustainability: The Case of Bulgarian Tourism

MARIYA STANKOVA*

South-West University 'Neofit Rilski', Blagoevgrad, Bulgaria

16.1   Introduction

Bulgaria is a country with beautiful and fascinating nature, ancient cultural and historical heritage left by old-world civilizations, and magical music, dances and rituals. In all their diversity, those resources provide various combinations for the tourist offerings. Tourism development in Bulgaria dates back to the pre-World War II period, but gained momentum after the war (Ivanov and Dimitrova, 2013). Over the years, Bulgaria has been a holiday destination for the former Soviet bloc (Madanoglu, 2012), but after its collapse and during the transition period (after 1989) it faced the challenge of finding the right path of development. Today, tourism, as one of the leading industries in the Bulgarian economy, is characterized by dynamic development and high rates of growth, clearly expressed since 2000. Its contribution to the growth of the gross domestic product (GDP) is indisputable, and this makes it an efficient tool of social economic growth, as is apparent from the statistical indicators of the Bulgarian National Statistical Institute (NSI) (2015). The merits for its development could be attributed to a large extent to private entrepreneurs. Nowadays, over 99% of tourism accommodation is private or shareholders' property. Another factor influencing tourism favourably is the increasing interest of Bulgaria to foreign investors. The big hotel, restaurant and tour operator chains and companies are beginning to expand into the country and contribute to its active inclusion in the process of globalization of the tourism industry.

Indeed, tourism development over the recent years has affected other industries of the national economy positively, too, like construction, agriculture, food, the wine and tobacco industries, transport, etc. And, at the same time, tourism is among the industries of the national economy that are expected to recover quickly from the 2008 economic crisis and to report sustainable development. Considering that, this paper

*E-mail: mzlstan@yahoo.com

investigates the possibilities of, and the best approaches to, developing Bulgarian tourism in a sustainable manner. The total concept also implies the establishment of conditions to increase Bulgaria's competitiveness as a tourism destination, in order to achieve economic growth through tourism, aimed at improving the quality of life in Bulgaria and preserving its natural and cultural heritage for the future (Marinov, 2008). Vagionis (2002) underlines that, nowadays, Bulgaria is a country that can be considered as having completed the 'transition period' to the free market economy and is now part of the European Union (EU), and so has access to the EU's support structures and funds. In these conditions, reconsideration of the concept of Bulgaria's sustainable tourism development discloses new dimensions and directs research to different issues and key players. And, since tourism has hands-on contact in key areas such as employment, regional development, finances, transportation, taxation, education, new technologies, etc., the vision for its sustainable and competitive development should embrace the idea of forming a sustainable tourism industry, based on clear, detailed and economically practical strategies.

16.2   Literature Review

Sustainability and its principles refer to the environmental, economic and social aspects of the development of tourism, in which a proper balance of the three divisions is to be achieved. In this way, sustainability is guaranteed on a long-term basis. Hence, sustainable tourism should: (i) optimize the use of natural resources, which are key elements of tourism development, by saving major ecological processes and protecting the natural heritage and biological diversity; (ii) respect the social cultural authenticity of the hosting community, preserving its cultural heritage and traditional values, and thus contributing to intercultural understanding and tolerance; (iii) provide reliable, long-term and fairly divided economic activities ensuring social economic benefits for all interested parties, including a steady employment rate and opportunities for income and social services of the hosting community, and thus contributing to the reduction of poverty. According to the opinions of several specialists, a determined attitude and increased attention to the approach to sustainable development on a global scale demands specific actions from the tourism industry with regard to the critical condition of the environment (Kamenov *et al.*, 1996). These can be achieved only through purposefulness and coordination of the actions of all engaged parties. For that purpose, actions with regard to travel supply and consumption should be avoided if there are any doubts that tourism activity could cause irreversible damage or lack of balance between the components: economic effect, social effect and environment (Kamenov *et al.*, 1996).

In tourism, the implementation of theoretical formulations of sustainable development provides the succession of the economic activities put in place and establishes prerequisites for achieving positive results, while at the same time ensuring that the environment in which they are implemented is not destroyed. In that regard, four different conceptual approaches can be used, as presented in Table 16.1. The choice and application of each of them are subjected to the general concept of sustainable tourism development in adherence with the idea of the coordination and mutual subordination of the economic, social, ecological and cultural aspects of development,

Table 16.1. Approaches to the implementation of sustainable development principles. (From Kamenov *et al.*, 1996.)

Systematic approach or determining the source of the problem, analysis and synthesis of the influence on the environment and social development, and undertaking counteractions to eliminate or reduce the negative influence.	Interdisciplinary approach or applying the knowledge of various subjects allows a greater thoroughness in the implementation of principles.
Cooperative approach or integrated application of principles.	Critical approach or confrontation to proposals.

as well as of the harmoniousness of the natural and reproduced components of the tourism product, of the preservation of the cultural and natural heritage, of overcoming any discrepancies in and achievement of social equality in the hosting community, and of stimulating the civil initiatives and partnerships at all levels engaged in the planning and development of tourism.

The search for and achievement of a balance between the three major aspects of development – economic, sociocultural and environmental – underlies the concept of sustainable development (McKercher, 1993). To maintain a balance between these processes, which, in essence, go in different directions, requires the establishment of partnerships between those in business circles, the natural environment and the local communities connected with urbanization and globalization. The pressure exercised by these two key processes of modern society influences the role of relationships within the community. Mainly negative changes are observed in established economic, social and cultural relationships, in the contacts between governmental and local structures, the private sector, non-governmental organizations and even in neighbour and family relationships. To a great extent, this is due to the deficiency of financial and natural resources, to legal restrictions, to the re-evaluation of values and social norms, as well as to the increased demographic pressure (Peattie and Montinho, 2000).

The manifestation of the processes described has a certain connection with tourism and its development as a priority industry of the global economy. In the search for new ways of sustainable development over recent years, prerequisites have occurred for the general reorientation of existing tourism policies and strategic approaches to implementation. A very strong trend has been presented in the policies implemented by the World Tourism Organization (UNWTO) and the EU, aiming to overcome the economic backwardness of certain regions and to solve the social, cultural and environmental conflicts that currently exist. Sustainable tourism development, however, can be achieved only as a result of a well-considered summary of purposeful actions. In that sense, clarification of the problems studied with regard to the travel destination can be structured in a three-stage process of strategic approaches.

16.2.1 Conceptualization of sustainability: terminological clarification

A study of the rich literature on sustainability clearly shows that there are many publications focused on the issues of sustainable development and overcoming accumulated economic, social and political problems. However, a significant part of the literature is focused on private issues, and that referring to tourism and the tourism industry is still on the periphery of scholarly interest. The category conditionally marked as first studies the processes of globalization and the consequences of its occurrence with regard to economic and social life (Bauman, cited in Cunha, 2009). These processes of globalization are related mainly to the deregulation of the economy during the second half of the 20th century and to the weakening of the national sovereignty of countries. This is regulated by EU Directive 2004/35 of 21 April 2004 (European Union, 2004) on environmental liability regarding the prevention of and compensation for environmental damage, as well as by the law on liability for the prevention and removal of environmental damage (refer to the Bulgarian Official State Gazette No 43 from April 2008). The second category is still under consideration, scientific discussion and theoretical interpretation. In general, this category covers the restrictions on the uses of environmental and natural resources, which modern human society has aggravated over the last decades of the past century. Manifestation of this category is determined by globalization and the impact of market factors. But at the same time, its establishment, forecasting and management are directly related to sustainable development. This statement is supported by reports from the Club of Rome, in which, even in the middle of the 20th century, opinions were expressed on the negative trends expected with regard to world economic growth (Meadows *et al.*, 1972).

Trying to achieve objectivity, it should be mentioned that many of the forecasts made years ago have already become a reality. And countries will have to face this in their development. The threats to their social economic development, and to the development of humankind in general, have increased rapidly. These threats were discovered and brought to the attention of the general public early as 1992, in Rio de Janeiro, at the remarkable UN conference on development and the environment. With the preparation and announcement of Agenda 21, environmental, resource and social political restrictions and threats to the development of humankind were defined and specific decisions were made to limit them and bring them under control. The general outlines of the concept of sustainable development were approved, too. Today's reality, however, depicts a world that has not progressed to sustainable development yet, but has become even less sustainable and subject to procrastination. The withdrawal of state regulation of the economy, which has become a worldwide trend, does not contribute to the solution of natural resource and economic problems. More and more frequently, leading specialists recommend in their analyses the replacement of market 'self-regulation' mechanisms, which have been unable to overcome the environmental crisis by serious regulation and financial state support (EU Directive 2010/30).

It is obvious that a variety of positions and viewpoints occur in the interpretation of sustainability and sustainable development. But it should be recognized, however, that this clash clears out those manifestations that are apparently both balanced and oriented towards the three time dimensions: past, present and future. In the conceptual frame of the studied issue, it is essential that the literature used encompasses international and Bulgarian authors, articles and gathered feedback; analytic information from the Bulgarian National Statistical Institute should also be used. Reflections on the topic also take into account the Scottish Executive Social Research report, expressing the existence of two key conceptual approaches to sustainability

(Scottish Executive Social Research, 2006): 'Strong sustainability (or a planet over people approach); and weak sustainability (essentially a willingness to pay approach)'.

According to the World Tourism Organization (UNEP and UNWTO, 2005), *sustainable tourism* brings together the management of all the resources in a manner that satisfies economic, social and aesthetical needs with preserved cultural integrity, fundamental environmental processes, biologic diversity and life maintenance systems. As a part of the definition of sustainability, sustainable tourism can be described also as a process that meets the needs of particular tourists and the hosting community, protecting and improving their needs in the future. Sustainable tourism should also maintain a high level of tourist satisfaction and ensure a meaningful experience to tourists, raising their awareness of sustainability issues and promoting such tourism practices among them (UNEP and UNWTO, 2005).

16.3   Methodology

Research on the challenges in the sustainability of Bulgarian tourism, within the theoretic aspects, implies investigation of the history of Bulgarian tourism, as well as identifying the current situation, and examines the challenges facing sustainable tourism development. The cluster approach is applied to a specific Bulgarian tourism destination, assuming that the usual unit of analysis is the destination (Plog, 1974; Cho, cited in Jafari, 2000). In this framework, clusters are looked at as a conception and organization form of association of business structures and establishments, as well as specific networks of mutually connected, but still remaining competitors on the market, companies, specialized suppliers, firms and organizations providing services and the related administrative authorities and non-governmental institutions within a particular area/region (Ministry of Economics of Bulgaria, 2004). Some other points of view are taken into account, such as that of Zakova (2007), expanding that a cluster could also be considered as an original self-organizing production system within which the companies cooperate in vertical or horizontal 'chains' in order to gain extra added value and to improve their competitive powers. Thus, created formation combine groups of various sectors/branches that have a certain previous experience in mutual cooperation as horizontal clusters (companies at the same level of production and marketing) or as vertical clusters (companies at consecutive levels of production and marketing).

Taking this formulation as an initial one, it is important to mention that with the establishment of a cluster, an effective interaction between the uniting parties is achieved with regard to innovations, design, quality, product development and marketing. The formation of a cluster brings a significant reduction in expenses for the members of the network, and as a form of business cooperation it becomes a stimulus for the development of assets, technologies, infrastructure and joint investments – effects that could not be achieved by one organization alone (Zakova, 2007). In addition, the methodological background is provided by the use of inductive reasoning as the main method of research, assuming that each study can be viewed as a series of inferences leading to new knowledge. In this case, referring to judgements that follow from other, already accepted as true, propositions relevant to the problem discussed.

16.4   Results

In the 1980s, Bulgaria was developed successfully as a tourism destination and, according to the assessments of foreign as well as local authors, was comparable with the tourism of already developed destinations like Spain, Greece or Croatia (Mintel International Group Ltd, 2007). The quantitative summit in the development of tourism was reached at the end of the 1980s. In 1988, the places offering lodging had at their disposal around 600,000 bedrooms and sleeping accommodation; the country was visited by 8.3 million foreigners and realized roughly 60 million overnight stays overall (one-third of whom were foreigners). There were around 150,000 people employed by the tourism industry (one-third of them annually), and income was evaluated at more than US$360 million (National Statistical Institute, n.d.). Typical peculiarities for Bulgarian tourism during the socialist period were the unbalanced productive structure (sea holidays predominate), manifested special conception, which included many tourist resorts that isolated tourists from the local environment, high seasons and undeveloped tourist infrastructure. Furthermore, the orientation of the East European market, in combination with highly developed social tourism, reflected on service equipment standards and price level, helping to form a preference for organized and particularly group tourism (international and internal), projecting an image of a cheap destination. Concerning mass tourism, there was inadequate resource usage for effective development of tourism as 'export of place' (limited part of the additional tourist services expenses). Property belonged to the state, and the tourism sector management was strongly centralized; but in spite of all this, there was a manifestation of departmental approaches and conflicts. At the same time, there was a system for tourism development planning (including specialized institutes and groups), but quite a few of the plans' recommendations (especially from an environmental protection point of view) were not preserved (Stankova, 2003). The whole development of tourism is motivated ideologically and economically, and there is very often conflict among goals. Most of the limits to the sustainable development of tourism existing nowadays were revealed in the period to 1990, but resolve will be strengthened during the next few years.

After 1990, tourism development was characterized with the following, more important tendencies: the industry reached a crisis, due to external changes (a change in market conditions, the conflicts in the Persian Gulf and former Yugoslavia), as well as to inner factors: 'decomposition' of the existing ruling system, lack of distinct plans for the industry's adaptation to the new conditions, abrupt worsening of living standards, high prices and currency dynamics, instability of internal policy, the interference of corporate interests, and the entry of many new people with professional experience in the industry. For the period between 1988 and 1996, the registered overnight stays decreased from 62.3 to 16.4 million, or 3.8 times (foreigners decreased 3.4 times and Bulgarians 4.1 times) (National Statistical Institute, n.d.) (Table 16.2).

After the drastic downturn reported in 1991 (2.2 times compared to 1990), a hesitant growth in foreign visitor accommodation can be noticed, and a reversal in the decrease in Bulgarian overnight stays. Tourism was slow to suffer from the economic and social crisis during the years of change (after 1989), and appears to be escaping it faster in comparison with other sectors. Regardless of the unfavourable tendencies, the Bulgarian tourism industry turned out to be sturdy and less pliable to

Table 16.2. International tourism in Bulgaria, 1980–1996. (From National Statistical Institute (Bulgaria) and Bulgarian National Bank data.)

Year	Number of foreign tourists without transit (million)	Number of foreign tourists with overnight stays (million)	Number of overnight stays of foreign tourists (million)
1980	2.9	2.7	16.0
1985	3.6	2.8	18.0
1990	4.5	2.1	12.7
1991	4.0	0.7	4.7
1992	3.8	1.0	5.6
1993	3.8	1.1	7.5
1994	4.0	1.0	6.4
1995	3.5	0.8	5.4
1996	2.8	0.8	5.9

the unfavourable external factors, and confirms the maxim that the 'tourist industry succeeds in crisis periods and flourishes in periods of progress'. A great part of the inherited disproportions and problems went deeper – unbalanced use of the tourist resource potential, homogeneous product, special-time conception, low equipment and services standards, unprofessional management, and others. There is a serious change in the approach towards tourism management – on the level of enterprise and from the tourism policy aspect (above firm) – stipulated by the common approach towards market economics, the decentralization of state property administration, the fast development of private tourism enterprises (due to considerably small investments in tour operator and agent activity, high and often unjustified expectations for the success of hotel and restaurant activities, lack of other opportunities for economic activity and incomes) and privatization. Changes in the property structure created a fragmentary structure of the tourism industry, which was typical for countries with market economics, where small and average-size businesses dominated. This process was conditioned by the formation of many new private companies until 1996. According to some assessments, the entire number of real, functioning private companies was round 5000. More than 1000 new private hotels offered more than 15,000 bedrooms. In 1996, 14–15% of hotels' turnover fell into the private sector, as did 24% of the turnover of the nutrition, trade and the amusement businesses. With the acceleration of privatization during 1997–1998, privatized building sites reached 99.9% after 2007. Separately, private companies became a major factor in tourism; it is hard to speak of the presence of national and local tourist policy until 1996. Several attempts have been made to develop tourism law, but most projects are inadequate in view of the conditions nowadays. The national tourist policy is typically pragmatic (reacting to concrete problems without specific proposals); an institutional basis, which is typical for countries with market economics and for a great number of companies in the tourism industry, is missing (this basis should provide, as well as tourism, interaction with other economical and non-profitable activities on a national, regional and local level, as well as interaction of the public sector with the private sector); the instruments are extremely limited (the supply control system is falling apart, marketing and destinations are becoming extremely limited, etc.). Tourism management on the part of the authorities is reduced to state property administration (with a strong accent on almost permanent changes of enterprise management).

Changes to the tourism policy can be noticed in 1996, but especially during 1997. The basic tendencies are connected with: a change towards conceptual policy (working out of national conception, attempts for strategic planning on a local level); shifting of the state administration burden from direct property administration towards questions that concern regulation, and paying much attention to private, including small, businesses (this process is conditioned to a great extent by accelerated privatization); the initiation of and encouragement for local tourist organizations to form part of the state organ in tourism; legislative regulation of the norms and conditions concerning economic tourist activity and the institutional base of the tourist policy by the tourism law (approved by the Parliament on the first reading); specifying stable financial sources, concerning tourist policy on a local and national level (funds for tourism development); regularization presupposes local conditions and views, including further assignation of serious responsibilities concerning the involvement of local authorities in the development of tourism. The tendencies pointed out give reason to expect an end to the existing model of tourism development and to search for new alternatives with regards to products, and then markets, and a new tourism policy model incorporating sustainable tourism.

A significant growth in tourism (up by 15%) was recorded for Bulgaria during 2000–2004, while world growth was between 3% and 5%/year. This growth, albeit at a slower rate, has been maintained in the years following, from 2009 to 2013 (Table 16.3). And, today, it is a fact that tourism is one of the major industries with a large contribution to the foreign currency revenue of Bulgaria.

16.4.1 Modelling capabilities of sustainable development

From the point of view of sustainable development, the concept for a national tourism policy was developed in 1996, as well as the governmental programme, 'Bulgaria 2001'. From the 1990s, a set of specialized non-governmental organizations have emerged whose base activity involves aspects of tourism sustainable development and the search for mass tourism alternatives (Bulgarian Association for Agricultural and Ecological Tourism, Bulgarian Association for Alternative Tourism, the 'Blue Flag' movement, and others). Unspecialized departments, engaged very actively with the

Table 16.3. Arrivals of foreign citizens to Bulgaria 2009–2013. (Adapted according to data from the National Statistical Institute, 2014, and the Bulgarian Industrial Association and Union of the Bulgarian Business, 2013.)

Year	2009	2010	2010/ 2009 (%)	2011	2011/ 2010 (%)	2012	2012/ 2011 (%)	2013	2013/ 2012 (%)
Total	7,872,805	8,374,034	6.4	8,712,821	4	8,866,552	1.8	9,191,782	3.7

problems of tourism (in its alternative forms), are the Ministry of Environment (eco-tourism, tourist utilization of protected territories), Ministry of Agriculture (country tourism), Ministry of Culture (cultural tourism), Ministry of Public Health (development and protection of resorts and their resources), Ministry of Regional Development and Public Works (tourism as a factor of local and regional development and urbanization of territories, with manifested tourist functions, especially the Black Sea coast). Some specialized tour operators have appeared, although not in great numbers, offering extremely alternative opportunities for tourist travel and encouraging local activities directed towards sustainable development (State Agency for Tourism, 2009). In the first half of 2014, a new Strategy for Sustainable Development of Tourism in Bulgaria for the period 2014–2030 was adopted. It systematizes the vision, strategic objectives, priorities and activities that are to lead to the establishment of sustainable schemes for the development and management of tourism activities in the destination (Strategy for Sustainable Development of Tourism in Bulgaria 2014–2030; Ministry of Economics and Energy, 2014). Given that the newly adopted strategy aims to provide the ongoing competitiveness of Bulgaria as a tourism destination, management efforts should be directed towards investigation of the challenges facing sustainable tourism development. A good opportunity in this direction can certainly be found in the implementation of the cluster approach, applied in this case to illustrate specific Bulgarian tourism destinations. Following the conceptual tourism chain, a base model of tourism destination management (Stankova, 2009) can be developed in the format of a public–private partnership. A structural plan follows the sequence shown in Fig. 16.1.

The major objective of the model presented is to provide the sustainability of the product produced by the tourism companies and the interim chain of organizations on the basis of the resource potential available within the territory. To implement this, a decomposition of task by major directions will be carried out, namely – supply (offering), coordination of offers (performance of offers), market research, structuring the marketing and price strategy, tourist attendance. The proactive approach (Tribe, 1995; Cooper et al., 2013) is to be applied as a leading concept in order to secure the maximum efficiency of management.

Implementation of the partnership formed on the principle setting of the cluster approach can be positioned in south-west Bulgaria, based on the ski tourism destination of Borovets, in the Rila Mountains. It is conveniently located and has good prospects, due to a series of prerequisites. On an international scale, the resort is known to the European ski and biathlon federations, it is popular among winter sports fans in a number of Bulgarian traditional markets like the British, German, Russian, Scandinavian markets, etc. Based on its closeness to the countries from which considerable tourist flows originate, as well as on the convenient transport links abroad, its geographical position is assessed as favourable for developing both domestic and, more attractive, international tourism. The superstructure available and the relatively good infrastructure secure the partnership strategy and reveal great choice options (Filipova, 2010).

The model introduces cooperation between tour operator and hotels. It consists of cooperation to increase the degree of occupancy of the best hotel/s, to attract customers by encouraging loyalty and inducing the desire to repeat purchase due to the staff's personal and professional approach and from verbal recommendations. At the same time, the tour operator undertakes to add new elements to the product,

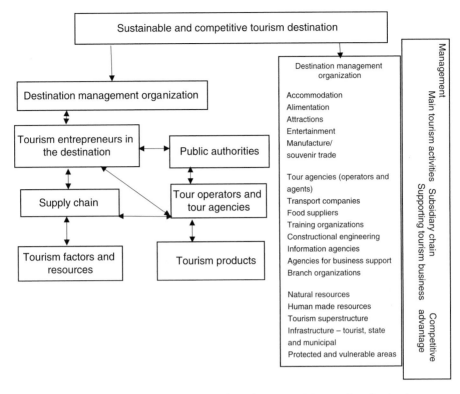

Fig. 16.1. Model of public–private partnerships for competitive tourism destination management. (From author's own elaboration.)

increasing its usefulness and improving the qualitative parameters of the existing product. One part of the scheme is the tour operator's participation in publicity campaigns, with the obligation to present the attractions of staying in a mature destination, based on consumer attitudes (Kozak, 2001).

16.5   Conclusion

From a theoretical point of view, tourists have some general notion of the product purchased at which their appraisal of the weight of the separate component – the hotel, for example – within the whole of the 'travel package' is rendered difficult (Stankova and Rizova, 2012). The 'feeling' about these elements can, to a certain extent, be intensified through placing the focus on other parameters such as the attractiveness of the destination or the type of transport vehicle. Therefore, regardless of the efforts exerted by the hotel staff to satisfy the guests, if the other components comprising the core of the tourism product fail to achieve the same level, total satisfaction will be incomplete. This reconfirms the old rule – the quality chain has the strength equal to that of its weakest link.

In tourism, the concept of quality should be considered as an issue of exceptional importance for sustainable development. In the situation of the modern tourism market and the frantic competitive struggle for the creation of a unique product and experiences, sustainability is a necessary condition, but also a competitive advantage. Achieving the competitive edge in the context of sustainability requires the balance of all the individual elements, both with regard to destination and tourist companies, as well as in relation to tourists consuming the tourism product offered. In the hypothetical example discussed, the problem is to guarantee an equivalently high quality of the product as a whole if supplied separately by different business entities. The solution consists, to a large extent, of the sustainable combination of the concept of quality with the cluster approach and the processes of integration. To a certain degree, the model presented, orientated primarily to the improvement of sustainability, would contribute towards increasing trust in the Bulgarian tourism product, both abroad and in the country. In the not too distant future, the partners who have adopted such a policy inevitably will offer a product of better quality. The resources invested by them in the partnership will improve the standard and style of the service they provide.

Acknowledgements

The research and findings drawn were presented to experts from the Rila National Park in connection with the preparation of strategic documents concerning the sustainable management of the protected area, due primarily to the need to establish the effectiveness of the solutions proposed for the Borovets resort, located in close proximity to the national park. In this regard, the vital support and multiple contributions of Stefan Kirilov, Director of the Rila National Park, should be acknowledged.

References

Bulgarian National Assembly (2008) Official State Gazette No 43, April 2008. National Assembly, Bulgaria.

Cooper, C., Wanhill, S., Fletcher, F., Fyall, A. and Gilbert, D. (2013) *Tourism: Principles and Practice*, 5th edn. Pearson, Edinburgh, UK.

Cunha, D.F.S. (2009) Economic crisis and possible legal and social perspectives. *Rev. direito GV [online]* 5(2), 343–358.

European Union (2004) Directive 2004/35. Available at: http://eur-lex.europa.eu/legal-content/EN/TXT/?uri=CELEX:32004L0035 (accessed 16 October 2014).

European Union (2010) Directive 2010/30. Available at: http://eur-lex.europa.eu/legal-content/EN/TXT/?uri=CELEX:32004L0035 (accessed 16 October 2014).

Filipova, M. (2010) Peculiarities of project planning in tourism. *Perspectives of Innovations, Economics and Business* 4(1), 57–59.

Ivanov, St. and Dimitrova, M. (2013) Chapter 4. Bulgaria. In: Costa, C., Panyik, E. and Buhalis, D. (eds) *European Tourism Planning and Organisation Systems. Vol. II. National Case Studies*. Channel View. Available at: https://www.academia.edu/930047/Tourism_Management_and_Planning_in_Bulgaria (accessed 21 March 2014).

Jafari, J. (ed.) (2000) *The Encyclopedia of Tourism*. Routledge, London.

Kamenov, K., Todorov, T. and Penchev, P. (1996) *Sustainable Development*. ABAGAR Publishing, Veliko Tarnovo, Bulgaria.

Kozak, M. (2001) Repeaters' behaviour at two distinct destinations. *Annals of Tourism Research* 28(3), 784–807.

McKercher, B. (1993) Some fundamental truths about tourism: understanding tourism's social and environmental impacts. *Journal of Sustainable Tourism* 1(1), 6–16.

Madanoglu, M. (2012) Contemporary challenges of Bulgarian tourism. *E-Review of Tourism Research*. Available at: http://ertr.tamu.edu/files/2012/09/264_a-1-3-1.pdf (accessed 21 March 2014).

Marinov, S. (2008) Strategic goals for enhancing the competitiveness of Bulgaria as a tourist destination. Paper presented at the 4th International Conference of ASECU 'Development Cooperation and Competitiveness', pp. 383–393. Available at: http://www.asecu.gr/files/RomaniaProceedings/41. pdf (accessed 21 March 2014).

Meadows, D.H., Meadows, D.L., Randers, J. and Behrens, W.W. III (1972) *The Limits to Growth: A Report for the Club of Rome's Project on the Predicament of the Mankind*. Universe Books, New York.

Ministry of Economics and Energy (2014) Strategy for sustainable development of tourism in Bulgaria 2014–2030. Available at: http://www.fpdd.bg/en/page/strategic%20docs#sthash.MqpUnREr. MoL8NqwK.dpuf (accessed January 2014).

Ministry of Economics of Bulgaria (2004) Klusterite – instrument na novata politika za ikonomicesko razvitie [Clusters – tool of the new policy of economic development.] Power point presentation in Bulgarian language. Available at: http://textil.stfi.de/download/sites/download_script.asp?filename=732_134.ppt (accessed 22 October 2015).

Mintel International Group Ltd (2007) Country Reports No 1, Europe. Travel and Tourism Intelligence. In general information to the tourism sector in Bulgaria. Available at: http://www.oecd.org/industry/tourism/40239491.pdf (accessed December 2013).

National Statistical Institute (2015) Realen bruten vatreshen product na covek ot naselenieto I temp na prirast. [Real GDP per capita and growth rate.] Available at: http://www.nsi.bg/bg/content/11472/реален-бвп-на-човек-от-населението-и-темп-на-прираст (accessed 22 October 2015).

National Statistical Institute (n.d.) Arrivals of visitors from abroad to Bulgaria by purpose of visit and by country of origin. Available at: http://www.nsi.bg/en/content/7056/arrivals-visitors-abroad-bulgaria-purpose-visit-and-country-origin Time series: TUR_1.3_For_en.xls (accessed 22 October 2015).

Peattie, K. and Montinho, L. (2000) The marketing environment for travel and tourism. In: Montinho, L. (ed.) *Strategic Management in Tourism*. CAB International, Wallingford, UK, pp. 17–37.

Plog, S.C. (1974) Why destination areas rise and fall in popularity. *Cornell Hotel and Restaurant Administration Quarterly* 14(4), 55–58.

Scottish Executive Social Research (2006) Sustainable Development: A Review of International Literature. Available at: http://www.gov.scot/Publications/2006/05/23091323/0 (accessed January 2014).

Stankova, M. (2003) *Tour Operator and Transport Activities*. SWU Publishing House 'Neofit Rilski', Blagoevgrad, Bulgaria.

Stankova, M. (2009) *Enhancing the Management of the Tourist Destination*. Editorial House 'Avangard-Prima', Sofia.

Stankova, M. and Rizova, T. (2012) Tourism destination management by applying cluster approach. *Thematic Collection of the Papers of International Significance 'Improving the Competitiveness of the Public and Private Sector by Networking Competences'*. Faculty of Economics, University of Niš, Serbia, pp. 291–311.

State Agency for Tourism (2009) National Strategy for Sustainable Tourism development 2009–2013. Available at: http://bulgariatravel.org/data/doc/Strategy_final_02.2009_3_7430.pdf (accessed 15 January 2014).

Tribe, J. (1995) *The Economics of Leisure and Tourism*. Chapman and Hall, London.

UNEP and UNWTO (2005) Making Tourism More Sustainable – A Guide for Policy Makers. Available at: http://www.unep.fr/shared/publications/pdf/DTIx0592xPA-TourismPolicyEN.pdf (accessed January 2014).

Vargionis N. (2002) Alternative tourism in Bulgaria: diversification and sustainability. Available at: http://www.oecd.org/cfe/tourism/40239624.pdf (accessed 5 March 2014).

Zakova, E. (2007) Clusters – Ways of Their Formation and Operation. Overview of Clusters in Bulgaria. Available at: www.arcfund.net/fileSrc.php?id=2234 (accessed 12 April 2014).

17 Conclusion

ANDRÉS ARTAL-TUR[1]* AND METIN KOZAK[2]

[1]Technical University of Cartagena, Cartagena, Spain; [2]Dokuz Eylul University, Foca, Turkey

Destination is the place where tourism occurs. Tourism supply meets demand in the destination. Environmental and cultural resources, attractions and the hospitality industry are all located in the destination. The tourism industry touches the ground at the destination. As a result, enormous pressure is put on destination resources. The development of the mass tourism model extends that pressure all over the world. Many families and firms, either in developing or developed countries, depend on the revenues generated through the tourism industry. The extension of tourism activities results in a negative impact on the life conditions of the local population. In this context, it is necessary to continue improving our understanding of the phenomena of destination sustainability. This has constituted the main aim of the present book, with a strong focus on the environmental and competitiveness dimensions. We have endeavoured to direct the attention once more towards these pivotal fields of research, providing new tools and knowledge to confront the big challenges appearing for tourism destinations.

The analysis has comprised three main parts, including destination competitiveness, the role of the environment, and the general framework of sustainability. All three topics are clearly interrelated in the tourism industry. Sustainability is no longer possible without a holistic strategy about the environment and natural resources. No sustainability is possible without stating a competitive strategy for the future. But no destination will remain without a forward-looking sustainable strategy. All three issues become clearly endogenous in the dynamics of the tourism destination, this being the central idea guiding the present work.

Part I has focused on the analysis of factors influencing the competitiveness of destinations. The contributions have shown a number of interesting results. In terms of indicators, and employing a wide range of them in order to identify the most effective factors fostering destination competitiveness, researchers have shown the

*E-mail: andres.artal@upct.es

© CAB International 2016. *Destination Competitiveness, the Environment and Sustainability: Challenges and Cases* (eds A. Artal-Tur and M. Kozak)

prominence of specialization at destinations. Environmental and sustainable strategies could be the answer to this pace of specialization that destinations need to follow. The demand for green and responsible tourism is not only a growing trend of consumers, but a necessary condition for the future of the industry. The diversity of the supply of services and the role of service quality continues to stand as the second variable in importance when one wants to improve the performance of a destination. Moreover, the analysis of the competitiveness pillars by focus groups of professionals and tourism experts indicates the leading role conferred to the activities of destination management, marketing and promotion, coordination of stakeholders, sourcing of good information to monitor the destination, and planning activities in general. The level of accessibility and the quality of tourism services were also pointed out as relevant issues in the competitiveness of a destination by the selected experts participating in the study of Brazil.

Subsequent chapters of the book add a more qualitative view in the study of competitiveness. They have pointed to other emerging sources in the creation of destination-based competitive advantages, including that of creativity and the role of visual semantics in promotion and communication actions. Creativity is yet to be recognized as a driving force for urban and cultural development in tourism, while the capacity of communication policy in shaping the international image of a destination, and by then of building new competitive resources, is an interesting view in this branch of the literature. Results on case studies for both issues have shown the role of climate, street life, accessibility, urban connectivity and gastronomy offer in attracting new visitors to creative destinations in urban contexts. Security issues and a relevant supply of cultural and leisure activities have been also pointed out as important dimensions. Mid-sized destinations are increasingly preferred to big urban locations when choosing a new residence, given the negative externalities arising in the latter case. Historical downtown areas and other urban spaces that facilitate the social and professional interaction of people are highly demanded by this emerging class of visitors.

Regarding the capacity of visual semantics and communication tools in reshaping the competitive features of a destination, the investigation has shown new ways of defining tourism destination imagery. It has shown the possibilities that visual semantics add to changes and transformations in the design and marketing of new tourist products, helping in this way to renovate the traditional supplies. Visual promises reveal the scenic beauty of destinations as a frame of reference. The connotative functions of the images communicate multiple concrete and symbolic possibilities, one of the most salient being the representation of social interactions with local residents, leading to the generation of a social image of the destination. Marketing and communication are then highlighted as useful tools in promoting the image of the destination, hence leading to the creation of new competitive advantages.

Part II of the book has elaborated on the environmental dimension of tourism, proposing ways of implementing that central subject in the daily practice of the tourism industry. The investigation started by wondering about the level of awareness shown by the industry stakeholders on the environmental impact of their business, and the corresponding practices to mitigate that activity. Two major issues were investigated, including green economy practices and the effects of climate change and global warming on infrastructures, facilities and destinations in general. Regarding the case on green economy practices conducted in South Africa, the findings showed that there was generally a lack of understanding of the concept among tourism businessmen. The main green economy practices do not go beyond that of water- and energy-saving initiatives. Most of the tourism managers interviewed showed a lack of knowledge on current government policies and incentives launched to promote green economy investments. The results also showed the need for increased awareness on both the green economy concept and its meaning and how it will benefit the industry. They were not aware on how to plan the developments of new labour skills necessary for the implementation of green economy practices. Among the key constraints for implementing these initiatives, the lack of information on green economy meaning and processes and the expected high costs of engagement were identified.

In the case of Turkey, interviews on the degree of consciousness about the effects of climate change and global warming were conducted among tourism managers. The objective was to understand how these central actors of the tourism industry perceived the effects of such a central issue on three dimensions: their personal life, the business they lead and the destination environment in general. Results have shown that managers perceived, as the most important ones, the consequences of climate change on the performance of their own business, followed by general concerns on the necessary commitment to be applied to protecting the general environment, and in third place they showed concerns about the impact of changes on their own personal life (physical health, sustainability of the industry and jobs, decrease of value of affected properties). A deeper analysis segmenting by profile of the interviewed manager is unlikely to reveal big differences between males and females, but a slightly higher level of awareness of older managers of the impact on their own business (hotels) and of more educated ones regarding the effects of climate change on their personal life and mental concerns. In general, some degree of consciousness was found in stakeholders, but given the profound impact of climate change and global warming on the tourism industry in the near future, the study called our attention to the need to place a higher emphasis on bringing this matter to the very frontline of the literature and the policy arena.

In this context, education emerges as a central matter in protecting the environment, leading to changes of attitudes for the future. Educational institutions are well suited to provide environmental awareness to society. As pointed out throughout the book, education can provide the basis for the required process of gradual change, including awareness, knowledge, attitudes, skills and participation. Environmental education provides the foundations for understanding the physical environment, creating motivation and guiding the discovery of suitable solutions to environmental problems. It is also involved, and plays an effective role, in environmental movements of a social and political nature. Moreover, in the case of tourism, one of the main challenges for the new century seems to be the inclusion of environmental consciousness in the curriculum of tourism education. This would allow enhancing awareness of the impacts of tourism, leading to a pro-environmental attitude not only among tourists themselves but also the host community, the commercial sector and the government.

Results have shown the existence of a degree of backwardness still present in the educational programmes of developing, but also developed, countries, in order to actively promote environmentally related modules, workshops on the environmental side, field trips for oriented educational purposes, or campaigns related to environmental issues and values. As noted by the results of the investigations in this book, a few students have participated in these types of activities, but attention is drawn to the need to improve both the number of activities and the motivation of students to pursue them. In general, the results have identified some weaknesses still present in the educative process when promoting the environmental awareness of students. In this way, the book recommends the promotion of university and public sector partnerships capable of facing the necessary 'ecologicalization' of institutions and organizations in various social systems (and scientific disciplines), still making slow progress in developing nations, as a means to paving the way to (tourism) sustainable development in the near future.

Following this reasoning, the book has investigated how a government can face the challenge of developing a truly green destination by building on policy tools. In this way, tourism activities can be used to improve the awareness of people of the effects of climate change, focusing on the case of the Caribbean. In this context of extreme interdependence between business and climate conditions, the governments in the Caribbean should be facing the challenge of improving the understanding of stakeholders and related personnel on the necessity of undertaking real measures against the sources of global warming. The same industry, which receives multiple international tourist visits, could be playing an instructive role regarding such a global issue. In this way, Caribbean governments have a good opportunity to build on the tourism industry to actively face the challenge of climate change.

Throughout the investigations, particular key issues have been identified when developing a strategy against the advance of climate change and environmental decline. They include the maintenance of a risk management framework, the implementation of training programmes, the integration of climate change issues in tourism policies, the development of preventive regulations and the establishment of a network, physical and virtual, designed for the dissemination of practical experience and background information. The need for behavioural changes at the tourist level has also emerged as a critical element of the strategy, as well as the promotion of structural changes in the tourism industry. The capacity of governments in providing the correct incentives to tourism entities has been found to be pivotal throughout the whole process. The need to build on a general framework that can serve as a road map in the adoption of a mindful environmental strategy at destinations has been the main conclusion of this part of the book.

Another relevant action in order to promote the green dimension in tourism relates to the capacity of environmental management to build new competitive advantages for the hospitality industry. This practice is very useful as it aligns the profit-seeking character of the industry with the mindful environmental behaviour that the consumer/tourist increasingly demands. Research results in this book have shown that environmental management constitutes an outstanding competitive advantage for the destination; for example, in the case of the hotel industry. Such an issue has been clearly recognized by managers as usually being present not only in their daily practice but also in their mid-term strategy. In particular, we have tested for the role played by two main types of environmental management techniques, namely environmental quality management and environmental impact management. Testing exercises have not permitted us to identify with more clarity which of these two sources of managerial advantages excels in this process, according to the managers' responses. This remains an open question of research for the future.

Part III of the book has been devoted to the central subject of destination sustainability, including the environmental, sociocultural and economic dimensions of the question. Regarding the topic of demand seasonality, the methodology applied in the investigation has helped to identify segments of travellers more prone to come in low- and mid-season periods of the year, helping in this way to offset the high seasonal pattern arising in some coastal destinations. The use of a double segmentation by the origin and travel motivation of tourists has been very useful in capturing some features of tourist behaviour not visible in a merely descriptive analysis of data. Culture appears as the most promising activity in fostering arrivals out of high-season periods, with a higher relevance for international inbound flows. As shown in this case, cultural tourism is a cornerstone in reducing the seasonality of destinations, helping to diversify the profile of visitors, thus promoting specialization in sustainable activities at destinations. Other important conclusions in this regard highlight the role of coordination of domestic tourism industry stakeholders, in order to reduce excessive dependence on international tourism operators, and the necessity to develop new tourist products particularly designed to attract new visitors coming out of season. The importance of developing promotion and communication marketing plans for a destination, and the need to keep these activities ongoing, appear to be important tools in shaping the image and reputation of destinations.

From the point of view of the economic sustainability of destinations, this book has investigated the impact of expenditure and tourists' length of stay in defining an optimal revenue policy at nature-based destinations. Those on a shorter length of stay show high-expenditure behaviour per day, while those on a longer stay accommodate their daily spending to the length of the stay. Moreover, both types of tourists present very dissimilar behaviour according to the activities pursued on the trip. Those on a shorter length of stay follow a typical leisure stay with low geographical mobility across the destination, all-inclusive and package-related holidays and the characteristics of a mass tourism model. To the contrary, those on a longer length of stay move around the destination, explore its natural and cultural richness and interact more positively with the local population. In general, visitors on longer stays show a more sustainable profile in environmental terms, while those on shorter stays provide higher economic sustainability. Taking advantage of both types of behaviours in an optimal way should be the objective of destination management organizations (DMOs), as prescribed in this book. In the case of a nature-based destination, it becomes a central issue, as we have shown. Providing information on this issue is the role of researchers, in order to facilitate this task for destination managers. In the case of small city tourism, the investigation highlights the need to focus on sustainable activities for medium- and high-income visitors, in order to pursue a more balanced development of these types of urban enclaves.

Finally, the role of networking in leading heritage-based tourism has been identified. Networking enhances collaboration, cooperation and joint action at the destination. Cooperation inside the network increases knowledge sharing and enhances the awareness of sustainability between stakeholders, who further communicate the importance to individuals outside the network, i.e. the tourists themselves. Meeting the challenges brought by modern times brings some inevitable inconsistencies to the policy of heritage protection. Therefore, the biggest emerging challenge is to reconcile the old with the new dimensions, but to embrace these changes through professional, ethical and active management, ensuring long-term sustainability of these types of heritage-based destinations. As a corollary, the last chapter of the book has explored a broader view in implementing tourism sustainability while developing an emerging destination, the country of Bulgaria in the former Eastern Europe. Not repeating the past mistakes of the surrounding EU destinations is important for these emerging actors in the tourism industry. Tourism development must be capable of evaluating the relevant cultural, historical and societal assets existing at the country level.

In general, as shown by the book, managing the sustainability, environmental and competitiveness challenges of destinations is always a complex task. However, tourism destinations at the very edge of the new millennium have a responsibility to face these. The survival of the tourism industry depends on how we confront these challenges. In taking this route, stakeholders will have to lean on new developments from academia and industry practices. This book presents a number of these new developments, with important case studies highlighting the most promising realities of these pivotal issues. This is taking a new step towards a more sustainable tourism industry, but, as we have shown, we are just at the very beginning.

Index

Page numbers in **bold** refer to figures and tables.